"IMPRESSIV⟨ **W9-DHR-425**
—*San Francisco Chronicle*

'By telling my story, I was finally able to present another reality that was Vietnam. Another view of both the Vietnamese as a human, compassionate people, and a first-time look at the many heroic American soldiers who were the embodiement of the human spirit we all know exists in our country."
from—

DON'T CRY, IT'S ONLY THUNDER

"POWERFUL. . . . The beauty of this heartrending book is that it shows how much good just one individual can do in a world that seems to fight back almost every inch of the way." —*National Catholic News Service*

PAUL G. HENSLER, the subject of this book, has lived the story. He has continued the work he started in Vietnam by helping place Asian children in foster homes. He has also co-produced a film about his experiences, *Don't Cry, It's Only Thunder.*

JEANNE WAKATSUKI HOUSTON is the author of *Farewell to Manzanar,* a much acclaimed account of Japanese-American detention camps in the United States during World War II.

Heart Warming Stories from SIGNET

DON'T CRY, IT'S ONLY THUNDER

PAUL G. HENSLER
with JEANNE WAKATSUKI HOUSTON

A SIGNET BOOK

NEW AMERICAN LIBRARY

SIGNET TRADEMARK REG. U.S. PAT. OFF. AND FOREIGN COUNTRIES
REGISTERED TRADEMARK—MARCA REGISTRADA
HECHO EN CHICAGO, U.S.A.

SIGNET, SIGNET CLASSIC, MENTOR, PLUME, MERIDIAN and NAL BOOKS
are published by New American Library,
1633 Broadway, New York, New York 10019

First Signet Printing, January, 1985

1 2 3 4 5 6 7 8 9

PRINTED IN THE UNITED STATES OF AMERICA

Acknowledgments

To complete this book I had to rely on a great deal more than my own recollections. I have asked for and received more assistance than can be acknowledged here. But there are a special few who were most instrumental in helping me complete this manuscript. I am especially thankful for the experience of working and learning with Jeanne Wakatsuki Houston, who gave life to many pages of empty words. I also want to thank these generous friends: George Ow, Dr. Jim Brill, James D. Houston, Betty Barton, the cast and crew of *Don't Cry, It's Only Thunder,* Pan American Airways, and Father Peter Prayoon Namwong.

Some names in this book have been changed to protect and honor those who do not wish to remember.

Paul G. Hensler

September 15, 1983
Santa Cruz, California

Contents

List of Illustrations

Prologue

"Brother Paul, there's a long-distance phone call for you from California," Father Walsh said softly, then left the chapel where I had been meditating. Snapping out of my peaceful contemplation, I hurried up the stairs to the phone desk, wondering who would be calling me from California.

The voice on the other end sounded vaguely familiar, the heavy accent identifying the speaker as Vietnamese.

"Paul, this is Dr. Chi. Remember me? We met at Carlton University. You spoke to one of my Political Science classes."

"Oh yes. How are you?"

"I'm good. Listen, I'm working with the State Department here at Camp Pendleton. We're trying to deal with the first big group of refugees from Vietnam, and we have about fifty unaccompanied children who are in need of supervision. Could you possibly get away from your studies for a while and come help us?"

I didn't need to think twice. "Yes, I'll be there as soon as I can catch a plane."

It was the summer of 1975. I had spent almost three years studying for the priesthood with the Missionary Oblates of Mary Immaculate, in Ottawa, Canada. Since 1970, when I left Vietnam after two and a half years of army duty there, I had chosen to put my experiences behind me and move forward into the next phase of my life. Vietnam remained a submerged memory, surfacing rarely, and then only as a superficial reference point in conversation. I had never told my family, my Brothers in the house of studies in Ottawa, or anyone the whole story of my time in Vietnam. So the call from Dr. Chi provoked more than a memory of a pleasant meeting with the learned professor and his family . . . it was a call from the past, a detonator of the time bomb of memories that had lain dormant, waiting for the fuse to be lit.

Still the past did not explode instantaneously before me. The memories percolated to the surface—sporadic and diffused. On the plane from Ottawa to California, I began to think about Vietnam. Five years had passed since I said good-bye to the nuns and orphans in Saigon. For many reasons, but especially because of my experiences with them, I made the decision to study for the priesthood with a missionary order where I would eventually be able to work with children again. I believed my life's work would involve children somehow but had not anticipated the opportunity to do so would come so soon. When I received that phone call, Dr. Chi's voice might just as well have been Sister Hoa's. I responded spontaneously. I knew it was more than a call to help refugee children. For me, it confirmed my decision to leave my studies toward the priesthood . . . something I had been considering for a long time.

Ten thousand refugees were crammed into the hastily built tent city on Camp Pendleton Marine Base, and each day more arrived from Vietnam. These were the first people evacuated by the Americans when Saigon fell, and most were wealthy Saigonese connected to our government. As I walked through the alleyways between the tents that first day, I was taken back to a similar scene outside Saigon in 1969. My first trip into the city took me past the poorest refugees who were fleeing the fighting in the country. They built their impoverished shacks and lean-tos on any available piece of dirt and waited for help or death, their children lying malnourished and sick in the doorways. But here the families all looked happy and well fed. Their children ran about playing, laughing, free.

Brown faces with dark almond eyes smiled at me. There were no begging hands out, only smiles and long lines waiting for the delicious American food. Vivid images, charged with heavy emotions, flashed through my mind as I walked among the refugees . . . the first large group of Vietnamese people I had seen since I left Vietnam five years ago.

* * *

I was named the Director of the Unaccompanied Children's Center by the International Red Cross and the U.S. State Department. My job was to supervise forty "unaccompanied" children who had arrived at the camp without parents or blood relatives. In most cases the children had been smuggled onto boats or aircraft by desperate parents who wanted them to be free from the new and feared Communist Government.

This left the children, except for a few who were provable orphans, unadoptable in the United States. There were no death certificates proving they were truly orphans and no documents showing parental permission for adoption. The only course left for most of them would be a foster home situation, and until these arrangements could be made they remained under my supervision.

I plunged into my new job, appreciating the active involvement with Vietnamese children again. It was so much like being with the orphans in Saigon, playing games, organizing schedules, and even yelling at the few tough guys in the crowd. I loved it. It made my decision to leave the Oblates right and good. I realized, too, that my studies for the priesthood had not been wasted. After two and a half years of work with the orphans of Vietnam, I had only just begun to mature; later, within the disciplined and ritualized Oblate community, my past experiences were slowly forcing me to come to terms with that part of my life.

But in confronting those powerful memories head-on, putting them into some order of understanding, I found myself alone. I was so far ahead of my Oblate Brothers, who had passed painlessly from adolescence to their religious vows, somehow missing the experiences of love, sex, death, and real life. Their call to the religious life was from God, unchallengeable and pure. My call to serve as a priest was from gathered experience and faith. After a year of graduate studies in theology, I found myself too anxious to challenge my Brothers and God as He was being taught, about life as I knew it to be. Not life sanitized and made more palatable by poverty, chastity, obedience, and the belief that prayer was the answer to all the world's problems. But life as it was lived by the children, the orphans of Vietnam. And life as it was suffered through by the poor of every country including our own. There was a time for prayer, of this I was sure, but for me action was the answer to the immediate problems of the Vietnamese refugees and their children.

Day after day my work at the Unaccompanied Children's Center brought back the greatest memories of joy, collected during two and a half years with the orphans in Saigon. These children displayed the same simple gratitude and trust, the thirst to be held, tickled, loved, and the same painful sadness in parting as they began to move toward foster homes and sponsors. It was so much like an exact replay of my time in Vietnam, happiness mixed with their lack of family or future, but happiness was the only thing I could give them. I wanted and needed to learn how to give them more.

And then one day another beautiful yet painful memory walked back into my life. Her name was Anh. She was around twelve years old, not very pretty, silent and very frightened. She had arrived in the camp with a family and was falsely identified as one of their children. One of my children in the center came back from lunch and told me she had seen a girl being beaten. When I questioned the man identified as her father, I found that the girl was not his daughter but was in fact his slave, purchased three years ago in Vietnam. I notified the State Department and had the child put under my custody.

Afraid her "owner" might seek reprisal against her, she clung to me, never letting me out of her sight. Her gentleness reminded me of another little Vietnamese girl—one of my favorite children in the Saigon orphanage—named Thom— whose attachment and caring for me had taught me how precious a child's unconditional love could be. Anh was not beautiful, as my Thom had been, but there were many other likenesses—an awareness of others, sensitivity, and an obvious backlog of painful, traumatic experiences revealed in her sad, dark eyes. But what was truly chilling because of its uncanny similarity was Anh's refusal to speak. Thom also did not speak, having been shocked into silence by war and the vision of her parents dying in her arms.

What seemed like a strange coincidence—or what Sister Tuan would have called fate—set off a strong desire to recall as much as I could about my experiences with the children in

Vietnam. Wasn't I doing it again, reliving a vastly watered-down version of my time there? Sister Hoa had said I would forget . . . and when it was time, would remember . . . when the lessons were clear and understandable.

I began writing down my memories. I remembered scenes, dates, dialogues, insights, feelings, even smells. In doing so, I relived those experiences in my mind and felt again the pain and joy in my body.

Finally, I began to understand what I had experienced when I was a nineteen-year-old boy trying to be a man. I began to know what Vietnam really meant for me.

Honolulu
March 1983

PART I

— 1 —

Triage

A Dustoff chopper (or flying ambulance, as they were called in Nam) swung its tail around so that its open door was broadside to the triage area. Overloaded with wounded, whose bandage-wrapped arms and legs hung out the door, the chopper set down hard on the asphalt landing pad. When the stinging dust finally cleared, I moved closer and watched the triage medics start unloading the stretchers of wounded Americans.

The first two men carried off the chopper screamed as they were placed on waiting stretchers, their arms flailing about trying to grab someone, anyone, who would listen to their pleas for morphine or their mother. The third stretcher off the chopper made my eyes water with stark terror. His head lay to one side, his eyes cold and dry, staring directly at me. It was like walking by a master's portrait in a gallery or museum, the eyes of the painting following you as you walked by. His midsection was a massive jumble of hamburger, his legs were bent grotesquely, and the toes of his boots were turned completely around backward. I took several steps forward, my eyes unable to believe the damage done to this boy's body. I had been helping out on the wards in triage and the emergency room for several weeks but had never seen such brutal death. I grabbed my stomach in violent sympathetic pain, fighting to keep my lunch from churning back to daylight.

The medics dropped him at the side of the triage area and ran back to the chopper. No sheet over his body, no prayers, no one to care for him. The living were more important at that moment and needed immediate attention. The dead would wait patiently without complaint.

Another stretcher team came toward me. A hand grabbed my arm, dragging me along. The man on the stretcher was eighteen, maybe nineteen, his long blond hair matted with blood, his eyes closed, and his teeth clenched in pain. Nothing seemed wrong with him except maybe a cut under all the blood in his hair, until the stretcher bearers jostled the litter as we entered the emergency room and I saw his right leg below the knee roll away from the upper part. He screamed and nearly tore through my arm with his fingernails.

One of the triage teams, dressed in surgical scrub gowns—a doctor, two nurses, and a medic—swarmed around him. Practiced hands soothed him, cut his bloodied uniform away, drew blood, injected 0.5 cc of tetanus toxoid, 10 milligrams of morphine, probed his head wound, and then began on his mangled leg. More orders yelled above the emergency room din. A surgery room scheduled, orthopedic tools called for. Medics passed absorbent gauze, needles, clamps, sterile water, scissors, a grotesque-looking stainless-steel saw, and finally the soldier's amputated leg was dropped to the floor with a horrible thud, like a piece of freshly split firewood.

His hand slowly relaxed its grip on my arm, but I was now holding several tubes of blood and his medical chart so I stayed close to the bed, stepping aside only to allow one of the medical team more space.

I was watching, listening, staring at the shredded leg, but I kept seeing the dead man being dropped outside. In a few hours his parents would know, but never see, thank God, the damage done to their son. The Army Mortuary would mark the coffin, "Remains Unviewable," sparing his parents the horror within. What would my mother do if she saw all six-foot-four inches of her skinny son Paul rearranged by an enemy hand grenade?

Brian O'Shea, my friend and medical instructor, entered the room, took the tubes of blood from my hands, and handed me an intravenous-injection setup. With a quick smile he was gone to get the lab started on a type and crossmatch so the soldier could begin getting a badly needed transfusion.

Brian was only twenty-one but already a seasoned veteran,

having been in Vietnam for more than five months. We met
at the Headquarters Medical Clinic in Phan Rang when I reported for my first series of in-country inoculations. Cholera,
plague, typhus, tetanus, all required protection in a country
where disease sometimes claimed as many lives daily as the
war. He was gentle with the needles, something I had always
feared, and the first person since I enlisted in the army to ask
me more than my name, rank, or serial number.

We became fast friends and I began volunteering most of
my free time at the hospital, helping out where I could and
watching him work with the wounded in triage, emergency,
and on the wards. It was where I wanted to be assigned, what
I wanted to be doing, but then anything would have been
better than stacking outdated medical supplies in a dusty,
horrendously hot army tent.

Brian was highly trained, a diligent worker, and a respected member of the hospital staff.

I was "fresh meat" in Nam, in a medical support company, an outsider who wanted to be a member of this elite
team but, more importantly, an outsider who constantly felt
uncomfortable around such a close, already established
group of friends.

The soldier was quiet now as the morphine infiltrated his
body. I moved quickly, washing his arm with an alcohol
sponge, and easily inserted the Intracath needle into a large
vein on his forearm. "Good shot, Hensler," a medic said
across the table. Brian had trained me well. The dextrose
and water began to run into the soldier freely and would help
reduce his body's traumatic loss of fluids.

Brian returned with two units of blood, complaining that
the bags were hours from expiring but thankful there was
blood to give him. As I hooked the blood into the IV line I
had just started, the triage surgeon signed the soldier's orders for drugs administered and surgical procedures to be
performed, then moved on to the next patient.

"Hold his leg up," Brian said as he began to wrap layer
after layer of Curlex gauze around the bloody stump. The
boy's eyes popped open as the rough bandage came in contact with raw exposed nerves and his hand shot up into the
air, searching for something to hold onto.

"Talk to him, Paul. Maybe he'll hold still so I can finish this dressing."

I looked down at the boy, who smiled at me, the morphine pulling him toward the only legal high in Vietnam, then took his hand in mine.

What could I possibly say to this brave eighteen-year-old who lay naked before me, no lies possible, and whose amputated lower leg was being dumped into a trash can, muddy combat boot still laced to the foot? Less than an hour ago this kid had been blown up, flown in, fixed up, and messed up for life. Five minutes ago he had unwillingly joined the Veteran's Hospital system forever and here I stood, trying to think of something to say that would make him feel better.

"Hey, Doc." His soft voice scared me. "Doc . . . tell me the truth . . . you fixed my leg, right?"

He only had to lift his head to know the truth, but he stared straight into my eyes. The slightest change in my face, the direction of my stare or expression, and he would know.

"It's still there. I can feel it," he said.

I looked quickly at Brian. He shook his head no.

"Tell him the truth," Brian whispered, wanting the boy to think I was the doctor. I caught on.

"I'm sorry. The bone and blood vessels in your lower leg were too badly damaged. We couldn't save it. . . . You just lay still and let us finish, okay?"

"Sure, Doc. . . . Sure. . . . I'm okay." He answered, closing his eyes tightly. Tears appeared, one dropping down his cheek. He pulled his hand away from me and covered his eyes with his forearm. Even now, his leg gone, in intense pain from a thousand damaged, raw nerve endings, he didn't want us to see him crying.

"Thanks, Doc," he said as two litter bearers picked up the stretcher to take him to surgery. Now I was crying.

Brian turned away from the sink, drying his hands.

"You still wanna go downtown?" he asked with a smile, throwing me the wet towel so I could wipe the blood from my hands and quickly, without him seeing, the tears from my eyes.

"Yeah . . . sure."

"Come on, Hensler, none of that bleeding heart bullshit now. There're too many to cry over. . . . I'll make sure

here are no more cases waiting, then we can hit the road,"
e said, slapping me on the arm, happy, I suppose, that the
ast few minutes had not totally freaked me out or sent me
unning.

"I'm used to it," Brian would say when I asked him how
e handled his work, mentally. But I believed it to be his way
f avoiding conversation or any expression of emotion about
he nonstop horror show he witnessed every day.

I could never get used to it. Like the raw nerve endings in
he boy's leg, each incident struck something deep inside me.
Each innocent face I saw contorted in pain, every bloody
and I held, that transmitted the fear of death and thanked
ne with a squeeze for my reassuring grip, were day by day
eing catalogued in my mind. And day by day they were
uilding up to an emotional confrontation that would de-
nand answers. "I'm used to it" would not work much lon-
er for me.

While waiting for Brian I went outside and walked directly
o where the dead soldier had been left. He was still there,
vaiting, staring through dull piercing blue eyes toward the
rilliant sunset. I bent down, waved the flies away from the
lried blood on his face, then gently lowered his eyelids. Dip-
ing my finger into a mud puddle next to the dead boy's
rm, I touched the reddish-brown water to his forehead and
nade the sign of the cross. "I baptize you in the name of the
father, and of the Son, and of the Holy Spirit . . . Amen." I
ooked around quickly to be sure no one was looking and
hen thought, why the hell do I care what the others think?

Dear Mr. and Mrs. Hensler,

We are sorry to report that your son Paul was blown all over South Vietnam today, thirty thousand miles from the warmth of your embrace.

— 2 —

Cao Van Trong

As Brian drove the army jeep toward Phan Rang City, about fifteen miles from the base, there was a relaxed silence between us.

The day's events were forgotten, my questions for Brian put on hold, tomorrow's duty unimaginable, for we were both a short distance away from the fulfillment of our most recurring erotic fantasy: getting laid for the first time. We had made an agreement two days earlier—that is, once we both admitted to having the same nagging ailment, *virginity*—to rectify the situation with the help of two whores, a little dope, and lots of beer.

"Hey man, slow down." I grabbed the windshield brace. "I don't want to lose my life on the way to losing my cherry," I yelled over the jeep's whining engine. Oh Jesus, I thought, men don't lose their cherries, only women do. What a stupid thing to say.

"We've got a nine o'clock curfew out here. We gotta get in and out . . ." He looked at me with a wide grin.

"Get it, Hensler, in and out . . . ," he said laughing.

"I get it, watch the goddamned road," I shouted, grabbing the steering wheel. He swerved back onto our side of the road, almost sideswiping an old farmer riding a water buffalo. The old man must have been asleep or dead because he didn't even flinch as we passed within three inches of him and his four-legged Vietnamese John Deere tractor.

As we turned off the main road toward the city, the open dry land quickly began to disappear under cardboard and tin refugee huts. The closer we got, the more crowded and

27

packed the huts became, stretching as far as the eye could see from right up to the edge of the road.

Naked children, old women, mangy dogs, beggars, and the pungent smells of sewage and camphor smoke surrounded us.

The children waved and ran alongside the jeep, chattering, laughing, begging for a handout.

"Candy, please, my mother very sick. My daddy die in war . . . please, G.I., give me money."

Their high voices piped over the din of the jeep's motor and noise of the marketplace we were approaching. I noticed their thin brown faces, the upper lips chapped and shiny from their runny noses. I was taken aback by the swollen stomachs and festering sores that cratered their arms and legs. Like a pack of hungry dogs, they stuck together and chased after us, hope for some money or a candy bar spurring them on.

Standing along the edge of the street were more tiny children, small-boned and delicate-looking, many carrying babies on their hips almost as large as themselves.

Brian honked the horn, carefully negotiating the jeep through an open market where toothless, spitting old women squatted behind their neatly laid out piles of hard French rolls, foul-smelling fish, vegetables, fly-covered meat, and tall, stark white cones of rice.

This was the closest I had come to the Vietnamese people. My eyes darted from face to face—the colors, the children. The stark poverty was unbelievable. These were the people whose democracy we were defending? Whose territorial integrity we were dying for and for whom we would hold back, at any cost, the Red Tide of Communist aggression? As I looked across the faces all I could think was someone had made a terrible mistake. The boy I had baptized this afternoon had died trying to keep these poor sickly looking people free?

We drove out of the slums and into the center of Phan Rang City, much like going from a garbage dump to a flower garden. Beautiful trees lined the streets and I could smell the scent of flowers as we passed the flower market. The buildings were a mixture of French and Chinese architecture. That was one side of the street. The other side also had

French architecture, but most of it was lost behind cheap sleazy bars, massage parlors, and assorted rip-off joints, all servicing the horny Americans and their dollars.

Pretty little women, and some pretty ugly women, all in the worst mixtures of Western fashion, buzzed around drunk soldiers, whispering, cajoling, promising unimaginable acts of sexual pleasure followed by the price. Large signs, under which young girls waited, dressed in short white mini uniforms, offered: Saigon Massage, Happy Massage, and in large red letters over every parlor, SPECIAL MASSAGE.

One of our company clerks, drunk and slobbering, had cornered me in the Enlisted Men's Club and insisted on telling me in explicit detail about the secret pleasures of SPECIAL MASSAGE. "No," he sneered, "it ain't no slant-eyed Oriental teenager walking up an' down your greasy spine." And "No," he went on, "it ain't the use of no exotic oils smeared all over ya by a naked beauty." "Then what the hell is it?" I asked innocently. He laughed out loud, spitting beer across the bar, then said, "Usually it's some old toothless mamasan who dumps about a quart of this foul-smellin' cream in your crotch, followed by some quick up and down motions with her hands. Let her fingers do the walking an' there ain't no need for talkin' . . ." He laughed at his little poem. "You look like you just been shot, Hensler. You get the same rush but no chance of the Black Syph . . ." "Oh" was all I could say. The Black Syph?

After parking the jeep we decided to cruise the bar side of the street and pick the cleanest whorehouse we could find.

Mary's Bar was darker than Tom Sawyer's cave and the New York Bar had only one drunk sailor sprawled in its doorway. The Brother's Shelter was a neat little place with great ambiance, but twenty pairs of uninviting dark eyes lodged in huge muscular faces of black skin told us to retreat with speed.

As we continued down the street, we were suddenly surrounded by four or five little girls, smudged faces smiling up at us and dirty little hands holding baskets of roasted peanuts.

"You buy, Joe? Only ten piaster." They giggled and jostled each other, moving in very close. They were around nine or ten years old. Their features were dainty, and the skin under the grime was warm brown. It would not be long before they would be selling more than roasted peanuts in the streets. One of the girls, bigger than the others, was unmistakably half American. Her hair had an auburn cast and her skin was coppery. Their smiles were relentless, and I found myself responding to their friendliness.

"Get the hell away!" Brian suddenly yelled, scaring the smile off my face and scattering the little girls in every direction.

"What the hell'd you do that for, O'Shea?"

"Those cute little girls are all primo pickpockets, Hensler. The best in the country," he said, checking to see if his wallet was still in his back pocket. "And you gotta watch these guys, too," Brian said, pointing at two little boys walking toward us carrying small wooden boxes. They stopped in front of us, flashing twin smiles. "You like shine, Joe? Only fifty cents American." As one boy knelt down and tried to get Brian to put his scuffed boot on the second boy's box, Brian nudged me with his elbow. "Watch this," he said in a whisper. He leaned down close to the boy in front of him and for a moment I thought he was going to belt him.

"*Di Di Mow,* you little rodents," he screamed at the top of his lungs, once again scaring me as much as the boys, who fell over each other as they ran away.

"I'm not sure which I hate more, begging kids or us for making them beg. Man, this country sucks," he said, pulling a joint out of his fatigue shirt pocket.

In relief I stood watching him light the skinny joint. Brian didn't smoke. We had joked about probably having to get loaded so we could get laid. And I had never heard him raise his voice or speak angrily to anyone either, although I had seen many times when he had every reason to explode. His gentleness and compassion for all who came under his care at the hospital had never wavered. At the same time, he avoided my questions and even chided me for getting emotionally involved with the wounded.

I felt uneasy as we continued walking. Brian was my only friend among a couple of hundred guys in my company and the first person I had ever opened up to in my life. A true friend was like gold to me now, but maybe once again I had trusted another too quickly. Perhaps the potent marijuana would make him tell me of the hidden anger that seemed to simmer inside him, or maybe I would just hear a blast of painful words from a dope-loosened tongue like, "Why do you give a shit, Hensler?"

Brian stopped my thoughts by handing me the joint. Cupping it in my hand, I took a deep drag. My first toke of the illegal killer weed and already the word addict flew around my head.

"Let's try this place," Brian said, leading me behind a blackout curtain and into another bar.

It was so dark inside it took several minutes for our eyes to adjust before we found the bar and ordered two beers. Not much of a place but nicer than the other bars we had seen. Tables and booths lined the gaudy red walls on which were hung felt paintings of nude Oriental women, army, navy, and marine company plaques, and signs offering big discounts to infantry men just in from the battlefields.

About six other soldiers sat in various corners of the disinfectant-smelling room with bar girls wrapped tightly around them. A tall lanky marine, still carrying his M-16, got up from his chair, picked up his girl by the waist, and carried her into the back room.

"This is the place, Hensler," Brian said, lighting a second joint. He took two hard drags and handed it to me.

"I'm ready," I lied. The dope was burning in my lungs but gently drawing my mind into relaxation. I wanted today to be the day. Yet I wasn't sure. Neither of us were the type to bullshit about sex like those who spat out the names of six exotically perfect, silicone-breasted local girls they had conquered in a single evening—with a rating for each. I had spent many a day watching Brian inject millions of units of penicillin into the asses of guys who the night before had conquered the same reluctant girl we might end up with in a matter of minutes.

The heavy marijuana tar coursed through my head, blurring my thoughts. I looked at Brian, who was watching the activity around the tables, and realized it was to maintain his friendship and respect that I was about to *do it* for the first time. Okay, O'Shea, I'll prove to you that I'm no bleeding heart. I'll walk right up to one of those girls, pick her up like the marine had done a few minutes ago, and drag her into the back room where I'll . . . ?

"You like sit down? I get you numba-one girls," mama-san asked from behind the bar. She was the boss, bartender, and bouncer and a pretty woman for fifty years old. The slinky silk pajamas she wore were a little tight for her rice-fattened hips, but then not every G.I. in Vietnam was eighteen.

"Sure, mamasan, and make sure you bring us your best and youngest girls," Brian said as if he had been in here before.

"No sweat, all my girls numba one. You go sit now," she said with a smile, then screamed in guttural Vietnamese to a horde of hidden whores in the holding room.

Because it was only a few degrees cooler inside the dark bar than out on the street, we picked a table under a slow-turning ceiling fan. The loud whine of Vietnamese disco music blaring from a hidden cassette player was strange and shrill to my ears and drowned out any attempt at conversation. Almost immediately, two young girls appeared from the back room dressed in flimsy pajamas and made a beeline for our table. We eyeballed each other, smiles crossing our faces. "Here it comes," I said. "The moment has finally arrived."

A small heavily made up face leaned on my shoulder, almond eyes dark and luminous. I could feel her breasts rubbing against my shoulder blades as her right hand snaked down to my crotch. "My name Mary," she said in a soft seductive whisper. "You try me, I show you happy time. You like I sure." Tiny fingers played across the zipper of my pants, searching for a sign, urgent and active, like the practiced hands of a deaf mute, screaming some desperate message in sign language. My body, lulled into lethargy by a mixture of dope and beer, but mostly fear, refused to respond. I felt panic rise in my chest.

I looked from my crotch over to Brian. His macho act wasn't any better than mine. An older prostitute had her arms twined around his neck and was urgently cooing into his ear. "Come on, Joe. I show you really good time. Anything you like. Come with me now, you pay later." Her voice was whiny and edged with impatience as she tugged gently at his neck. She seemed a little older and more experienced than my girl and probably figured we were scared, drunk, stoned, or a mixture of all three. She spoke in quick Vietnamese to my girl and then both of them sat down on our knees, each one's left hand automatically going for our zippers. "You guys cherry," Brian's whore cried out. Brian looked at me and we both shrugged our shoulders. "No sweat, we wait till you ready," she said with an admonishing grin. I looked around the bar quickly. Now they all knew. "You buy us Saigon Tea, okay?" and before we could answer she called out to mamasan for the National Whores cocktail, a mixture of tea and water, known throughout the country as a ripoff drink but a required purchase if you wished to keep the girls at your table.

As Brian tried to smile at the girl on his lap and avert his stare from mine, I knew he felt guilty about dragging us into this. The truth was out. I wanted to push the whore off my lap and tell him I didn't care about remaining a virgin, that I wanted to save it for the girl I marry and not give it to a woman I did not love, to some poor little girl who chewed a wad of Juicy Fruit gum while she was being slammed against a wafer-thin mattress by one sweaty soldier after another. "Thanks, Joe, you pay ten dollar American, please."

I wondered how we could get rid of the whores without losing, in their eyes and ours, any more of our sagging masculinity—and money.

I felt a tug at the arm of my fatigue shirt and with relief turned my attention away from the table. A small dirty hand held a three-by-five index card in front of my face. Dressed in a ragged shirt and torn short pants, a boy about ten years old stood before me. His legs were filthy and covered with sores. He shifted his weight from one hip to the other, using his feet to chase the flies from the open sores.

The whore sitting on Brian's lap tried to push him away, but he held his ground, dodging her hand like a trained pugilist. The card returned to its steady position in front of my face and I read the neatly printed message: MY NAME CAO VAN TRONG, MY FAMILY WAS KILLED BY VIETCONG. PLEASE GIVE ME MONEY FOR MY LITTLE SISTER SO WE NO STARVE. GOD BLESS ALL AMERICAN G.I.

"Hey Joe, you give me money, please," the boy pleaded.

His smudged face cracked with a well-practiced smile, stained white teeth appearing beneath his chapped lips, and he looked me unwaveringly in the eye. I don't know if I was responding to his bravery for entering this den of whores, his index card message, or in gratitude for the interruption, but I reached into my pocket and retrieved a few dollars in Vietnamese money to give him. Before I could put the bills into his hands, the whore sitting on Brian's lap reached across the table and slapped the boy across the chest, knocking him to the floor.

"They lie too much!" she said. "This boy no orphan, he just thief who steal from G.I. You save money for Mary and me."

The boy stared at her with cold hard eyes, spat out a couple of Vietnamese curses on her dead ancestors, picked up his card, and moved to the next table.

Encouraged by the sight of money, the whores resumed what they thought was seductive enticement. "You come with us now, we teach you first time. No worry, Joe, same price, only five hundred piaster."

Knocked out of my intimidated state by the slap delivered to the boy, I stood up, dumping my girl on the floor. "Forget it, ladies. We have to get back to the base. No boom-boom today."

"Right," Brian yelled, also dumping his girl as he jumped to his feet.

The abrupt movement to stand up sent my head spinning and I felt a sudden urge to throw up. The local marijuana was all the barracks talk made it out to be. I tried to get my balance. All I needed now was to throw up or trip over something and this misguided fiasco would have its glorious finale. Suddenly, someone grabbed my right wrist and ripped my watch from it. I fell against the table, momentarily stunned. The orphan boy had slipped by the whores, who were trying to get us to sit back down, and quickly and deftly relieved me of my wristwatch and was out the door before I could regain my balance.

By the time Brian and I got out to the street, the boy had rounded the corner two blocks ahead of us. My nausea had passed, replaced by an adrenaline rush of anger. "God bless all American G.I.'s my ass." The new Seiko was a cheap one, easily replaced at the base exchange, but I ran after him, somehow believing if I caught him I might regain some of my shredded dignity.

Brian followed in our jeep on the street, and I cut through the marketplace. The low-strung myriad patchwork of canopies forced me to run bent at the waist. I kept my eye on his small figure as he wound his way through the dark passageways and stalls of fruit, meat, and vegetables. He knew the market well and moved quickly, nimbly skirting around the hawkers and merchants. My breath burst from my mouth in painful gasps, and my back began to spasm from its bent position.

He disappeared. Frantically, I jumped over baskets of cackling chickens, scaring them into a frenzied flurry of feathers and dust. I soon arrived at the open street, just as Brian drove around the corner.

"Did you see the kid?" I shouted.

Brian hadn't. We both looked up and down the empty street. I was panting, reeking of beer and pot which exuded from my pores with the sweat that soaked my fatigues and ran down my face. Brian, stoned, calm and recovered from the whorehouse debacle, drove off to search the alleyways behind us.

The street was deserted and very quiet. A half-demolished church, the largest building on the block, stood out from the other structures, most of which were completely destroyed and burned out. Surrounded by a cement wall, its height too high for anyone but an Olympic pole vaulter to negotiate, the church had to be where the child had gone. I ran toward the building.

The large wooden door of the church closed heavily behind me, as if blown by the wind . . . or pushed by someone? I pulled the .45 from my pants leg pocket and waited for my eyes to adjust to the darkness. A chill shot through me. What the hell was I doing in here alone? I had heard a thousand horror stories, from Brian, in triage, and around the wards. Vivid drug-induced flashbacks shouted out, rupturing desperately needed sleep or screamed from the center of a nightmare. Vacant buildings, booby traps, snipers, bouncing

Bettys hidden below floorboards that blow you up, out, and away. A Betty's the quickest way to buy the FARM.

I was instantly sober, and I cursed myself for my stupidity. My life for a goddamn watch! I started to back toward the door, scanning the rubbled interior. My eyes had adjusted to the dim interior, and except for my labored breathing, a dead silence blanketed the broken pews and fallen beams.

Seconds seemed hours as I backed away slowly. I relaxed enough to notice a marble altar which still stood intact at one end of the church. How many times had I knelt before a similar one in my hometown in New Jersey? Pillars of light shone down through the damaged roof, spotlighting broken blocks of cement and part of the altar. It reminded me of the light pouring through the stained-glass windows of Holy Cross Church where I was blessed, baptized, baffled, and bored. But here there were no colors . . . just golden columns, made luminous by the reflecting dust and shadowed by patterns from the jagged holes in the ceiling.

A scraping noise jolted me into the knee-firing position! I could see a large piece of plywood leaning against the side of the altar begin to move. It teetered on its edge and then fell to the floor with an almost silent whoosh, launching billows of dust into the still air. I closed my eyes and pulled on the trigger. The safety was still locked on. I snapped my eyes open, and at that moment a small naked infant stumbled out from behind the altar. He caught his toe on the plywood's edge and fell hard on his chin. The air was split with his high-pitched wail, and I remained frozen on my knee, the gun still pointing at him, my knuckle turning white against the locked trigger.

A small figure draped in white quickly emerged from behind the altar, scooped up the baby, and raised an arm in surrender.

"Please, no shoot! Only baby and me. No shoot, Joe," a girl's voice called to me.

The white blur of material with the baby in its arms walked carefully toward me. It was a very young Vietnamese nun. Her bare feet pushed the pebbles aside as she walked a well-worn path through the rubble-strewn floor. Suspicion shot through me. Could this be a trick? Was there a grenade under her habit? A gun under her veil?

Stopping fearlessly close to me, ignoring the shaking pistol, she held out her hand to help me to my feet.

"I sorry baby make you scared," she said, bending to dust the red clay dirt from my knee.

She backed up and straightened her habit. It was dirty and wrinkled, stained by spilled food and diaperless babies. She looked to be sixteen or even younger. Her face was beautiful, the eyes soft and sad, imploring me to lower the gun. She bounced the baby in her arms, never taking her eyes from my face, smiling, as the infant pulled at the soft skin of her cheek.

"You okay, Joe? You know, this baby like walk. He walk, walk, walk . . . all day. Never stop."

"What are you doing here, Sister?" I asked, still holding the gun pointed at them.

She looked around as if I was talking to someone else, then down at her dusty feet.

"We have no other place. American soldier come to our village. Fight. We must run." Her eyes filled with tears.

She turned around to face the altar and called out in loud Vietnamese. My heart began to race, and I pointed my gun toward the opening the plywood had covered. A second nun, much older and very tall for a Vietnamese woman, emerged with a dozen children quietly trailing after her!

The older nun snapped in quick Vietnamese, bringing the young nun running to her side. They conferred with urgent voices as I scanned the tiny faces, searching for the thief.

The children were a motley group, tattered clothes, no shoes, runny noses, and the beginning signs of malnutrition. Hiding behind the skirts of the nuns, they peered at me, afraid yet curious. It was probably the closest they had come to an American soldier who was not firing his weapon in a hateful frenzied rage or throwing things at them from passing trucks.

One child, a girl around eight years old, stood apart from the group, staring as if she knew me. Her face was round, open, and trusting. Suddenly, she was beside me. She slipped a tiny hand into mine, the one that didn't hold the pistol, and smiled up at me.

For a moment the building fell into complete silence, a dozen pair of almond eyes were riveted on me, watching

what I would do. Kiss her, kick her . . . or smile? I smiled
and as I dropped the .45 into my pocket, all hell broke loose
Like the crack of the starting gun for a fifty-yard dash, it sig
naled, as did my smile, friend. In a flash I was surrounded by
ten little children who quickly checked me out, especially the
hairy arms and hands, something missing in most Oriental
races. There was laughter and whispered fascination with
this tall, lanky, blond-headed American. The little girl still
grasped my large fingers trustingly, not joining the others,
not uttering a word, just gazing up at me, unsmiling, in a
way that made me almost uncomfortable. Likewise, I felt my
smile disappear. Her eyes were deep and looked wise beyond
her years. They seemed to be saying, "I know you" . . . or
"I know something about you."

The older nun silenced the children and looked at me with
a strict face. Her erect, ramrod posture made her appear
taller than she really was, and I felt myself shrinking.

"Why are you here?" she asked in perfect English.

"I'm looking for the little boy who stole my watch," I said
almost apologetically. "He ran in here. I saw him."

I put out my hand to indicate his height. As I did this, I
noticed my wrist was covered with blood, scratched by the
metal watchband as it was torn away. The young nun
reached for my hand to examine the wound, concern cloud-
ing her face, but was pulled back by the older one.

"As you can see, there is no boy here. So, you can go. The
children do not like the American soldiers."

"Where is he, Sister? Or do you want me to find him myself?" Her stern face reminded me of the very proper Sisters
of Mercy who were my childhood teachers. I was used to
dealing with them and pushed my cause further, adding a
tone of defiance to my voice. "I know he's in here. I know
he's one of your kids."

"He's not a kid! He's a man!" she shouted back and immediately slapped her hand over her mouth, realizing she
had given him away. For one instant her eyes were vulnerable. Then she quickly recovered her composure and asked
quietly, "What did he take?"

"I told you. He stole my watch, and I want it back." I
raised my voice, confident I would be able to intimidate her
now. I had the upper hand.

The young nun looked nervously at me, then at the older nun, before she ran back and disappeared behind the altar.

"He steals for us. You must understand. We have nothing . . . no food, no money, no place to sleep but this very cold, damp church. They are homeless orphans. Some of their fathers are American soldiers. Look at them." Her words shocked me but were true. I looked at the children quickly: pale skin, wisps of reddish-blond hair, eyes a little rounder than normal, and even one nose and cheeks peppered with freckles. Children of whores and the offspring of quick desperate romances in a war zone.

I looked back at the older nun, her face showing the strain of little rest . . . poor food and too much responsibility for their care. An imposing woman . . . perhaps fifty years old, her strength emanated from her like rays from a sun lamp, warm and constant, but dangerous up too close.

The young nun reappeared from behind the altar with the young thief. He was still sporting his infectious grin but stayed close behind her. She held my watch in her hand and was reaching up to give it to me when the older nun snatched it from her!

"What kind of watch is it?" she asked quickly, breathing hard, her eyes now blazing and fueled by a desperate survival instinct.

"Come on, Sister, enough games." I held my hand out to her.

"Is the watch valuable to you?" Her voice was hard. She allowed a silent pause . . . waiting for me to catch on.

"Okay, Sister, how much?" I felt defeated. "How much for *my* watch?"

"Your money will help us buy food. Please do not be angry. He steals so the children will not starve. He does not steal for himself."

I gave her twenty dollars. She still didn't return the watch.

"Just twenty!" She was disdainful. "That is only enough to feed us for two days!" She looked at me as if I had grossly underpaid an overdue bill. Echoes of the whining prostitute's entreaties reverberated in my head, and suddenly I was ready to pay double.

The young nun stepped forward, trying to smooth over the transaction.

"You know food costs too much in marketplace. They no can give free food to Sisters. Too many refugee come here."

The older nun shook her head sternly at the younger nun and said some words in Vietnamese. She quickly began to gather the children to return to their hiding place behind the altar, but the little girl holding my hand seemed reluctant to go. I knelt in front of her and asked her name. She just looked at me, then smiled. I hadn't learned any words in Vietnamese and figured she hadn't understood my English.

The young nun spoke. "Her name Thom. She no can speak anymore. She hear you but no can speak." Thom finally let go of my hand and followed the young nun and children back to their sanctuary.

"Please help us, young man." The nun was now imploring, her face softening, her eyes challenging me to live up to some unexplored image she seemed to see in my baby face. "We do not like to beg, but there is no other way. Please, young man, I know you are not like the others," she said, holding her hand out again.

She knew nothing about me, and yet standing there looking into her eyes I felt naked and ashamed.

I put another twenty-dollar bill in her hand.

"God will bless you for helping us."

She turned quickly and joined the others, who waited for her by the altar. The children laughed and cheered when they saw I had backed out the church door.

By the time I walked out into the street again the sun had set, and miraculously Brian came cruising around the corner.

"Christ, where the hell have you been?" he said, pulling the jeep to a stop in front of me. "Did you catch the kid?"

"Yes. Now let's get out of here," I answered and then looked away from Brian as we headed for the highway.

I was afraid to tell him about what had happened in the church. Afraid he would call me a wimp, and at the same time I really didn't care what he would say.

I felt vaguely different, clear and quiet, like the air feels before clouds gather to produce a storm. It was a strange ending of an afternoon that started with horror, then half-hearted plans for losing my virginity. Instead, I lost my watch and forty dollars. My first steps toward achieving manhood began not in a whorehouse but in a church and were only an initiation, a foreshadowing of what was to come.

"So, where's the watch . . ."

I didn't answer.

"That little kid suckered you out of it, didn't he?"

I looked at Brian's expectant, angry face and began to laugh. Brian looked back toward the road and started to shake his head.

"No. He didn't sucker it out of me. Someone else did," I said and laughed even louder.

— 3 —

Med Cap

Driving back toward the base, I told Brian about the nuns, described the orphans, and explained how the boy was attempting to feed the others by trading what he stole for food on the black market.

"And the nuns condone this?" he asked.

"They said it was the only way they could get their food besides begging."

"And you believed them, Hensler?" he asked accusingly.

"Why do you always call me by my last name, Brian? It's Paul, remember?"

He looked at me quickly, then smiled.

"Sorry, but are you sure they were real nuns? You know these people . . ."

"They were real all right," I said, interrupting him. "There was this older nun who reminded me of Sister Marie Jean, our principal at Holy Cross school. Even when I didn't do anything wrong, which I never ever did . . ."

"Right!!" he said, making a half-fumbled sign of the cross.

"Like I was saying, no matter what I did, somehow she could always make me feel guilty. Just like the nun in the church back there."

"Maybe she could smell the scent of the whores," he said, breaking into hysterical laughter, honking the horn, and swerving the jeep back and forth on the empty highway.

"Wait, wait, Brian. You haven't heard the best part yet."

"So, go on."

"I felt so guilty that I paid her forty dollars for a watch that only cost me seventeen and then forgot to take the watch back from her.''

"We can still go back for it if you really forgot to ask her for it.''

"What'ya mean 'if I really forgot'?''

"Come on, Paul. That old lady knew she had a sweet little Catholic sucker in her church the minute she saw you.''

I didn't have a quick flip answer to throw back at him. He was right. The nun was right. That beautiful little girl and those kids knew also. They made a connection with something inside me that was planted years ago by my parents, like the face of the dead soldier was now planted in my mind, never to be forgotten.

"You should have seen those kids, Brian. They looked pretty sick.''

I should have changed the subject, but I wanted to tell him how I felt when I saw those kids. And more, I wanted him to tell me it was all right for me to be sensitive, that I wasn't just stupid. I couldn't find the words.

Brian's face went soft, and he grew quiet. After a few minutes he said, "Like I said before, this war sucks. The worst thing is the kids. They don't have any say in this mess, but they're the ones who are always jumping rope right under one of our bombs.''

Now I was really confused. "I can't figure you out, man. You're the greatest medic in that hospital, then you scream at a bunch of little kids like some kind of jerk, and now you're telling me that you really feel sorry for them.''

"Don't get me wrong, Paul. Those street kids are turned bad by assholes like those guys in the whorehouses.''

"We were in that bar too, Brian.''

"Neither of us really wanted to be in that place, and you know it,'' he said, looking over at me.

"Then why didn't you say something?'' I asked.

"Let's forget about it, all right?''

"Brian, that's what you say every time I ask you a question, or you say 'I'm used to it.' I'd really like to know how you feel about . . .''

"You want to see the kids I really feel sorry for? Kids that really need a handout? Are you working Saturday morning?''

"No," I answered.

"Then you drag your ass over to the chopper pad behind the hospital at 5 A.M. and wait for me. You're going on your first Med-Cap mission."

"A what mission?"

"A Medical Civilian Assistance Program is what the name stands for, but save your questions until Saturday, okay?" he said.

"Yeah . . . Sure."

The Med-Cap team began to gather at the chopper pad about 5 A.M. I was early, but then I liked the early mornings in Vietnam when the air was the day's coolest and the sky was void of clouds or attack aircraft. First to arrive were two Navy Medics, or "Squids," as they were called. Brian arrived carrying medical supplies, which I helped him stack under the back seat of the Dustoff chopper. He rechecked the medical kits to be sure that nothing was forgotten and then told the pilot we were ready.

We sat in a small circle, drinking coffee, waiting until there was enough light for safe flying. Brian explained that the military had initiated the voluntary Med-Cap program as, first, a goodwill gesture and second, to keep the villages surrounding the military bases in Vietnam dependent and friendly. In exchange for free medical attention, it was hoped the locals would inform the military when the Vietcong visited their village or hamlet. The Squids said they had never heard of a village turning in the Vietcong and had many times even treated the Vietcong for gunshot wounds inflicted by our side. Before I could question the logic of healing the enemy so they could go on fighting, the chopper's turbine screamed into action.

At exactly 6 A.M. we ascended three hundred feet into the crisp morning air and headed for the South China Sea. We would be going to the village of Vinh Hy about 150 miles up the coast from Phan Rang.

It felt like we were riding on a magic carpet, floating along close to the ground, the deep verdant jungle out one open door and the sparkling blue South China Sea out the other. We flew over small villages, camphor smoke circling up toward us from breakfast fires, dogs and chickens running

from the unfamiliar sound of the chopper's air-cutting rotors. Fishermen heading out to sea in their long boats waved,
while farmers prodding their water buffalos through the
muddy rice paddies ignored us.

The chopper literally dove into Vinh Hy, a small village
pushed up against a steep green mountain on one side and
fronting a spectacular beach on the other. I felt as if we were
landing at Waikiki Beach or some beautiful resort in Mexico.
The locals were obviously used to the chopper's noisy and
turbulent arrival as they covered their faces and held down
the drying mats of rice and fish.

Before the swirling sand could settle, the villagers began
lining up outside a small hut which doubled as both class-
room and dispensary. The Squids were set up and seeing patients within minutes, explaining that they tried to move
through the line before news got out to surrounding villages,
bringing the residents from miles around to the free clinic.
Brian and I started another line for the children while the
Squids looked at the older patients.

I immediately understood Brian's feelings for these children. Pathetically poor and dangerously malnourished, they
were much more in need than the peanut girls and the street
thieves. As I looked at them, I was reminded of television
shows about the starving children of Africa. Like those children, it was not only because of war that they suffered but
also because of illiteracy and the lack of birth control. Eight
children from the same family stood before us, the father off
fighting for who knows which side and the mother trying to
squeeze one more drop of breast milk into her crying new-
born's mouth. The children, covered with sores, skin rashes,
and all in desperate need of dental care, still managed to
smile as we cleaned their abscesses and shot them full of penicillin. Brian tickled them as they passed in front of him, and
some returned two or three times for more of his happy treatment.

The adults quietly stepped up in front of the Squids,
nodded yes when asked if their arms, legs, stomach, or head
hurt, were given iron pills, diarrhea medicine, and a pat on
the back as they walked away.

At noon we closed the portable clinic and decided to take a
swim before heading back to the base. The chopper pilot, co-

pilot, and Squids were naked and in the water without a second thought. Brian and I were not too sure about stripping in front of fifty old people and children who were already in hysterics over the stark white American asses mooning them from the water. We finally gave in and joined the others, followed by the children.

It was like washing away time and the war and every unforgettable experience I had gone through since my arrival in Vietnam. The water was warm and inviting as we dove and swam and wrestled with each other and the children. Brian and I pretended to be sharks, sneaking up on the children from underwater. Then we would pop up, grab a shrieking child, and toss him back and forth. It was like being back with my brothers and sisters on the Jersey shore. We used to spend every summer day playing in the sun, our father, the shark, terrorizing us or teaching us to swim.

In an hour it was over, our chopper pulling up and away from Vinh Hy village. But for the first time I had something good to remember. Something to remind me of laughter and fun when we worked feverishly to keep alive another boy like myself.

— 4 —

Bad Tidings

After another uneventful day in the supply tent, I showered and walked over to the hospital. The fighting, wherever it was happening, had obviously increased, for as I entered the postoperative ward, a sea of white bandages filled every bed and overflowed onto the floor.

Nothing in my nineteen years of upper-middle-class Catholic childhood could have prepared me for this daily bombardment of visual horror. All nine of my brothers and sisters and myself had been carefully insulated from the harsher realities of life. The pain and suffering of the poor in our own country, and in places like Vietnam, were used only as playful lessons why we should never waste food. The savagery of modern war, or its reasons and political justifications, were never discussed at the Hensler dinner table.

Joan Kolarsic, one of the first female army nurses I met in Vietnam, rushed up to me.

"Hensler, I hope you're here to help out cause I'm short-handed tonight and that guy in bed six is driving me crazy," she said with the residual twang of a fading southern accent.

"Where do you want me to start, besides bed six?"

"Give two, five, and nine each a million and a half units of penicillin, then . . ." She looked down her list of doctors' orders.

"That's it for meds until nine. Then could you please tell the guy in six I'll be over the moment I get free."

"What's wrong with him?" I asked.

"He's going to die," she said. For a long moment she just

stared straight into my eyes. The words she had just spoken were repeated many times a day and seemed almost routine, but for some like Joan, they ripped away one more layer of toughness.

"He can have all the morphine he wants," she said, then walked away.

I gave the injections to two, five, and nine, who were resting comfortably. Number six was a young boy on a respirator. He looked like a young child, his face still free of a beard, maybe eighteen or nineteen years old. The right side of his chest had been blown away when a grenade he had hooked into his web gear was detonated by an enemy round. They had removed his right lung, most of his liver, his right kidney, and then closed him up, unable to repair the damage to his intestines and spinal cord. The surgeons had done their best but the damage was too massive to correct.

I walked up to his bedside and gently touched his hand. His eyes opened slowly.

"Is there anything I can do for you?" I asked. He did not respond. "Do you want something for pain?"

He nodded yes slowly, then grimaced as the respirator forced air into his left lung, pulling against the stitches in his chest.

When I returned to his bedside with the injection, he was trying to write something on a small pad of paper. I pulled the sheet off his right leg, washed a spot of skin with the alcohol sponge, shoved the needle deep into his thigh, and drove the plunger smoothly down the barrel of the syringe.

He turned the note pad so I could read it. "I'm scared," it said, then he grimaced as the morphine stung into his tissue.

"I know," I said but could not imagine the fear racing through this boy's mind.

"Is there anything I can do for you? Write a letter to someone?" I asked.

His eyes searched my face, finally focusing on my eyes. I handed him the note pad and pencil. He paused for a moment, then wrote, "I'm going to die, right?"

"Yes."

I had been with enough men now who had died, who appreciated knowing the truth about their condition. They could tell by your face if you were lying to them and became angry, seeing it as the final betrayal. Knowing the truth seemed to help the men come to terms, to write in a letter or say aloud what they needed to communicate of themselves. In the last hours they could speak the truth without fear, bravely telling of their confusion about killing, unfinished business, or the love for another, never to be realized.

His eyes were flying around like large brown marbles bouncing off the walls of a pinball machine, the morphine confusing him, scaring him, making him afraid of the final loss of consciousness. He scribbled quickly now, afraid he would not finish. "Help me to believe. Ask Him to forgive me for killing."

"Just by asking He already forgives you," I said.

He nodded his head.

"How long?" he wrote.

"I don't know. A few hours maybe. Can I write a letter for you?"

He nodded his head yes, but as I reached for the pad he slowly shook his head no.

"I have no one," he wrote. His eyes stopped dancing, and he stared at me, tears beginning to spill down his pale cheek.

"Hold me," he wrote, then looked back to my face.

I held his hand for ten hours until he died. He would close his eyes for a while and suddenly pop them open to make sure I was still there. Then he would smile at me and drift off again, reassured. The respirator continued its pulsing rhythm until its alarm sounded, and I felt the veins in the top of his hands slowly deflate. When Joan arrived to shut down the respirator, I placed his hand gently next to his body and walked away.

I sat in the hospital commissary till dawn, sipping coffee. I was numb and angry but mostly sad for the boy. "I have no one" rang in my ears over and over again.

I reported to my job from there, and after stacking supplies and delivering orders all day, I was ready to drop. At six

I mumbled, ''See you tomorrow'' to the supply sergeant and headed for the door.

''Hensler, Morris signed you up for guard duty tonight. First watch.''

''What?'' I said, nearly passing out on the tent floor.

''You report after chow.''

Six cups of coffee later I reported for my first watch and was now so wired I couldn't even sit down. It was a spectacular sunset, the bizarrely brilliant orange sky, beautiful and soft, in contrast to my dark feelings. The warm air and light felt seductive, luring me to relax and forget the young kid's hand.

In the guard tent after the first watch was relieved, I lay down and tried to sleep. My mind raced with images from triage. Torn limbs, gaping wounds, crying soldiers, and the boy. Holding his arms out to me. Hold me. Please HOLD ME.

Someone grabbed my arm and I shot to a standing position.

''Jesus, Paul, you okay?'' Brian asked.

''What are you doing here?''

''Joan told me about last night. I just wanted to make sure you were okay,'' he said.

We walked outside and sat against a sandbag bunker.

''Man, you look whipped. I should have let you sleep.''

''I can't. I wasn't asleep,'' I said, lighting a cigarette.

There was a long moment of silence between us. I could feel Brian staring at me, but I just looked straight ahead.

''Why do you let that place get . . .''

''I don't want to hear that bullshit, Brian. I don't know how to stop it from getting to me. I can't turn it off like you do. Not yet anyway.''

''Maybe you should stay away from the hospital for a while,'' he said.

''That's not the answer. It's not the work, and you know it. It's their faces. I keep seeing their faces asking me for the truth. Begging me to keep them alive or kill them.''

''I cried a lot too, Paul. When I first got here the hospital, the wounded, it all blew me away. I thought I'd be handing out malaria pills and treating the clap. No one told me I'd be closing the eyelids of dead teenagers or telling them they'd never walk again.''

"Then why do you come down on me so hard for feeling the same way you did?" I asked.

"Because I care a lot about you. I wish there was some way to keep you from . . ."

"From the truth?"

"Yes. Most people don't react like you, or like I did . . . We can't look at death and say, well, that's what happens when you have a war. We die a little every time one of these kids does and there's no way to turn it off. I don't know if it's a curse or a blessing to be sensitive, to cry, to care so much for people we don't even know."

"You still haven't told me how you deal with this place, with what's happening in this country," I said.

"I don't look at their faces anymore. I do Med Caps whenever I can and smoke a little dope so I can sleep. In other words, I still can't deal with it."

We sat in silence. The night air was cool. Suddenly I felt a wave of gratitude toward him. He had taught me everything I knew about hospital work. I wanted at that moment to tell him, to thank him, to say a thousand things, but the words to express my feelings would not come. They stuck in my throat like cotton.

"Thanks for telling me the truth, Brian."

"Ain't no big thing, Hensler, I mean, Paul. It's the only way."

There was another long moment of silence between us, but this time I was staring at Brian and he was looking straight ahead.

"There's something else, Paul. Something I believe we both feel but can't say in this gung-ho army. That is, not without someone calling us fags. . . . Do you know what I mean?"

"I think so," I said, lying and then instantly afraid that I had just admitted to some unspoken secret.

"It doesn't bother me to say it, Paul. I'll say it for both of us. I love you."

"It's true," I said, looking away from him.

Sensing I was embarrassed and may have taken his statement the wrong way, Brian said, "Listen, Paul, I'm not a fag, and I know you're not."

My chest tingled with warmth, yet I felt awkward. Here we were, two men sitting in the dark, a hundred more men only a few feet away and a war roaring in the distance, admitting a warm natural love for each other. I had never been able to say I love you to anyone. I couldn't even say it to my father. There was no way I could say it to Brian.

Brian jumped to his feet. "I gotta get going. You should sleep for a while."

"I'll try," I answered.

"You know, I watched you work with those kids on Med Cap, Paul. Your hands were meant to hold them. Not one of them was afraid of you," Brian said as he backed away to leave.

"And I saw you, too. You're the same."

"That's our problem, Hensler. We're the same."

He turned and was gone before I could think of a reply, but he was right. We were the same. I was no longer alone.

An hour later I was assigned to guard post number thirteen, physically exhausted but mentally excited and happy about my conversation with Brian. I could now work harder and, I believed, with less emotional strain at the hospital. My eyes wandered over the moonlit rice paddies beyond the barbed wire fence, a gentle breeze pushing at the rice stalks. They waved hypnotically, relaxing me, and I closed my eyes for a second to rest them.

A deep voice boomed above me, "Good morning, Private Hensler. You're under arrest!" I jumped to my feet and immediately started to sweat. Before me stood the Officer of the Day, a Warrant Officer from the motor pool. Not only had he found me asleep on guard duty, an offense punishable by death if the enemy had slipped by my post, but he had also taken my M-16 away from me while I snored away.

"I . . . um . . . sir," I stammered, fighting to awaken or return to my bad dream.

"Get in the jeep, Private," he said, giving me a shove.

We drove back to the company area in silence, where he instructed me to wait in my quarters until charges were filed and my company commander sent for me. Too exhausted to consider the implications of what had occurred, or what was about to happen to me, I fell onto my cot and instantly dropped into a dark, dreamless sleep.

—— 5 ——

Court-martial

I reported to my Commanding Officer at noon, starched fa
tigues, spit-shined boots, and scared to death. As I waited out
side his office, the company clerks stared at me and clicked their
tongues like old washerwomen admonishing a local boy for
missing church or worse. I didn't even know them, except for
the day I reported to the company and gave them my assign
ment orders. Nor had I met the company commander, al
though I knew what he looked like, having greeted him in
passing with a courteous salute. And now I stood before him
feeling dirty, accused of a serious crime, soon to be branded a
criminal, sent to prison then discharged from the service, an
embarrassment to my family and community forever.

"You have been charged with dereliction of duty, a viola
tion of the Uniform Code of Military Justice, Article 113.
You will be tried by Special Court-Martial as soon as a panel
can be convened. Until you are notified of the date of court-
martial, you are restricted to your quarters, leaving them to
report to your duty station, the mess hall, and the latrine
only. Do you understand, Private Hensler?" Captain Pier
son said, without ever looking directly at me.

"Yes, sir."

"You're dismissed."

"Thank you, sir," I said, then turned neatly on my heels
and marched back to my tent.

For the next five days my mind tortured me. Executed me
by firing squad. Hung me in the center of the company area
where my comrades spit at my dead gray body. Dragged me
naked behind a tank to a mass grave for the Vietcong. And

en kept repeating the image of the front door of my fami-
's house in New Jersey being slammed in my face.

On the sixth day Brian was waiting for me when I returned
om twelve hours of burning human waste, a job usually re-
rved for some poor Vietnamese laborer with fifteen chil-
ren.

"Paul, I'm going to speak for you and tell them what you
ere doing that night, why you were so tired."

"What ya gonna say, Brian? We were sitting up till three
lking about how much we loved each other?" I said,
ripping off my foul-smelling fatigues.

Brian looked at me, then started to leave.

"Wait, Brian. I'm so goddamned scared. Please . . . I'm
orry."

He came back and sat on my cot.

"Listen. Whether you know it or not a Special Court-
Martial is not as bad as a General Court-Martial. It'll be
kay. You should also tell them about the hospital and what
ou've been doing over there."

"You really think that will help?"

"I don't know, but you can't just sit there and let them
ang . . . sorry . . . punish you for nothing."

"I fell asleep on guard duty, Brian. They could . . ."

"Bullshit, Paul. You fell asleep guarding six trucks and a
ile of furniture for the Officers' Club—in a noncombat
one."

"Thanks, Brian. I'll tell them that."

At 9 A.M. on the 30th of May 1967, I marched into the
ness hall tent, stopped in the center of the empty room, fac-
ng a table behind which sat three men. Captain Pierson,
Warrant Officer Dunne, who filed the charges against me,
nd another captain I had never seen before.

I saluted and said, "Private E-2 Paul G. Hensler, report-
ng as ordered, sir."

"You may be seated, Private," my CO said.

Brian entered the tent and sat alone at the back.

Captain Pierson rose and began reading from a long blue
aper.

"Before this Special Court-Martial Board, convened at
Phan Rang, Republic of Vietnam, pursuant to Court-Mar-
ial Appointing Order Number 5, this headquarters, dated

30th May 1967, will be arraigned and tried: Private E-2 Pau
G. Hensler, RA 11-755-055, United States Army, 529t
Transportation Company. The charge: Violation of the Uni
form Code of Military Justice, Article 113. Specification: I
that Private E-2 Paul G. Hensler, United States Army
529th Transportation Company, APO San Francisco 96321
on or about 0545 hours, 19th May 1967, at Phan Rang, Re
public of Vietnam, being on post as a sentinel on post num
ber thirteen was found sleeping upon his post.''

"How do you plead, Private Hensler?'' Captain Pierson
asked.

"Guilty, sir.''

"Is there anything you would like to say, Private Hensler
before this board determines sentence?''

"Yes, sir . . . Sir, I realize I have committed a very seri
ous offense . . .''

"Stand up, Private, when you address the board,'' Cap
tain Pierson shouted, stopping me cold. I jumped to my fee
and stood at attention.

"As I was saying, sir, I realize I have committed a very se
rious offense, but I would like to explain why I was so tired
and fell asleep. The night before I pulled guard duty, I was a
the base hospital, helping out in Intensive Care . . .''

"You were what?'' shouted Warrant Officer Dunne, in
terrupting me.

"I was volunteering my off-duty hours. Helping the
nurses, sitting with patients, writing letters for them
and . . .''

"Hensler, you're assigned to the 529th Transportation
Company as a supply clerk. You're not a goddamned candy
striper. Your main duty is to this company . . .''

"Let him finish,'' Captain Pierson said, stopping Dunne';
angry tirade. I looked at Warrant Officer Dunne, trying to
figure out why he hated me. I had never seen the man until
he said, "Good morning, you're under arrest.''

"Go on, Private,'' said Captain Pierson.

"That's all I have to say, sir, except that the night before I
fell asleep I sat up with a marine until he died. I then pulled
duty all day and guard duty that night . . . I tried to stay
awake, sir, but I guess I couldn't,'' I said and then sat down
slowly. I blew it. I felt faint. They're gonna hang this little

candy striper by the balls, and that son-of-a-bitchin' Warrant Officer is gonna be holding the rope, I thought.

The board mumbled among themselves for what seemed like ten hours. Captain Pierson finally rose.

"Come to attention, Private Hensler," he ordered.

"It is the finding of this board that to the Specification and Charge, you are guilty. . . . Our preliminary sentence is as follows: The board orders that Private Paul G. Hensler, RA 11-755-055, 529th Transportation Company, Phan Rang, Vietnam, be confined at hard labor for six months, forfeit sixty-four dollars per month for a like period, and be reduced to the grade E-1. Final sentencing will take place after a short recess."

It's over. I will not live through six months in the Vietnamese sun cracking rocks. As the board rose to their feet, some of them beginning to talk about a dance at the Officer's Club that evening, Brian yelled from the back of the room.

"Excuse me, sir, but I would like to speak on Private Hensler's behalf."

"Identify yourself to the board, please," Captain Pierson said. The board sat down.

"My name is Specialist 4th Class Brian O'Shea from the Hospital Company, 44th Medical Brigade."

"Thank you, Specialist. You may proceed."

Brian walked forward until he was standing next to my chair.

"I have known and worked with Private Hensler for several months now and believe that with explanation you will find him not only highly motivated but an example of the superior attitude required of all of us to sustain this war effort," Brian said eloquently, and with a quick squeeze of my shoulder he continued.

"Although the hospital staff is totally capable of handling the workload produced by the escalation of this war, there are not enough ward personnel to deal with the psychological and emotional problems of the wounded and dying. Private Hensler has been volunteering his off-duty hours at the bedside of these men and has dramatically increased the morale of the ward personnel and patients."

"What is your MOS, Specialist?" asked Warrant Officer Dunne.

"I am a 92B10, sir."

"You're simply a medic then, right?" said Warrant Officer Dunne, looking quickly at the rest of the board.

"I am a highly trained member of the hospital staff, Mr. Dunne. There is nothing simple about my work," Brian fired back at him.

"What I'm getting at, Specialist . . . what is your name again?"

"O'Shea."

"Specialist O'Shea . . . What I would like to know is, what qualifies you to make very broad statements about the escalation of the war effort in Vietnam, and secondly . . ."

"That's enough, Mr. Dunne," said Captain Pierson. "Specialist O'Shea, do you have anything else to say specifically regarding the charges against Private Hensler?"

"Yes, sir. As Private Hensler told the board, the night before he was to pull guard duty he was asked by one of the nurses in ICU to sit with a young man who had been fatally injured in combat. The boy was eighteen years old and very frightened. Private Hensler stayed at his bedside for over ten hours until he died. That is all I have to say to the board, except one soldier who had no one else in the world did not die alone. I hope Private Hensler is there if I or any one of you are ever in the same position."

The board remained silent as Brian turned and walked out of the mess hall. There were no party discussions this time as they stood and filed quietly out the door.

Brian was waiting for me as I walked out into the blinding noonday sun. He grabbed my hand and shook it hard.

"I told you it would be okay."

"What makes you so sure?" I asked.

"Just trust me, Paul. I gotta get to work, so you come over later and tell me what they decided."

"If you get a postcard from Long Binh Jail, you'll know their decision," I yelled to him as he ran toward the highway.

Ten minutes ago I thought I was dead and here I was joking about Long Binh Jail. Somehow I wasn't scared anymore. Brian had spoken the truth. I could only hope that the truth meant as much to the board as it had to the boy.

An hour later I was once again standing at attention in front of the Special Court-Martial Board. Captain Pierson shuffled papers in front of himself, grabbed the long blue paper, and began.

"It is the combined decision of this Summary Court-Martial Board, Appointing Order Number 5, this headquarters, dated 30th May 1967, that in the foregoing case of Private E-2 Paul G. Hensler, RA 11-755-055, United States Army, 529th Transportation Company, only so much of the sentence as provides for restriction to the limits of the company and hospital area for two months, forfeiture of fifty dollars per month for two months, and reduction to the grade of Private E-1 is approved and will be duly executed."

I wanted to jump up in the air and shout.

"I wish to add the following advice to you, Private Hensler," Captain Pierson began, dropping the blue paper on the table. "Although I believe, more than some of the other members of the board, that you are to be commended for your work and willingness to learn at the hospital, your primary responsibilities are to this company, the 529th Transportation Company. You will be allowed to continue working at the hospital under one condition. If at any time in the future your section commander feels it is interfering with your primary MOS, you will be banned from any further involvement. Is that understood?"

"Yes, sir."

"You will report to Warrant Officer Dunne in the motor pool this afternoon to begin your extra duty."

"Yes, sir."

"You are dismissed."

"Thank you, sir," I said, saluting smartly and then quickly backing out of the room before anyone could change his mind.

When I arrived at the company motor pool, Dunne was waiting for me, hands on his hips, ready to explode.

"That goddamned hospital! You have no goddamned right being over there! I don't know why in hell you weren't restricted to your tent and the toilet. You are now assigned to me, Hensler, and I don't want to see you over there. Understand?'' he shouted, moving closer to me, saliva foaming at the corners of his mouth like a wild dog.

"Yes, sir," I answered.

"You will stay here and work with your own men and company. No more hanging around like a pussy with the nursies . . . shit . . . holding hands." That image seemed to push his anger beyond words and he began to sputter, spittle flying out of his mouth. "Do you understand me, Private?"

"Yes, sir, but with all due respect, I believe the court-martial board restricted me to the company and hospital areas, sir. I intend to continue volunteering every off-duty minute I have at that hospital, sir."

He stared at me as if I had slapped his face.

"You are already in very serious trouble, Private, but I'm going to help you straighten out. I'm going to keep you much too busy, doing every shitty detail I can think of. You will have no time for that hospital, of that you can be sure. Now go to the tool room, sign out a ball peen hammer, and report back to me on the double."

When I reported back to him he was standing next to a huge boulder that sat in the center of the motor pool, the 529th Transportation Company logo painted on one side of it.

"You see this boulder, Private?" he asked, slapping his hand on the boulder's surface.

"Yes, sir."

"I want you to make it disappear with that hammer."

"With this?" I asked, holding the hammer out in front of me.

"Correct. With that hammer. And when you finish with this boulder, I'll find you another one. This is your assigned duty now, Private Hensler. I expect to see you out here chipping away during your normal duty hours. Your extra duty will begin every evening at 1800 hours. Until further notice you are not to speak to anyone, eat with the men, or even shit with them. Do you understand?"

"Yes, sir."

"Then you may begin," he said, turned abruptly, and walked away.

For five days straight I beat on the boulder. For all my swinging and sweating, the boulder bore only ten or twelve white spots and a few scratches. The bloody blisters on my hands began to turn into calluses. I remained silent and beat on the rock rhythmically, lulling myself into a hypnotic trance, deafening my ears to the jeers and comments of passing drivers. I never left the rock even to pee, opening my fly and urinating right there in the middle of the motor pool.

At night I washed dishes next to an old betel nut chewing mamasan, who never quite understood why I was doing her work. Then I burned human waste and rounded out the day either on guard duty or cleaning the company commander's latrine.

About the sixth day, Warrant Officer Dunne got bored with thinking up extra duty and assigned me to the motor-pool tool room, where I cleaned and counted greasy tools. Some of the motor-pool personnel started to come around to the tool-room window to tell me they didn't think I was such a bad guy. As far as they were concerned, I had passed the initiation rites into their fraternity.

When I finished my two weeks of extra duty, I applied for a transfer to the Hospital Company. It was denied.

—— 6 ——

Brian

Six weeks after my court-martial, I received orders transferring me to another transportation company in Cam Ranh Bay. Although I had repeatedly requested a transfer to the Hospital Company, Warrant Officer Dunne refused to forward my request to Battalion Headquarters, stating that they could not authorize the additional training I would need for the transfer.

I walked over to the hospital to tell Brian about my new assignment and found he was out on another Med-Cap mission, this time to one of the inland villages. My restriction had kept me from going on any of the missions, but Brian always gave me a full report on his return. Today they were late. No one had heard from the chopper and I decided to go to the operations center to see if they knew where the team might be. Frequently the choppers were diverted to pick up or transfer wounded from one evac center to another, but normally the Med-Cap team would radio in their delay and new approximate time of arrival.

When I was about ten feet from the operations center, its door burst open and two medics ran out.

"What's up?" I yelled at the first medic.

"A Med-Cap team's been shot up."

"O'Shea's team?" I yelled as he passed me.

"Yeah. A troop ship's bringing them in. Be here in five minutes."

Before I could ask if they knew how many were injured, or who was injured, the medics had entered the emergency room to alert the triage team. I walked slowly to the chopper pad to wait, praying silently for the first time in years.

Please, God, let him be alive. I promise you anything, just let him be alive. Let one thing in this lousy war turn out okay. The triage team gathered behind me to watch the sky and wait for their friends.

In the distance I could hear the clacking of the choppers' huge rotors, a sound every soldier in Vietnam knew and would never forget. Its air-splitting clap, clap, clap was a welcome sound on the battlefields and meant troop replacements, resupply, medical evaluation, or protection from above. Tonight its clattering sound was ominous. The air was taut with tension, each one of us hastening the chopper to land, yet dreading to know its cargo.

Brian was on the second stretcher out. He was covered with blood and dirt, and lying on top of him was a Vietnamese child, also covered with darkened blood. He moved his arm up the child's back. He was alive, and so was the little girl, who looked about four or five years old. She tightened her grip on Brian's fatigue shirt when we surrounded the stretcher. She had a gaping wound of the neck, but the bullet had luckily missed the carotid artery, which pulsated weakly in the center of the wound. As one of the nurses lifted the little girl off Brian, his mangled left hand fell away from his stomach. His bloody hand was a mass of twisted tissue and bone. "Oh, thank you, God," I thought. "It's only his hand."

As we were carrying his stretcher to the triage area, Brian lifted his head and vomited a gush of bright-red blood. Immediately one of the nurses suctioned his mouth to make sure his airway was clear. We began to cut away his blood-soaked fatigues, and I started to cry. His body looked like Swiss cheese, with horrible gaping gunshot wounds running from his chest over his heart down to his groin. Brian looked at me as I rushed to start the IV. He knew. The doctor listened to his lungs and slowly shook his head no. A nurse was watching his blood pressure, trying to read the dial through tears which dropped onto her green surgical shirt.

"Would you like some morphine, Brian?" the doctor asked.

Brian slowly shook his head no.

Several more members of the triage team entered the room now, having finished with the other wounded. His friends gathered around him. A medic covered Brian's chest with several towels as he searched the faces in the room. He smiled at me weakly, then wrapped his right hand around my wrist. He seemed so calm, almost ready. There was no anger in his eyes, or pain, only peace.

"Will you make me a promise, Paul?" His voice startled everyone in the room because of its strength.

"Sure. Whatever you want," I said, trying to dry my eyes without him seeing.

"Promise me you'll take the little girl to the nuns."

"What?" I was watching him but not listening.

"The nuns in the old church. Promise me you'll take her to them when she's okay," he said. A new trickle of blood appeared at the corner of his mouth.

"I'll do it. I'll take her there. Don't worry . . . Please Brian . . . ," I said, taking his hand in mine, unable to finish the sentence.

"I hope . . . Paul," he said, starting to struggle with the blood and mucus in his throat, "you never forget me . . . that you never forget what we learned . . . and never let anyone tell you you're not a good person, Paul. All of us are great. Right?" he said, his eyes sparkling with a radiance that lit his face.

The nurse indicated to the doctor his pulse was weakening.

"Brian," I said but again could not continue. I wanted to say to him then, say the words that had stuck in my throat before, "I love you, Brian. I respect you." But again, standing there watching the life slip away from him, I couldn't say it. He gave my hand a gentle squeeze.

"I meant what I said," he said weakly.

"I feel the same . . . but how can you be so calm?"

"Nothing hurts," he said softly, and then he was gone.

— 7 —

Sucked In by God

The little girl filled the emotional gap left by Brian's death, and although it was against all regulations to treat Vietnamese civilians at any military hospital, six-year-old Nguyen Mai became the star patient of ward five. She was very scared and asked for nothing, lying quietly, not quite able to comprehend the attention lavished on her, probably the most food and care she had received in her life. Even the ambulatory patients, men who had been wounded by her people, came to her bedside with small gifts, an extra soda or a game they hoped would make her laugh.

I stayed away from the hospital, except to visit Mai, putting in my time at the supply tent and waiting for my day of transfer. Surprisingly I was not angry over Brian's death. Just sad that perhaps many more would die, alone, before the fighting ended. The military strength in Vietnam grew day by day, the fighting escalated, the number of dead and wounded increased, and who could I tell? Who would listen to a nineteen-year-old private who felt that *nothing* was worth the death of one man or the maiming of thousands of teenagers? I wondered as I walked through the wards if I was the only one who hated this war. When I sat with the little girl at night, it would all reverse on me. That's why I would never make anyone understand—because I myself was years from the answer. She was six and had already seen and suffered through more of life than most adults. It was all very simple, team A against team B, and the goal posts were graveyards; she was the football.

One of the young army doctors who was doing his internship in Vietnam (an experience no medical school could hope to duplicate) performed some experimental plastic surgery on Mai's neck wound. By taking a patch of skin from her buttock, he was able to neatly cover the exposed muscle tissue and the carotid artery without an ugly scar. Five weeks after she had been wounded, Mai was ready to leave. The nurses and doctors gave her a little going-away party, at which she wore a beautiful Chinese dress one of the corpsmen had brought her from his R&R (Rest and Recuperation) leave in Hong Kong.

With her gifts neatly tucked into a pillowcase, Mai and I drove toward Phan Rang City. She watched me closely for a while and then moved over to sit next to me. I put my arm around her like I used to hold my little brothers and sisters and pretended to steer the jeep wildly, bouncing and shaking until she finally laughed out loud.

I retraced my chase through the city streets and after a half-dozen wrong turns found the old church. Carrying Mai in my arms I picked my way through the debris-littered floor and walked behind the altar. Their possessions were there, some clothing, cooking utensils, and a couple of blankets, but no children or nuns. The shrill screech of children's laughter from behind the building led me out the back door of the sanctuary and into a walled-in courtyard. It looked like an elementary school playground with the children chasing each other back and forth across the cracked cement. The younger nun, her habit tucked up under her belt, skipped easily over a thin rope being swung by the watch thief and another little boy. The older nun was sitting on the ground with four of the little ones, tickling and singing to them. Her thin face looked gentle and soft, almost childlike in her concentration to entertain the babies.

The young nun spotted me, untied her skirt from her waist, and ran over to greet me.

"Hi, Joe. What happen to little girl?" she asked smilingly, taking the child from my arms and inspecting the bandage on her neck.

"Her village was attacked by the Vietcong. I think her parents . . . Can you take her?"

"I know what you say. Can do. We take care of her," she said, pinching the little girl's cheek, trying to make her smile.

Suddenly the older nun was beside us. "We do not have

enough food to feed her. We hardly have enough for the children now." Her face had quickly lost its soft look, replaced now by a stern, schoolmarm set, eyes penetrating and accusing.

I could feel myself immediately stiffening, ready for the onslaught of guilt this erect noble-faced woman managed to draw out of me.

"I already gave you some money, Sister . . . I'm sorry, I don't know your name."

"My name is Sister Hoa, and this is Sister Tuan," she said, pointing to the younger nun.

"Sister Hoa, I did give you some money and my watch . . ."

"That was more than a month ago and enough for only a few days," she said, taking another step toward me. "Just look at the children here," she said, pointing across the courtyard. "Do they look like they are well fed? Do they look healthy to you, young man?"

"Sister, I'm just doing what . . ."

"I would like to take the child, but we are desperate now and can barely feed the children that we have."

"Please, let me finish what I was going to say, Sister," I said, raising my voice. She took hold of the wooden crucifix that hung around her neck, fingering it gently, waiting for my tongue to totally entangle me in her web.

"I promised a friend I would make sure the little girl was taken care of, and that's why I brought her to you. My friend didn't give me any money, Sister, and I'm only a private . . ."

She continued to look at me, her face unchanged. My excuses obviously had not worked.

"Please, young man. I know you are a Christian. Look hard at us. We do not wish to steal from you, and we are very tired of begging in the market and getting only food meant for the pets of the rich."

Bull's-eye. I had seen the refugee-swollen streets, where thousands begged their meals and where a nun's habit had no effect. It meant nothing in a country slowly dying from within. I gave her all the money in my pocket, about twenty-two dollars and thirty cents. I even pulled out the linings to show her there was no more.

"I knew you would help us. I know God will reward you for your generosity," she said, quickly pocketing the money.

"Do me a favor, Sister. Don't ask God to do anything for me, okay? I'm already in enough trouble."

"Oh, you must try trust Him," the younger nun said with a smile. "I think He the one who bring you to us. Maybe He have plan for you. You know I was . . ."

"Thank you, Sister," the older nun said, stopping her. "Tend to the children now."

"Yes, Sister," Sister Tuan said, ushering the children back to the jump-rope area.

"And I must tend to the little ones, but please stay and visit for a while if you like."

"I have to get back to the base," I said, feeling like I had just been had, then politely dismissed.

Sister Hoa stood for a long moment staring at me as if there were something else she wanted to say. Or perhaps she was waiting for me to offer my help or money in the future. Whatever she was thinking, I felt like I was sitting under the interrogator's lamp. The little watch thief broke the ice, running up between us and offering me his hand.

"My name Cao Van Trong. You mad I steal your watch?" he said with a wide smile. He looked like a puppy who had peed on the bed and knew vaguely he had done something wrong but hoped his innocent smile would help you forget it. I smiled at him and put out my hand.

"My name's Paul, and no I'm not mad at you." I clasped his thin hand in mine and he pumped it vigorously. Sister Hoa patted Trong gently on the head and walked away. The minute she was out of earshot, a torrent of broken English tumbled from his mouth.

"You no worry about Sister Hoa, she like sergeant. Very tough guy but not all time. I know she tell you I steal for kids, but Trong also steal for Trong. We friends now, I steal for you too!" As we sat down together on the steps he lowered his voice, then looked around quickly to make sure no one was listening. "I take you go numba-one boom-boom house. They have numba-one girls, not like Mama's. That place numba ten. No sweat, you no have pay me. Okay?" he whispered conspiratorially, as if we understood each other, man-to-man, the only males in this compound of women and children.

"How old are you, Trong?" I asked, unable to believe he knew what a whore was or did.

"Me *moi* . . . no, I ten year old. That how you say ten in Vietnam. *Moi.* No sweat, Fall. I teach you speak Vietnamese."

"It's not Fall. It's Paul, with a *P.*"

"Paul, right? Sure, I can speak numba-one English."

"Right. How long have you been with the Sisters, Trong?"

"Long time now. We come from Song Pha, it north from Phan Rang. Too many American come Song Pha, fight VC, so we run. We walk maybe fifteen day, and no place to stay. That why the children die. No food, no place sleep. We get cold and Sister Hoa get sick, too. Then we come Phan Rang, stay here," he said, starting to scratch one of the hundred mosquito bites that covered his legs.

"What about your family, Trong?" I asked, then immediately wished I hadn't. His face clouded and he looked down at the ground. I had just asked another one of my famous stupid, immature questions. Trong, like the other children playing around us in the courtyard, was an orphan.

"I'm sorry, Trong."

"No sweat. I man now. Soon I go to fight the Vietcong. I kill them," he said, a frightening anger filling his eyes.

The mute child Thom approached us now, carrying Mai. She sat down next to me on the step. Mai reached out for me, and I lifted her onto my knee. As was my way as a child to change a tense or uncomfortable situation, I became the comic. I began bouncing Mai on my knee, pretending we were driving crazy again. Trong and Mai began to laugh, while Thom clapped her hands together and smiled. I looked over at Trong with crossed eyes, and he rolled onto the ground, laughing uproarishly, slapping his bare feet on the cement floor. His laughter was contagious, bringing the other children over to see what was so funny, and I began to laugh too. For the first time since Brian's death, I felt my spirits lifting.

Entertaining the children, making silly faces, and bouncing Mai on my knee reminded me of my own family. It was impossible to keep from laughing when one or more of us were together in the same room. It became a contest to see who could say the funniest thing or be the most outrageous. One of my sisters, Margaret, never failed to amaze us with her impersonations of our parents or friends, comically but expertly mimicking their voices and mannerisms. In that environment of happiness and laughter, I grew up, and now with more and more children gathering around to watch me make a comical fool of myself, I was sharing those wonderful memories with them. It seemed I was giving them and myself an interim cure-all for the reality that surrounded us. Laughter.

Suddenly, I remembered I had left the borrowed jeep in front of the church and that I had to get it back before the motor-pool dispatcher missed it. I said good-bye to the children and nuns and walked quickly out through the church. I heard bare feet scraping over the cement and turned to find Sister Tuan and Thom following me.

"When you come back, Sister Hoa say bring milk . . . please." She smiled her childlike smile.

"I can't come back, Sister."

"You not come back see your little friend? And Thom like see you again." She pushed the beautiful little girl toward me to make the point.

"Sister, like I told you before, the only reason I came back today was to bring the little girl to you, and I'm sorry but I can't help you. Besides, I'm being transferred to another base soon so I won't even be here."

"Then maybe you bring milk for your little friend before you go away . . . Yes?"

"No, Sister." I took another step backward toward the door.

"Oh," she said quietly, her shoulders dropping in resignation. "Then Thom and I wish God to give you good luck."

I didn't answer as I got into the jeep and waved good-bye. They didn't wave back but stood there and watched me drive away from the curb. I looked once more in the mirror, and they had not moved, standing at the church door, Sister Tuan gently stroking Thom's long black hair.

The following Saturday I was back at the church. All week

long I had thought about them and what Trong had said to me. I stumbled through the church carrying two twenty-five-pound bags of powdered milk.

"Trong! Come help me." My shouts echoed through the stone building, and soon Trong appeared from behind the altar, several of the children and Thom following him. Sister Hoa appeared a moment later with a baby in her arms.

Just as Trong met me I dropped one of the bags and it landed hard on my foot. The children broke into screams of laughter as I hobbled around, feigning pain and howling like a wounded wolf. Their laughter invaded the reverent stillness of the old church, and now even Sister Hoa was laughing.

"We are most happy to see you again. Our prayers were answered." Her face was still severe and she looked tired, but I could feel the sincerity of her words.

"Well, Sister, I'm leaving for Cam Ranh Bay on Friday, so I thought I'd bring you some stuff before I left. It will help for a little while anyway."

"Yes, it will. And I am sorry you are going away. The children have been talking about you since you were here last week. Trong told me that when the war is finished he wants to be your brother!"

I looked over at Trong, who smiled back at me, a little embarrassed that Sister Hoa had shared his secret with me. Sister Tuan entered the church now, returning from a begging run to the marketplace. Her face literally lit up when she saw me.

"Oh, Paul, you come back," she cried merrily. "Sister Hoa tell me I crazy when I say, 'No sweat, Paul come back,' but I know; something tell me you like children."

"I came back to say good-bye. I'm leaving Phan Rang on Friday, Sister."

When I finished speaking, Sister Hoa moved closer to me, her bespectacled eyes on my face. I suddenly felt hollow in my stomach. I was happy about being transferred away from the tool room and Warrant Officer Dunne, who was still trying to figure out who borrowed the Commanding Officer's jeep a week ago, but for some reason I felt guilty about leaving them.

"Take us with you to Cam Ranh," she said softly. Everyone in the church fell quiet waiting for my response.

I was stunned by her request and stumbled with my answer. "What . . . I can't, Sister. I'm sorry."

"We cannot stay here any longer. The children will never be well until I can find some place dry and warm for them to sleep. Please. I am begging you to help us. You can find a way," she said, pleading now with tears filling her eyes.

"I'm flying there on an air force plane, Sister. They won't carry Vietnamese civilians. I have done all I can for you and the children, Sister . . . I have to go."

Every one of them was staring at me like I had just condemned them to death. Maybe I have, I thought, looking at their runny noses and open sores.

"All right, Paul." Her addressing me by my first name unnerved me. "We thank you for all your help and will pray that God will watch over you," she said and with a few quick words in Vietnamese led the group back toward the altar.

Once again I backed out the church door, and once again I felt like I had done something terribly wrong.

Dear Father Sullivan,

I went to church today, and like you told us right before our first Holy Communion, I didn't run, talk, chew gum, or spit on the floor, because it's God's house. Well, Father, I met God today in one of His more run-down houses. He talked like you . . . but He looked like Sister Mercy with slanted eyes.

— 8 —

The Catholic Convoy

As I drove back toward the base, I tried to convince myself I had seen the orphan group for the last time. I worked at feeling good about having done all I could for them and rationalized their condition to be unchangeable by anyone, at least until the massive war machines were stopped. A second later I remembered Brian telling me about the children he really cared for, like those we saw on my first Med-Cap mission. The kids at Vinh Hy were no different than the orphans, but their chances of surviving were better. Time, and a little Western technology, would keep them alive longer, healthier, and in a simple way happier. But the orphans were suffering and dying because of Western technology—war machines that took their parents away or made their tiny homes disappear in a flash of thundering fire and smoke. They were thirteen children and two Catholic nuns against a hundred thousand refugees—running and stealing to stay alive.

That night I decided to try and change the odds in favor of the orphans. The idea seemed impossible until I received orders to make a last round-trip supply run to Cam Ranh Bay. There would only be three trucks in the convoy. I could make a quick detour to the church, hide the orphans in my empty truck, and drop them in Cam Ranh Bay. I was afraid at first; another court-martial would be the end of me. Warrant Officer Dunne would probably volunteer to shoot me himself. But the more I thought about it, the more I believed it was right and surely what Brian would have done.

Six of us met in the motor pool, a driver and shotgun passenger for each truck. I quickly picked the smallest vehicle, a three-quarter-ton pickup, and followed the other two trucks out the main gate toward Phan Rang City. My passenger was a young guy, totally green, having arrived in Vietnam only a couple of weeks before. The way he nervously smoked cigarettes, chewed gum, and grasped the stock of his M-16 reminded me of my first trip from Cam Ranh to Phan Rang. The driver, a tired Southern hippie, had chewed tobacco and had terrified me with war stories about five-ton trucks being blown into scrap metal by Bouncing Bettys, a fifty-five-gallon drum of gasoline, sitting on an explosive charge, detonated by the slightest pressure. "Never did find that one dude's head," he said, drooling black tobacco juice down his chin. "They just threw a coconut into the body bag so's it looked right." He laughed as I barfed my lunch all over the Vietnamese countryside.

Just as we entered Phan Rang Village, I pumped the clutch and gas pedal at the same time, stalling the truck and scaring the hell out of my passenger.

"What's wrong, man?" he asked.

"Not sure. Just watch for kids with grenades," I yelled as I jumped down from the truck. He clanged his steel helmet onto his head, almost knocking himself out. I ran over to the other two trucks, pretending to be pissed off.

"What's up, Hensler?" the driver from the first truck yelled down to me.

"Plugged fuel line, I think. You guys drive out to the edge of the city and wait for me."

"Plugged fuel line, my ass, Hensler. You gonna go plug your mamasan real quick, right?" he whispered back with a stupid grin crossing his face. "You got ten minutes, then we go on without you."

"I'll catch up in five," I yelled, running back to my truck, dodging the shoeshine boys and dope peddlers. After pulling up the hood to feign repair, I noticed three shoeshine boys and one old woman standing at the curb with their hands up in the air. After doing a double take, I walked around the curb side of the truck slowly and found my combat-ready supply clerk pointing his M-16 at them, sweat coursing down his panic-stricken face.

"Put that thing up, asshole," I shouted, scaring him.

"Man, just look at them. They's Vietcong for sure. Just

like the pictures I seen in *Life* magazine," he said, spit gathering at the corners of his mouth.

"I said put that weapon up . . . Now!"

He released his white knuckle grip on the trigger and slowly lowered the rifle.

"First of all, they're not Vietcong, or you'd already be dead. Second, always put a clip of ammo in a weapon before you point it at someone, then they won't know you're an asshole."

He shot a quick glance down at the empty chamber of his M-16 and almost fainted dead away.

I pulled up in front of the church and ran inside. The nuns and children were eating a breakfast of bananas and rice and looked up at me surprised—but not shocked. Sister Tuan had told them I was sent by God. They seemed happy that He had decided to send me back to them so soon.

It was apparent they were used to moving on short notice, for within five minutes they had all their possessions, including their unfinished breakfast, loaded into the back of the truck. Once everyone was in position I told them to be very quiet, gave Trong the peace sign, winked at Thom, and then lowered the canvas flap to cover my Catholic cargo.

My front-seat passenger stared at me all the way out of Phan Rang, and only after we met the rest of the convoy and headed for Cam Ranh did he speak.

"You gonna tell me about the gooks in the back?" he asked.

"Gook in Vietnamese means shit. You call some old papasan a gook and he'll blow your balls off, and you tell anyone about the orphans I got back there and I'll let slip the heroic story of you holding a ninety-year-old Vietcong grandma at gunpoint with an empty rifle."

"Hey, man, I'm cool. I like orphans. Don't worry about me."

"What's your name?"

"Jody. And you're Paul, right?"

"Right. Just wanna get your name straight, in case."

He shot a quick worried look at me, then turned his attention back to the passing countryside.

* * *

Cam Ranh City had become as crowded with refugees as Phan Rang. I had traveled through the small city on several convoys but did not remember the conditions being this bad. Every square inch of the city was crowded with makeshift shelters, black-market stands, and even a few two-story refugee huts.

I let the two other trucks pull ahead through the crowded streets and finally made a sharp right turn down a side street.

"Hey, man, ain't the base that way?" Jody yelled, pointing behind us.

"Shut up and start looking for orphanages."

"What? Hey, why don't you just let me off here. I'll walk the rest of the way," he said, looking more worried.

"Keep a sharp eye out, man. I heard the Cong in this area disguise themselves as old ladies with black teeth," I said, flashing him a sadistic grin.

"Just fuck you, Hensler. Everybody makes mistakes."

Sister Tuan stuck her head into the front cab and shouted, "Stop, Mr. Paul," scaring Jody so bad that he hit himself in the forehead with the muzzle of his M-16.

We pulled up in front of a schoolhouse whose front courtyard was packed with children. Sister Hoa had only to speak to the harried matron for a moment to find out that their temporary orphanage was totally overbooked. We circled Cam Ranh City several times, stopping at every seemingly empty building, only to find it locked, full, or uninhabitable. After two hours of searching, I finally pulled the truck over to the side of the road and went back to talk to Sister Hoa.

"Please, you cannot leave us on the street. The children are sick already, and . . ."

"Then what am I supposed to do with you? I'm an hour late reporting for my pickup. The Military Police will be looking for me soon, Sister."

"Please, Paul," she said, knowing that calling me by my first name unarmed me. "Just one more time. Maybe near the back of the city we will find something. We have not looked there yet," she said, finishing with a coaxing smile.

"Sister . . . Oh, forget it. We'll take one more look, but if we don't find anything, I'm gonna leave you."

She didn't answer but continued to smile and gathered the

children closer to her. I looked across their faces, feeling my frustration mounting. She was fighting dirty. Using the children as her armor against me, and all I could do was stand there, looking stupid and feeling totally defenseless.

I circled the town again, checking all the back streets until I found myself on a dirty alley unable to turn around. When we reached the end of the alley, I tried to turn, hit a fence, ran over two parked bicycles, and panicked. Cursing and stomping on the accelerator, I crashed through a fence and ended up in a black-mud quagmire. Again I floored the truck before we sank too deep, and spewing rancid smelling mud up on our hood I spun out of the sewer into an open field. Now I was really pissed and drove like a madman over small gardens, chasing squealing pigs and sending chickens and a few locals running in fright. Every bump we hit sent us bouncing and lurching around the front seat, accompanied by squeals of fright and volleys of giggles and laughter from the children. Jody held on for his life and kept popping terrified looks at me, sure now that I was loaded on local pharmaceuticals.

After a breakneck tour of the Cam Ranh City garbage dump, we ended up in a large field with a single half-demolished building in its center. The structure turned out to be an old rice storage barn that appeared to have caught fire, burning out one end of the building and about three acres of field around it.

I stopped the truck at the side of the barn, and when I lifted the canvas flap to let my passengers out, billowing white smoke enveloped me. A bag of powdered milk had split open and literally coated the inside of the truck. Everyone except Sister Hoa was in hysterics, covered with white powder and looking like a herd of ghosts. Sister Hoa, peering over the tops of her milk-blocked glasses, was angrily wiping the sticky powder out of a crying baby's eyes.

"I think I found a place, Sister," I said, trying not to laugh as I helped the children out of the truck.

"You are lucky we can hold our breath. This bag broke a long time ago!" she said, stepping down and dusting herself off.

Jody came around the back of the truck and stopped with a

gasp. "And I thought you scared the shit outta me . . . Just look at them kids," he said, laughing, until I hit him on the arm to remind him of the nuns. "Oh, sorry, Sisters."

Sister Hoa took one long look at the old barn, pulled her glasses off, and turned back to me. "We can't stay here. This place is for animals to sleep . . . We are not animals." She planted her hands defiantly on her hips.

"This is it, Sister. This is the last stop. If you don't like this place, which happens to be the only empty building we've seen all day, then I'm sorry. You find a better place on your own."

"You would leave us here? The children will be very cold at night and get even . . ."

"Don't do this to me, Sister," I said, interrupting her. "No matter what I do, you make me feel like your problems are my fault. They're not, and you know it. Now I have to get to the base. I'm already two hours late. You stay here and maybe when I get back in a couple of days I can help you fix this place up. But for now, this is it, like I said before."

"Hey, man. You can't leave these people here," Jody said as he helped the last child out of the truck.

"Shut up and get back in the truck. We're leaving," I said, shoving Jody toward the cab.

"We wait for you, Mr. Paul," Sister Tuan said, trying to break the angry impasse. Sister Hoa turned abruptly, grabbed Sister Tuan's arm, and walked into the barn.

For one quick moment I felt I had finally won—or perhaps was right for the first time. As I started the truck's engine and waved good-bye to the children, who were already dirty from the sooty walls of the building, the victorious feeling left me. Somehow I sensed they were forever connected to me. One lecture from my mother, one memory of love, something indistinguishable but very strong, would not allow me to just turn away and forget.

As I drove toward a dirt road at the end of the field, I caught sight of Trong in my side mirror, his tiny legs pumping like pistons, running after the truck. I stopped, and he quickly caught up and jumped onto the washboard.

"No forget. We friends, right?" he said, then threw something in the window and disappeared back toward the barn. Jody jumped up off his seat, sure Trong had tossed a grenade in on us. He picked up what Trong had thrown. It was my gold watch.

— 9 —

Confined at Hard Labor

Fifteen minutes after reporting to my new company, the 410th Transportation Company (TS), in Cam Ranh Bay, I felt like Warrant Officer Dunne had gotten his wish that I be confined at hard labor. My new assignment was unloading huge freight ships of their military cargo from 6 P.M. to 6 A.M. six days a week. And I thought it was hot in the supply room! Teams of five men per cargo hold descended into the boiling bowels of the ship and shuffled pallets of cargo into the center of the hold, where they were winched up and off the ship. Two lucky men, the winch operator and a signal man, stayed topside in the cool night air and directed the cargo onto waiting trucks. Bombs, bullets, beer, and Band-Aids poured off the ships and were hauled away to bulging warehouses, the front lines, and, I was sure, the black market. When a ship was empty and riding high at the pier, we quickly lowered her back down to the water mark with military equipment: tanks, trucks, howitzers, and aircraft, grotesquely bent and twisted by modern war. As I watched a five-ton truck being tied down on the deck, its cargo bed twisted like a piece of licorice, I flashed on twenty men riding in the back, smoking cigarettes, laughing, telling jokes, and then being blown off the face of the earth.

For the first two weeks my body tried to die after every shift. All night long the calluses on my hands throbbed, muscles I had never used before bulged, and more sweat than the water I drank all night soaked my fatigues. The twelve hours of daylight were spent trying to sleep in a 110-degree oven tent with twenty radios blaring Beatles and blues. Cassette tapes from Ma, Pa, Billie Bob, Mary Sue, and a bark from Fido whispered their love to Johnny in Nam and nearly drove me crazy.

To make matters worse, the powdery fine-grained Cam Ranh Bay sand, whipped around by the slightest breeze, permeated my body, bed, breakfast, and breathing. It was either sweat in my sandy bed, sweat in the sun, or dig a hole in a sand dune and hibernate. Too many snakes out there for me. A few of us would hitch a ride to a pristine beach nearby and sleep under a palm tree all day, taking an occasional romp in the surf to keep the body temperature down. On our one night off a week, most everyone went to the Enlisted Men's Club, a movie, and a certain few, straight to the local whorehouse village.

Within three weeks I was bored to madness and began to think about the children and nuns. The orphanage was in an off-limits area, but so was the whorehouse village—the holes in its barbed wire fence big enough to drive a tank through. Every time I checked the time, my gold watch reminded me of Trong. It also reminded me of Brian, whose death was still painful enough to keep me from looking into hospital work again.

On payday, a rather depressing time for me, as I was now making a grand total of $105 per month, I went to the PX (post exchange or department store on a military base) and bought four cartons of cigarettes, two cases of beer, two cases of Coke, and two bottles of Four Roses whiskey, my total monthly ration. The guys giving me a ride toward Cam Ranh City never even questioned my destination. It was common practice to trade PX goods on the black market, bringing one enough worthless Vietnamese money to hang out in a whorehouse for a week or purchase a brick of primo local marijuana. The driver was a little shocked when I asked him to let me out in the middle of nowhere, but I could see the old barn from the road.

"Hey, man, is you crazy?" a thin black G.I. shouted over the rattling, rumbling engine.

"No, I want to walk for a while."

The driver and his second passenger watched me fumbling with the boxes and bottles, looked at each other, and shrugged their shoulders. "You all just have a real good time in the middle of that field now, you hear," he yelled as the truck pulled away.

I got about two hundred feet into the field, and the children spotted me. Trong led the group in a race to see who would reach me first. My spirits lifted with the sound of their high lilting voices, calling my name and chattering in unintelligible Vietnamese as we walked back to their temporary orphanage.

They had done what they could to fix up the old barn by closing the open end with thick matted palm. Half of the dirt floor was covered with their sleeping mats, each child's few possessions folded at the end of the mat, while the other half of the floor was still exposed but swept clean. The nuns had made a small partition with a torn blanket for their own sleeping area, and as we entered the barn Sister Hoa appeared from behind the blanket.

"I'm glad you have returned. We all prayed for you to come," she said, her eyes dropping from my face to the PX goods in my hands. Her eyes shone through her smudged glasses. I could tell she was thanking God and already planning what each of the items could be exchanged for at the market.

Before I had a chance to put the two cases of Coke down, we were on our way to the market. Trong carried the whiskey and cigarettes, I carried the Coke, and Sister Hoa marched ahead of us, her gait almost light and girlish, carrying the two cases of beer. Trong tried to imitate Sister Hoa's bouncy walk but quit the first time she turned to see what we were laughing at.

The marketplace was teeming with people, caged chickens, ducks, pigs, and was thick with a smell that jolted me into breathing through my mouth to avoid the assault on my nostrils. The midday heat accentuated every odor in the crowded two-block area, mixing overpowering wafts of acrid dried fish, sweet fruit, and black market French perfume. Trying to walk through the place was like stepping into a grocery store after an earthquake . . . only inches between the eggs and fish. One step off balance would cost you plenty.

Sister Hoa became the shrewd, tough commander, bartering forcefully with the vendors, and although I couldn't understand her quick Vietnamese, I could tell by the exasperated expressions on the stallkeepers' faces that at least two times out of three she got her price. One old lady even tried to exchange a little girl for a case of Coke. She was either an orphan or perhaps one child too many for some family. Sister Hoa gently stroked her hair as she spoke to the old woman, and by the disappointed expression on the child's face I could tell Sister Hoa was saying a polite "No."

Within twenty minutes my monthly rations had been exchanged for a live pig, three live chickens, fifty pounds of rice, ten smelly fish, two bottles of soy sauce, a bottle of fish sauce called Nuc Maum (the worst-smelling liquid on the face of the earth), forty cans of condensed milk, and two large baskets of fruit and vegetables. Trong and I gathered all the food in one pile and were ready to leave, but Sister Hoa had disappeared.

"Hey, Joe, you like ride?" a woman's voice asked from behind me. When I turned around, Sister Hoa was sitting in the passenger seat of a three-wheeled Lambretta, smiling playfully, and patting the seat next to her in the tiny cab of the truck. The Lambretta pickup truck was the workhorse of Vietnam but definitely not made for tall Americans. The driver and Trong were in hysterics watching me maneuver my long legs into the tiny front cab.

Puttering up the hill, the Lambretta loaded with food, we were like Santa arriving with a tropical sleigh full of presents. When I tried to pay the driver his prequoted fare, he looked around at the children and politely refused the money. "You tell me any time you like, I go here. No sweat. You like kid, so I give no charge," he said, flashing a wide toothless grin.

"Thanks, papasan," I said with a gentle pat on the back.

"No. You say, *Cam Un*. That thank you."

"O.K. *Cam Un*, papasan."

The old man drove away, waving to the children as he turned toward the road.

The atmosphere was active and light, the children laughing and playing tag in the field as Trong and I, aided by Sister Tuan's many suggestions, tied together a flimsy fence for the pig. Time flew, and before I knew it the sun was setting, leaving me only about an hour to report for duty. Sister Tuan invited me for dinner, and I told her perhaps the next time I would stay.

"You will like our food. Thom and I number-one cook," she said with a smile. I realized I had not paid Thom or any of the children much attention. Next time, I thought. I'll jump rope with them like we did at the church. Sister Hoa came out of the barn carrying a crying baby and quickly handed the diaperless little boy to me.

"I've got to go, Sister," I said, trying to hand back the baby. She seemed not to hear as she stared up at the roof.

"Will you come back again?"

"Yes, Sister."

"Soon?"

"On my next day off."

"Do you think you can help us fix the roof?" she gestured up with her thin hand, the long sleeve of her habit falling back to her elbow, revealing a thin ivory arm. Her upraised arm looked delicate, startlingly white in contrast to the tanned rough skin of her worn chapped hands. For a moment she was not the ramrod of righteousness and authority I had chosen to project on her; she seemed vulnerable, helpless, and suddenly very human. I wondered why and how she had become a nun, and why she had chosen the enormous responsibility of caring for the orphans of Vietnam.

I looked up at the roof. "The whole thing needs to be rethatched, Sister, and that will take a lot more money than I get paid."

She looked at my face, then at my watch. My stomach flip-flopped. Suddenly she took the baby from my arms and started to walk away. "You'll find some way, I am sure. See you soon," she said as she continued into the barn.

After saying my good-byes, Trong and I walked down the hill. His short legs double-timing to keep up with me.

"Paul, you want I take you go numba-one boom-boom house?"

"Not for a while, Trong. You heard Sergeant Hoa. I gotta save my money for a new roof," I said, slowing a little so he could catch up. "And thanks for giving me my watch back."

"Oh, no sweat," he said jauntily, as if he had made me a

gift of the watch in the first place. "I get many more. Cam Ranh have many boom-boom house, many G.I.'s go there."

I stopped walking and looked down at him as he came to a halt in front of me. I remembered how pissed off I had been at him when he stole my watch in Phan Rang. Any other dude, drunk or stoned, would have killed him! I wanted to lecture him, make him understand he could get hurt, but looking down at his proud face, feeling his eagerness to be accepted by me as a friend, not as a child, I held back my words. Instead, I pulled the watch off my wrist and gave it to him. He looked at me startled and uncomprehending.

"Thanks for giving me back the watch, Trong. But instead of going to the whorehouse and trying to steal another one, why don't you hold onto mine. You can give it to Sister Hoa so she can trade it for food, or maybe you should save it and we'll use it to buy some stuff for the roof . . . okay?"

He looked down at his feet, quiet and unresponding. Now what had I done wrong? These people were impossible to understand. When he looked up, I saw puzzlement in his eyes. I realized that he had not understood me. Why would I give back what I had chased him for, screamed at Sister Hoa over, and then paid forty dollars and forgotten? By giving me the watch he was showing me his loyalty, his desire to return to me something I valued. It was his token of our friendship.

Trying to salvage the situation, I said, "Look. You hold my watch for me until I need it again, okay? I have an idea for how to get some money."

Trong immediately brightened, and he slipped the watch over his thin wrist, where it hung like a huge medallion. "Okay, I hold watch for you, no sweat, Paul." His face was excited as he asked, "You got idea for you me make money? We be partners, right?"

Double lie. I had no idea how we could make a little money together, but assuaged by his happiness I lied. "Sure. But it's a secret. I'll tell you the next time I come here, but first you have to make me a promise."

"Sure. You tell me what, I promise."

"Promise that you won't go to the boom-boom house without me. Ever."

"Sure. But when I take you I know numba-one girl who like . . ."

I clamped my hand over his mouth and tickled him down onto the ground. "You go to the boom-boom house without me, and I'll tickle you till you die and go to heaven."

"Okay, okay, no sweat . . . But I no can go to heaven. Trong go to . . ."

Again I stopped him with some vigorous tickling. I saw a truck approaching and ran toward the road, calling back to him, "See you, Joe."

"Okay, Joe. You numba-one Joe," he yelled, as he got up from the dirt.

The truck slowed and I jumped into the back with several other soldiers. I waved at Trong, who flashed me the peace sign. He was silhouetted black against a golden orange light, standing like a small tree, erect and alone in the open meadow.

"Hey, man, who's the little dink?" one of the G.I.s asked.

"He's one of my kids," I said, still looking out the back of the truck.

"What? . . . How long you been in the 'Nam,' man?"

My lie to Trong about having a way for us to make some money unexpectedly turned into a truth a few days after my visit to the barn. One night when dinner break was called I decided to stay behind on the ship and skip the meal of reconstituted potatoes, tasteless meat, and yeastless bread. I wandered around the upper decks of the freighter, staring out over the silent bay, wishing I could stow away and wake up in America or any other country but Vietnam. I heard one of the winches operating on the stern deck and walked to the railing above the cargo hold. One of our team sergeants, a tall lanky Texan, was operating the winch by himself, a fairly difficult task without a signalman to direct the load from below. Without incident, a pallet of Hamm's beer appeared from the dark hold, dangled in midair for a moment, and then, instead of moving it toward the dock, the Texan carefully winched it out over the water. I quietly followed the pallet and looked down to find four Vietnamese men treading water next to the ship. Slowly the pallet lowered, hit the water, and, proving a basic principle of physics, floated. The swimmers unhooked the winch cables and quickly and quietly began pushing the heavy load into the darkness.

A couple of nights later I watched a repeat of the incident, except that the second time the pallet was lowered directly into a waiting boat. This guy really had balls. I decided to approach him, let him know what I had seen, and see if he would let me try the same thing. One pallet of Hamm's beer not only would fix the roof on the orphanage but leave them with enough extra beer to feed them for a month.

I walked down the stairs slowly, coughing a couple of times.

"Hey, Hensler . . . Why ain't you at lunch?"

"I can't handle that crap. It all tastes the same to me."

"I know what you mean. Why don't you walk up to the ship's galley. They'll give you something. Makes 'em feel like they're helping our guys in the war," he said offering me a cigarette and then lighting it for me. There was a long, very uncomfortable moment of silence between us. I had no idea how to get into the floating-beer conversation.

"What's wrong, Hensler? You wonderin' about where that beer's goin', right?"

"I think I've figured that out. I wanna know if you'll let me do the same," I said, a little surprised at my straightforwardness.

"As long as you don't screw up the market in whores' village. Help yourself," he said, flicking his cigarette into the bay.

"I've got other connections, so don't worry."

"I ain't worried. But if you get caught, it's your ass, and if you get me caught, I'll get your ass . . . You understand?"

"Yeah . . . Sure . . . Thanks."

"You better try for some food, Hensler. Your shift starts in ten minutes. Tell the cook I sent you. He gets free beer and broads at my whorehouse. You too, anytime."

"Which place is yours?" I asked.

"The Southern Comfort Bar, right on the beach."

"I know the place," I lied. "I'll stop by next time I'm in the village.

"Anytime, man. And remember, you get caught, I can't

help ya,'' he warned and backed away, flashing me the power sign, a raised clenched fist that I thought was used only by our black brothers. Maybe it was a warning. Cross this guy, or screw up his black market dealings, and I could be guaranteed making the headlines of tomorrow's *Stars and Stripes,* the military newspaper: THE BODY OF AN UNIDENTI-FIED, SKINNY WHITE SOLDIER WASHED UP ON THE BEACH THIS MORNING. IT HAD BEEN WEIGHTED DOWN WITH CEMENT COM-BAT BOOTS. Details, page 6.

The following Sunday I decided to stop at the market and buy some candy for the children before going to see them. A Red Cross truck slowed for me and I climbed up into the back. That is, I climbed into heaven. The back of the truck was loaded with fresh, fragrant, still-warm doughnuts, something I hadn't seen for almost eight months. I ate them until I couldn't swallow the dry delicacies anymore. As the truck passed the path up to the orphanage, I threw half a case into the brush at the side of the road so I could pick them up on my way back. When the truck entered Cam Ranh City, I waited until we were in a congested area of the city, then jumped off the truck with another case of doughnuts in my arms, and ran into the marketplace. I had just committed my first overt act of thievery, but I was convinced the children needed food more than a bunch of rear-echelon clerks needed the fattening pastries.

My expectations for the exchange of the sweet treats for food was more than met. I had a box full of diamonds! I held court in a corner space, holding up the wax paper packets with two doughnuts in each bag, while people pushed and crowded, offering me money, chickens, vegetables, fish, and fruit. Unfortunately, the only words I knew in Vietnamese were *stop, go, hello,* and all the curse words. It got hotter as the crowd moved in, and finally three little boys pushed through, grabbed a handful of doughnuts, and ran. Within a second, a free-for-all began. Doughnuts, chickens, and hands flew through the air. Then everything became quiet. The crowd parted and Trong and another one of the boys from the orphanage marched up next to me. He was shouting, pointing his fingers at the people and then me. Like a meticulous drill sergeant, he had the people in an orderly queue within moments. He paraded up and down the line, inspecting the merchandise they had to trade and presetting the price. "No, no," he would say disdainfully, "that chicken too old. No good." He argued for a minute more and like Sister Hoa got the price he wanted, eight doughnuts for one old hen.

With Trong's organized system we were quickly surrounded with a huge pile of food. I bought us all a Coke and pumped the boys' hands thanking them for their help.

"Paul, I tell you we make good partner. What else you like me sell?" he asked, his face wreathed with smiles, his stained teeth protruding like popcorn.

"I'll tell you when we get to the orphanage."

"Okay, partner, I get water now, see you later."

"Bye, partner," I said as the two boys disappeared into the crowd with their water bucket and carrying sticks balanced neatly on their heads.

"Uncle Paul-san," one of the kids yelled as the Lambretta came to a stop in front of the barn. Uncle Paul. I was nineteen and the rich uncle to thirteen beautiful children . . . Rich? . . . Never! Needed? Yes.

"Oh, Mr. Paul? . . . Again so soon you bring us food?" Sister Tuan yelled as she ran in from the field, followed by six children. She looked in the back of the Lambretta and began to jump around like a puppy. It amazed me that she was truly a nun. She was so ingenuously childlike, bubbling with energy and enthusiasm. Wiry and slight, her movements were birdlike and quick. Except for her soft feminine face, she could have been a young boy.

Next to appear was Sister Hoa, her habit newly washed and sparkling so white in the midday sun she was almost a blinding blur as she walked toward us. She watched the children and Sister Tuan unloading the food, crossed herself, and looked up at me with pious eyes, the sun glinting off the gold rims of her glasses. "Bless you, bless you, and you will stay and eat with us, correct?"

Up to now I had been a ride for them, the delivery boy sent by God, or the G.I. who might fix the roof. Today for the first time I was helping because it was fun and what I wanted to do on my day off. Now, all I wanted was to get to know them better, ask the thousand questions I had gathered since

I met them, and maybe they like Brian would get to know me. "That'd be great, Sister. I'll stay."

"That is good. Now you play with the children while Sister and I prepare our meal," she said and like my mother preparing for a big holiday meal began handing out chores to Sister Tuan and some of the older children.

"And Mr. Paul, we have a special treat for after our meal," Sister Hoa called to me as she entered the barn.

Trong arrived with the water buckets, suspended under each end of his bamboo carrying stick and sloshing over the rims as he hurried toward me. The walk from the village had taken him only twenty minutes, about ten minutes under the normal time, and his reddened face and sweat-matted hair said he must have run.

"So what took you so long?" I asked smiling.

"You try. I think you cannot do," Trong said, wiping the sweat from his face.

"I'll bet you a dollar I can," I said, pulling a crumpled dollar from my pocket.

"Sure, but I no have dollar," he said, pulling out an empty pocket.

"No sweat," I said, pushing him out of the way and maneuvering myself under the carrying stick. I simply could not lift the cans. They were two five-gallon cans of water and I could not lift them without feeling the stick was going to cut my shoulder in half. Trong helped me up, mainly so that I didn't spill the water he had carried so far, then put out his hand, dirty palm up.

"All right, Trong," I said, handing him the dollar, "what's the secret?"

"No secret. You just be strong like me," he said, popping into a Charles Atlas pose, with a wide smile on his face. I chased him out into the open meadow where a group of children were jumping rope.

Trong stood on a box opposite me, and we swung the rope in a high loop, a welcome change from the taut tiny arcs the other children turned for themselves. They squealed with delight as they jumped, always facing Trong, because I would make faces at them, causing them to miss. After each child had taken his turn, they insisted it was my turn.

"No way," I said, but they persisted, knowing I would give them a good show. The thought of my long legs and big feet trying to clear the rope convulsed them with laughter. It amazed me how easily they laughed, how a small amount of attention and caring extracted from them a devotion and love that was heartbreaking. The only adults in their lives were the two nuns. I was probably the only man they'd ever come close to, and what an example I was. Nineteen years old, just coming out of adolescence, scared and homesick . . . But at least I had a family to remember.

One of the boys brought another box so he could turn the rope with Trong. I tried to hop the first turn but my heavy army boots felt like their laces were tied together.

"All right, guys, I'll get it this time." My coordination was totally off, and my feet became entangled in the rope. I hopped around like a crane caught in a net, waving my arms like wings and howling. The children were hysterical, rolling on the ground, and the more aggressive ones, led by Trong, threw their arms around my legs, trying to knock me down. They were laughing so hard the tears streamed down their dirty faces, and finally with too many little bodies hanging on my knees I rolled onto the ground and began the free-for-all.

Someone called dinner; one second I was covered with laughing children and a moment later they were tearing for the barn.

I joined the line at the small washbasin, then was led by Thom to my place on the mat which was spread out for all the children to sit on. Two large pans of chicken and vegetables, a pot of rice, soy sauce, and some raw cilantro were set neatly in the center of the mat. The nuns filled each child's bowl with rice, added some of the broth from the chicken, and placed a pair of chopsticks onto the bowl before giving it to a child. Thom sat next to me, prepared my bowl, and then very slowly demonstrated how to use the chopsticks. I managed to spear rather than lift a piece of chicken and was about to put it in my mouth when I noticed that everyone was silently staring at me. Sister Tuan led the children in "Grace," sung in a beautiful chanting style. With "Grace" out of the way, I expected all hell to break loose, but unlike my large family, where the temptation to fire peas across the room was uppermost in our thoughts, the children just sat quietly and talked among themselves and with the nuns.

I copied the children, lifting the rice bowl to my mouth, and shoved the chicken and some rice in with my chopsticks. Not hard at all. The chicken was delicious, exotically strange to my meat-and-potato taste buds. The smells and taste of garlic and ginger were heady and pungent, the vegetables crisp and fresh-tasting. Fish sauce, hot peppers, soy sauce, all offered a variety of new taste sensations to the simple meal of chicken, rice, and vegetables. I, like the children, ate heartily, savoring my first home-cooked dinner since my arrival in Vietnam.

Thom watched me closely and filled my rice bowl each time I emptied it. She moved like a cat, graceful, lithe. Her constant stare, her adoring eyes, no longer made me feel uncomfortable, and I even felt warmed by her insistence on sitting next to me. I found myself studying her face. Her features were exquisite, her skin like tawny satin with an apricot glow. She was beautiful, and it saddened me she couldn't speak. Perhaps she could learn again. Sometime soon, I thought, I'll ask the Sisters.

After dinner the nuns went around the circle, telling me each child's name, pronouncing it slowly so that I could then say it properly. Mai, Linh, Tuyet, Trong, Ling and another Ling. Hi, Soung, Kiet, Thom, Nguyet, baby Sam, and baby Lei. Sister Tuan then interpreted questions asked by the children. Where was I from? How old? Why was I so funny all the time? Finally, from Trong, "Tell about your family." Before I could answer, Sister Hoa produced a large cloth-covered tray and set it in the center of the mat. The children whispered and rubbed their hands together, ready for the special treat she had promised. She pulled the cloth aside and there, stacked neatly in a pile before us, were about three dozen doughnuts.

"Jesus," I blurted out, remembering the doughnuts I had thrown at the side of the road. "Sorry, Sisters, but where did you get these?"

"Oh, the children found them on the highway. Another

gift from God, I think," she said with a quick wink of her eye.

Thom and I sat together outside the barn watching Sister Tuan chasing the children around the meadow. Sister Hoa came over and sat down beside me, still drying her hands. Neither of us spoke for a long time, savoring the beauty of the late-day sun and the happiness that rang out from the meadow beyond us.

"The monsoons will be here soon, Mr. Paul," she said with a quiet relaxed voice. "Do you think we can fix the roof?"

"I think so, Sister. I think I have a way to get what we need," I said, not really wanting to talk. It occurred to me that she had not asked me how I had gotten the food today, or what I had stolen—and traded. Nor did she ask about the money or stolen goods it would take to fix the roof. She merely accepted it gracefully, no questions asked. Whatever was stolen to feed them was a gift from God.

It was another one of those intimate moments for me, planted by the love of my parents, the sharing of good and bad times with my brothers and sisters. It had made it impossible for me to forget the children, and it drew me to their happiness. The food and stolen goods were my admission ticket to where I felt alive and needed. At home in New Jersey all of this was free; the love and security of my big family was taken for granted. Away from them I had to search and now had finally found a place of many similar joys.

"I must see that the children get to sleep soon," Sister Hoa said as she rose to her feet. "We will see you again soon."

"In a few days, Sister."

"That is good. The children will be pleased. God bless," she said as she walked toward the barn, her white habit whispering across the grass like a floating ghost. I said good-bye to Thom and began to walk down the road. Trong padded up behind me and grabbed my arm. "Wait. You no tell me what we do next," he said, trying to catch his breath.

"Can you swim, Trong?" I asked, making swimming motions with my arm.

"Like shark. What you want?" As he said this his face grew more intense, now the consummate business partner.

We sat down in the middle of the road and planned the great Hamm's caper with wild drawings in the dirt. When we finally parted, Trong was literally shaking with excitement and ran as if he were being chased back up the hill.

— 10 —

The Orphanage on the Hill

When lunch break was called, the stevedore crew left the ship quickly. My shift leader stopped by my side and pointed out to sea, pretending he was trying to show me something.

"I've got a bottle for the deck watch. We'll be in the main gallery, and all you've got is ten minutes to get what you want off this ship," he said softly, checking to make sure we couldn't be heard.

"Thanks."

"Forget that shit. You now owe me, Hensler." And with that he turned and climbed the stairs toward the bridge deck.

It was another balmy full-moon night, and I was sweating like a nervous teenager about to kiss his first date. I ran to the oceanside railing and found Trong and two little helpers sitting in a small paddleboat below. He grinned up at me and gave me the peace sign, our signal that he was ready. His smiling face comforted me, but I was still so nervous I cracked my nose on a thick support cable as I turned toward the winch. Bright shooting stars behind my eyes and a ripping pain in my nose took me to the edge of passing out. I stumbled around for a moment, fighting to keep on my feet.

After hooking up a pallet of Hamm's beer to the cables, I climbed up to the deck and sat down behind the electric winch controls. I had only watched the winch operators, a job coveted by the chosen few because it kept them out of the hot storage rooms below. I prayed that, like driving a car, there was nothing to it—I couldn't have been more wrong. With two handles, one for left- and right-line tension and the second for the up and down movement, practiced coordination—not one of my stronger traits—was the secret. The pallet banged against bulkheads, the ladder, other pallets of beer, and everything else down below before it finally appeared above the hatch entrance. Beer from punctured cans sprayed out over the deck like a spinning lawn sprinkler. I got it up; now how the hell did I get it over the side of the ship? As I sat there trying to figure it out, the load began to drop slowly from the weight on the cables. Gently I pulled the left/right handle and the load shot up into the air, now spraying me with beer. Two more gentle manipulations of the handles and the pallet began to drop and move toward the right. Before I could counter the movement, the pallet dropped too much and neatly ripped a section of the ship's cable railing clean off the deck. Suddenly, I heard screams from the paddleboat.

"Hey, Paul, what you do?" Trong yelled, being soaked by a shower of beer and railing parts. "Hey, this smell numba ten."

I said a quick prayer and began to lower the pallet slowly, but now I was really in trouble. There was no way for me to know when the pallet would be low enough for the boys to load the beer into their boat! Reverse, I thought; bring the load back up a little, and then check to see how far down it was to Trong's boat. I pulled the handles, both in the wrong direction, and then there was this terrible sound of cracking wood and screaming boys.

It was too late. I stood looking down at Trong and the boys, trying to hold onto both the boat and the beer. The pallet had landed in the center of the paddleboat, sinking it. The pallet bobbed in the water like a giant cork, but the boat poked its stern out of the water and with a final flurry of bubbles disappeared into the dark water. The other boys, either the boat owner or the sons of the boat owner, swore at Trong in excited Vietnamese. Trong finally grabbed onto the pallet and began to push it toward shore. The other boys, realizing that the beer would be their payment for the lost boat, began to help. Trong shot several quick glances up at me, his beady little eyes angry but determined. The three swam away from the ship's lights and disappeared into the shadows. I leaned on the railing for a while longer, wiping the blood from my nose, straining to hear the kids kicking and pulling the beer toward shore.

I thought of Trong, struggling out there in the dark bay and felt awed by his courage. He would be plenty angry with me tomorrow but quick to forgive his partner in crime. A shudder of warmth ran down my spine. Trong had become my only friend since Brian's death and in many ways was an easier friend to have. No heavy conversations, self-examination, or guilt. Only laughter and lots of lessons from a pint-sized ten-year-old. Maybe some day soon I could say the words I had been unable to say to Brian and now felt for my little partner. Trong would understand the words . . . I love you.

When I arrived at the orphanage the following morning, Trong was waiting for me. He was pacing back and forth outside the barn. I couldn't tell if he was fuming or trying to figure out how to explain what happened after he got to the beach. When he saw me, he stopped pacing and stood, his short arms folded across his chest. The children were all silently waiting for the confrontation, squatting in strategic ringside seats, whispering among themselves. Sister Tuan looked up from her dishwashing, and I could see she was holding back laughter as she smiled at me, then looked over at Trong.

Trying to change the mood of the situation, I ran up to him, scooped him up from the ground, and gave him a big bear hug.

"What happen your face, Paul?" he asked, pointing at the small cut on my nose and the beginnings of a black eye.

"And what happen your face, Trong?" I asked. He had a beaut of a shiner under his left eye. We both began to laugh, followed by the children who now swarmed around us. Sister Hoa came out with a semicold bottle of Coke for Trong and a cup of coffee for me. Trong sat me down on the rickety bench, handed me his Coke, and began to tell me the story of the failed beer caper.

"The boy who help want to take all the beer. I say no can do, so we fight, but they numba ten, fight two against one," he said, starting to box the air, showing us all how he overpowered the two villains. The children were really into the story, listening intently, all behind their little hero.

"I'm sorry, Trong. I wish I could have . . ."

"No wait, Paul," he said, stopping me. "I tell you more. They say I pay them for boat, their father will be very angry, so I say okay, how much you want? They say you give half. I say no can do and we fight again. One boy throw can of beer at me, hit me in eye, now I very mad." The children were in hysterics now as Trong got one of the imaginary boys in a headlock and was literally ripping his head off. "Then they start to cry so I say, okay, I give you ten case each. They say, sure." The children and I applauded Trong, who was really enjoying center stage.

"So how many cases did you bring back, Trong?" I asked.

"When we fight," he went on, avoiding my question, wanting to tell the story his way, "I no see other kid on beach. The box on beer no good, get wet, and beer now all over beach. They numba ten, steal beer. I cannot fight all them, so I take stick from tree and chase them." Suddenly his face grew serious as he got closer to the answer I wanted. "Now I take two Lambretta come here. I tell man I give ten can beer they bring me here. They say, sure. Can do. They lie too much. I put twenty case in one, about fifteen case in other, and we go. No way I can ride in two and no way I can see the one run away in the street. We go round and round but no can see, he di-di mow. Now I get only," he tried first to count on his fingers and then looked over at Sister Hoa.

"Nineteen case, fourteen can," she said with a smile.

"Yeh. Nineteen case!" he said, then sat down next to me. Thom brought some warm water and a small rag and began to clean the small cut on my nose.

"You did a number-one job, Trong. Nineteen cases will get us a lot of food," I said, wrapping my arm around his narrow shoulders.

"We no can fix roof, Paul."

"We'll find a way."

"You want watch?" he said, reaching in his pocket for it. "You can trade, maybe buy . . ."

"No," I said, stopping him. "You hold it for me."

"How will we fix the roof, Paul?" Sister Hoa asked.

"We could get a bigger boat, Trong."

"No way." Weary with the thought of another fiasco, he sat up straight, a smile creasing his dirty face. "Next time

you go boat with me." Color was flooding in his face again.
"When we go again?" he asked, squatting down in front of
me.

"Well, it will have to be real soon because my tour is almost up." I could see Sister Hoa stiffen with the announce-
ment. I had wanted to tell her quietly and make plans to
continue helping them with donations from the States. She
got up slowly and instructed Thom to take the children to the
meadow to play. When they were gone, she sat down next to
me and waited a moment before speaking.

"How much longer will you stay with us?" she asked,
looking out toward the children.

"Two more weeks, Sister."

Her hand flew to her mouth. She looked at me with
stricken eyes. "So soon. But we still have so much to do to
make this a real orphanage. Who will help us? Who will fix
the roof?"

"Maybe I can find someone, Sister."

"Someone who will love the children like you do?" she
asked, looking out at the children. Her words, as usual,
struck deep.

"If I extended my tour for six months, that would be
enough time to fix this place up." The words fell from my
mouth without my thinking them. I hadn't even considered
the thought. The last month had been filled with great experiences at the orphanage, but the risk of stealing and my donations of money were made easier by the excited thoughts of
going home and seeing my own family.

"That is good. I thank God you will stay with us, help us
for a while longer." She jumped to her feet. "I will tell the
others, and you must stay tonight for we must surely cele-
brate."

"Wait, Sister, I'm not sure yet." Panic running through
me, I got to my feet, but it was too late. She was running like
an excited schoolgirl, the happiest I had ever seen her.

That evening after another delicious dinner, Sister Hoa,
Sister Tuan, Trong, Thom, and I sat at the top of the
meadow watching the children playing tag. Thom sat close to
me, holding my hand and quietly watching me. One by one
the children, tired from the humid evening air, ran up to tell

us the score of how many times each one had been "it"—
then told us that we looked like ghosts, sitting above them,
silhouetted against the soft sunset. As dark settled over the
happy group, Sister Tuan led the children in a song, their
high singsong voices tinkling in the air like bells. I had never
heard them sing before and looked across their rapt faces,
smiling and winking at the little ones mouthing in imitation
of the elders. It was as if the nuns knew this little show would
force my indecision about extending. Whether they planned
it or not, it worked. In these few months they had become my
happiness, my peace, and the greatest feeling of being
wanted, or alive for a reason.

Thom squeezed my hand as if she were reading my
thoughts. I looked at her beautiful round face, the striking
dark brown brows that arched delicately above her large in-
telligent eyes. With her right hand she pointed at herself,
then made the sign of a heart on her chest, and then gently
touched her finger to my lips. I couldn't believe it. This was
her own sign language, and I understood it.

"And I," I pointed at myself, "love," made the sign of a
heart on my chest, "you," I said and gently kissed her soft
cheek. Her face lit up like a flare, and she clapped her hands,
excited that I understood her. That does it, I thought. My
little fantasy about taking Thom back to my family could
happen if I had more time to check into it.

"I'm staying, Sister. In six months this will be a number-
ten orphanage."

The entire group stared at me for a moment, their faces
registering confusion. Trong was the first to catch my mistake, and started to laugh, infecting the others who jumped
around laughing like there was something on me—a bug or
bird shit that I didn't see.

"You no say numba-ten orphanage. Numba ten very bad.
You say numba-one orphanage, that the best," he said and
continued to laugh.

"Oh. Number one, right?"

After saying good-night to the children and thanking the
nuns for dinner I looked around for Trong, my constant
companion. About one hundred feet down the road I saw
him, swinging a long bamboo stick at Thom, trying to chase

her back toward the barn. As I approached them, she ran protectively behind me.

"What the hell are you doing, Trong?"

"She like go with us to road. Only Trong walk with you. Every night same-same," he said, dropping the bamboo stick at his side.

"You hit her with that stick, Trong, and I'll never walk with you anywhere."

His face dropped about a foot. Our first angry words had been spoken, and hurt.

"No sweat, girl stupid. She no can steal beer for you. Maybe she die in water. Maybe she scream when she see big fish. I never scream. I fight. We mans and brave," he said, planting his hands on his hips to emphasize his point.

"We're men, you mean, and sometimes just as stupid as girls. But real men don't hit little girls with sticks," I said, planting my hands on my hips, imitating him. He looked at me with a cocked head, trying to understand. Thom stepped forward, took my hand, then put her other hand out to Trong. I gave him a shove toward Thom's hand, but he was not about to touch her.

"Come on, Trong," I said. "We'll all walk to the highway."

"No."

"Okay. See you tomorrow, partner," I said and started down the road. Thom looked up and smiled at me as we moved away from Trong. A moment later Trong ran up from behind and was just about to take Thom's outstretched hand when he changed his mind. With two more hops he was on my other side and grabbed my free hand. Trong, an eleven-year-old man, holding a girl's hand? "Never Happen."

— 11 —

Death from Above

My final orders granting me permission to extend my tour in Vietnam arrived a week later. None of my stevedore co-workers could believe I had extended for six more months of hard labor, but every time I visited the orphanage I knew that I had made the right decision.

Our major problem at the orphanage remained—how to fix the roof? The ships I had been unloading at night carried mostly bombs and munitions to supply the steadily increasing number of American ground troops (a depressing thought that seemed to keep the crews pretty quiet). We unloaded another ship carrying office supplies and truck parts, but I could not imagine how the hell Trong would get some general's desk and chair to the market. And what would mamasan at the vegetable stand do with ten thousand rubber gaskets for tank engines? Perhaps she could sell them to the Vietcong (my reason for not trading ammunition on the black market), but the Vietcong were still riding bicycles into battle—or at least that's what I was told by a drunken combat veteran right before he fell off his barstool.

The solution came one afternoon, in the strangest place, under the strangest circumstances. After buying my monthly ration of goods at the PX, I stopped at a relief station, or piss tube, as they were called—an outdoor urinal, actually nothing more than a drum full of rocks, buried in the sand, surrounded by a knee-high wall for privacy. I set my rations down outside and entered the empty station. Entering next was one slightly intoxicated navy corpsman, Seaman 2nd Class Stubbs. Now, in these rather crude circumstances people normally don't even look up from the task at hand, so I knew someone was there but not who.

"Why, you skinny little grunt," the person next to me yelled, scaring the hell out of me. I didn't know whether to run midstream or jump the wall. I looked over at Stubbs, and we both started to laugh. He was one of the Squids from the Med-Cap missions I went on with Brian.

"I'll wait for you outside, Stubbs," I said and backed out of the urinal.

"Sure, uh . . . sorry, Hensler. Be right there."

We drank a countless number of beers before I realized that I was almost too drunk to report to duty. Over black coffee, which he laced with brandy from his own bottle, he explained his reason for getting and staying drunk. One of his teams had been ambushed like Brian's and three of his close friends had been killed. It was instant memory recall for me and extremely unpleasant. Brian's death stayed submerged until someone reminded me of the loss. Stubbs had just been through the same experience, so I knew exactly how he felt. When tears filled his bloodshot eyes, I felt them well up in my own.

Using the old Hensler saying, that laughter is always the best medicine, and remembering his kind treatment of the children on Med Cap, I told him about the orphanage, the children and nuns, and about their present condition, leaky roof and all. It seemed to work, although he didn't find the parts about the children's living conditions too funny. He began to ask me in great detail exactly what was needed to fix the roof.

"That's all, just some corrugated tin?" he asked.

"Wha'ya mean, that's all? I've been trying to fix that roof since we found that old barn."

"You off Saturday?" he asked.

"No, but I can get it off. Why?"

"There's more dudes on this base that owe me penicillin favors than there are whores in the village, especially a couple of Seabees I know."

"You mean the guys who built all those runways in the John Wayne movies?"

"The very same. Tell me where this place is and we'll meet you there on Saturday or maybe Sunday," he said, pouring us another drink.

"That's all for me, Stubbs," I said, placing my hand over my cup. "I can't believe this, just meet us at the orphanage. That's all there is to it?"

"That's all. Eight A.M. Saturday. We ain't like the army man, with all that 'We can do. Screaming eagles all the way' bullshit."

"Cool it, man," I said, looking around the room. "We're in an army Enlisted Men's Club. Twelve of those screaming eagle assholes will pick us up and play grenade throw with our heads."

"So you say, man. So you say," he said, looking around the crowded room, sitting up in his chair and puffing out, like a posturing rooster, what little chest he had. He looked at me through blurry eyes, and we both started to laugh.

At five minutes before eight the following Saturday, the navy arrived, and none too soon. It had rained for the first time the night before, soaking everyone and everything in the barn. The large truck cut two deep trenches in the meadow as it labored up the muddy hill and stopped outside the barn.

"You Hensler?" the driver asked as he jumped down from the truck.

"Yeah. Where's Stubby?"

"Still recovering from a little binge, I think. I take it this is the building you need fixed up?" he said, pointing at the barn. Two more men appeared around the side of the truck.

"Yeah. As you can tell by those two wet and angry nuns, that's it," I said, trying to make a joke.

"We'll take care of it. Just tell the ladies to keep the kids outta the way, and we'll get to work . . . This here is Buzz and Dave," he said and just as abruptly started to unload the truck. I stood there with my hand out like a jerk until Trong ran up, grabbed it, and shook it as hard as he could.

"Hello, Joe, my name Uncle Trong. You like play with poor little orphan?" he said, smiling up at me with an exaggerated grin.

"No. I don't like little kids," I said, trying to keep a straight face, then jerked him up into my arms. "I like all kids," and tickled him into submission.

We all sat in a large group watching the men work, Thom

and Trong sitting next to me as usual, and for the first time, the little girl who came in with Brian worked her way closer and closer, until Thom lifted her onto my knees. I could feel her staring up at me but decided to allow her the time to check me out before trying to tickle her into friendship. Once tickled by me, they were friends for life.

There was a lot of animated chatter among the children, and I could imagine them explaining to each other what each board, nail, and piece of screen was for. This was as fascinating to them as a circus. All their short lives they had witnessed destruction—the exploding and burning down of their homes, schools, hospitals, and churches. For the first time they could see something being built . . . and it was being built for them.

Suddenly the children fell silent as a miracle began to happen before their very eyes—and mine too—for I knew nothing about this new addition. The Seabees had already put a new corrugated tin roof on the old barn, but now they were lifting into position next to it a new prefab, louvered, completely screened dormitory! Swinging screen doors and all. I had been so busy watching the children's reactions to the navy men, I had not seen their hammering and sawing on the walls for the new building. What the hell, I thought, miracles can happen. And by the expressions on the nuns' faces as they looked from the new building to me, God was working overtime this bright beautiful morning.

Five hours after they started, the Seabees climbed down from the new building and began to load their truck. The children and nuns applauded, then set about moving into their new home. Sister Hoa and I approached the three men with cold beer she had kept on ice for them.

"You will be truly blessed for your kindness toward the children, and you can be sure of a place in our prayers," she said, shaking each one of their hands.

"Uh . . . thanks, Sister, but you should be thanking Corpsman Stubbs. He's the guy who got us to do this," Duke said, a little embarrassed about why they owed Stubbs such a big favor. "And Hensler, tell Stubbs that building should pay us up for the rest of our tours."

"Oh, sure. I'll tell him, and thanks, for . . ."

"Sure. No sweat." He seemed uncomfortable with the whole scene. "We gotta get back."

"Come back any time, gentlemen, eat with us and visit with the children," Sister Hoa said with a gracious smile.

"We're pretty busy, Sister, but, we'll see," he said, backing toward the truck.

The Seabees never came back to visit but several times stopped at the roadside at the bottom of the hill, honked their horn to get the children's attention, and then would toss C-rations, blankets, dried milk, and crackers to the side of the road. With another blast of their horn they were gone, no thank-yous necessary.

Every time I returned to the orphanage the nuns had changed something or improved another area. The barn was used for cooking, eating, and classes Sister Tuan had begun. Reading, writing, and arithmetic were taught and recited for two hours a day . . . no hookey allowed. Trong was the only exception. He simply refused to sit with the little girls. He preferred to make the water run so he could wander around town for a while. The new building became the sleeping dormitory.

Other new additions were added, sneaked in when I was not there. First a half-black, half-Vietnamese boy the nuns named Tu. He was adorable with tightly curled black hair and large black oval eyes. His skin was creamy-coffee-colored, and he was quite husky and large for a Vietnamese child. Sister Hoa said one of the prostitutes from town had left him at the road with some money. A little girl appeared next, also of half-American parentage, with long lovely brown hair and beautiful almond-shaped green eyes. Sister Tuan had found her abandoned and crying in the marketplace. Both children clung to Thom and Sister Tuan, who carried them about on their hips until they were comfortable with the other children. It did not seem to matter to the nuns where the children came from or who their parents were. They arrived, received a few days of special attention from the nuns, Thom, and big brother Trong, and then were left with the other children, another member of the family.

The next task to accommodate the growing family was to dig a well. Trong made two water trips to the city a day, but it was never enough. Bathing with collected rainwater helped, but one day of hot sun and the rain barrel looked like it was growing cabbage. We searched around the barn and found one area where a well might have been, but it was now our outside latrine. Sister Tuan heard Trong and me discussing the well problem over tea and was shocked that we had not asked her about it from the first.

"You like find water?" she asked, staring at us with her hands on her hips.

"Sister, why else do you think Trong and I have been digging all these holes?" I pointed to the series of exploratory pits.

"You know, Paul, girl know nothing," Trong said laughing and ran from Tuan's playful punch.

"You dig there," she said, pointing to an area where the pigpen was. "Water over there under dog."

"And just how do you know water over there under the dog, Sister?" I said, getting to my feet. We had adopted a small puppy who seemed to survive on the rice and vegetable scraps and when he saw us pointing at him he took off for the open meadow.

"Dog always sleep on ground where cool."

"Sister, the water is more than twenty feet underground."

"I no can explain. My English no good, but you trust me. Trust God," she said then walked away to continue her chores.

About ten feet under the goddamned dog we found water! Cool, clear water. Both Trong and I were too embarrassed to shout with the discovery; we just quietly kept digging the well. At dusk we quit and joined the others for a delicious meal of pork, a la Sister Tuan. As we were eating, I watched her politely excuse herself, walk to the new well, look in, and then grabbing her rosary say a little prayer over it.

With the completion of the well, the "orphanage on the hill," as we had named it, began to look sharp and clean. With my rations, a little help from Stubbs and the Seabees, a rare egg now and then from our skinny, rice-fed chickens, we somehow managed to get by. Except for the roar of fighter jets and air force planes, which started to pass overhead alhost every day, the orphanage's setting was pastoral and serene, seemingly far removed from the war.

As time passed, life for me at the base and the orphanage became more engaging and meaningful. I was more emotionally fulfilled than ever before in my life. At nineteen years of age, it was an enormous ego boost to be needed by twenty-five children and two adults, one of whom was old enough to be my mother.

My relationship with the nuns was slow to develop, but through them I was finally able to learn about some of the children. The nuns avoided any personal questions and normally changed the subject by telling me about their original orphanage in Song Pha. The small village of Song Pha was located about a hundred miles north of Phan Rang and within an area beleaguered by constant bloody skirmishes. They described a beautiful orphanage that housed more than a hundred children and one day was hit by mortar fire. Fifty-one children and an elderly nun perished in the fire storm that swept through the nursery and dorms, and another sixteen children were critically burned. The Sisters and children who could travel, Trong included, marched south, sleeping along the roads and begging food until they found the church in Phan Rang. The next experience they recounted was when the tall, crazy G.I. chased Trong into the church.

Thom was not one of the original orphans from Song Pha. The nuns knew nothing about her background, having found her standing by the roadside, a village burning before her. In shock, and unable to communicate with the nuns, she stood like stone, watching what was probably her home and her family burning in the searing inferno. She never spoke a word, but because she was so sensitive and her hearing so acute, Sister Hoa guessed that she had been shocked into silence and one day would speak again. That was all they knew about their favorite little girl. When the trauma had finally worn off she blossomed under the nuns' care, her staring blank eyes came alive, and happiness reentered her life, especially when she cared for one of the younger children. "She is a loving gentle child," Sister Hoa told me, "who holds a very special affection for you." When I asked her why, she could not answer.

Their avoidance of my endless questions, especially ones

about them personally, started me wondering how they an
all the Vietnamese felt about the American involvement i
the war. An answer of sorts slipped out one night as we sat o
the hill after dinner. Watching another spectacular sunse
mirrored on the bay, I felt myself at one with the surround
ings, immersed in the landscape, part of the hill I sat upon.
turned to Sister Hoa, sitting not too far from me. "Sister
this is such a beautiful country. I feel almost a part of it."

She looked at me strangely, her eyes half spheres of blac
jade. "It was beautiful once . . . until *you* arrived. And I d
not understand how *you* can feel a part of a country you ar
slowly destroying."

I was stunned by her words, physically taken aback by th
cold intensity with which she delivered them. Sister Tua
looked at me uncomfortably and Thom was squeezing m
hand, trying to soothe the panic she felt run through me.

"I don't believe you said that, Sister. It sounds lik
you are blaming me for this stinking war," I said, turning t
face her. "You know goddamned well that without m
you'd . . ."

"Survive," she said interrupting me, "like we have for s
long now."

"What did I do wrong, Sister? Why does it sound like al
this time I have been helping, you really hated me?"

Her face softened. "I do not hate you, Paul. None of u
hate you. But in my heart I hate all Americans, for what *yo*
are doing to my country."

"Then why do you keep saying *you,*" I said, raising m
voice. "I don't carry a gun. I haven't dropped any bombs o
your people."

"That is true. Forgive me, please, but you must believe i
is not you I blame," she said, getting to her feet. "I am onl
human, understand. I am fifty, Paul, and tired of death." *A*
tear dropped onto the bib of her habit. She did not try to hid
her pain as she continued, "Someday you will know what
mean . . . Good-night." She walked away quietly.

The glorious sunset had lost its glow. I sat dejected an
confused. Why was I lumped into the group called the en
emy? The Vietcong were the enemy, not the Americans.
felt a barrier had shot up between us, or perhaps it was al
ways there and I had just recognized it for the first time.

oked at Sister Tuan, avoiding my gaze, smiling and hum-
ing to a child on her lap. Did she feel the same way? Even
hom's hands, patting my arm, and her concerned eyes
emed foreign, fake to me. Did she think I was someone
se? Trong too? And the children? I looked across their in-
ocent faces, some responding to my sweeping stare with a
ink. No, the children didn't hate me . . . only because they
ad not learned to hate yet.

As Trong and I walked down the road in semidarkness, he
ook my hand. I decided to put Sister Hoa's outburst of
ords aside and forget my anger. They would ring true
omeday I was sure, just like my parents' endless lessons,
nd when they did, maybe I would understand them.

In less than twenty-four hours I would learn in the most
ainful way, exactly what Sister Hoa had meant.

I had taken a part-time job at the base cafeteria to add a
ttle money and whatever I could steal to the orphanage
itty. Two days a week I made doughnuts for the small snack
ars all over the base but had no way to get them out of the
itchen. On my third day of work, the answer came. Hens-
er, take the truck and deliver them doughnuts to here, there,
nd everywhere. Yes, sir, and away I went! At each delivery
oint I shorted the order by twenty doughnuts, so that when
 started over the bridge to Cam Ranh City and the orphan-
ge, I had about two hundred golden black market nuggets
n the back of the truck. I whistled and sang, excited about
ow the children's eyes would pop when they saw their favor-
te treat. As I drove around the last series of curves before the
rphanage turnoff, I began to see black swirling smoke rising
rom the area near it. The grass around the buildings must
e on fire, I thought, and drove faster. The clouds of smoke
illowed ominously around the hill, and as I churned through
he mud toward the hill I could see that it was not the grass. It
was the orphanage itself. I stopped the truck about fifty feet
from what was left of the barn, shut down the engine, and
slowly got out. The barn was gone and most of the new building. Small fires still burned, and through the gray curtain of
smoke I could see the nuns and children standing in the center of the field.

I walked through the burned grass toward them, stepping

over smoldering timbers and burning clothes. They were a crying, tears streaming down their soot-covered faces. Befor them in the grass were six little bodies covered with shee and towels. Some of their arms and legs sprawled out fro under their coverings, twisted and burned back into the feta position. I felt sick as the smell of burning grass and flesh su rounded me and held me in a trance. Trong appeare around the end of the barn, pulling another body away fro the burning building. As he tugged at the seared rigid leg the bone snapped with a loud pop and he fell to his knee screaming. I ran over and picked him up, holding him tigh to my chest. His arms encircled my neck, and soot from hi face smeared onto my cheek. We joined the others and sat i a large group, huddled together, the children shaking wit the loss of their little friends.

I couldn't cry. No tears would come, although I felt lik my heart was about to burst. The ever-strong Sister Ho. looked at the building, unable to control her sobs, then too my hands in hers and began to pray. We knelt there in th green open field praying. For the first time in years I begge God to take the children to His arms and to protect th others. My hands were sweating as I said, "Why, why, why Christ?" over and over again silently. I still couldn't cry and I knew He wouldn't answer me.

We dug seven graves. All of us, with our hands and sticks pulled the dark red earth into mounds. The nuns continue to pray, the children watched. By sundown all the children were buried, with simple bamboo sticks to mark their graves. Sister Hoa said a short prayer over each little hill.

Trong and I tried to salvage what remained of the barn. The tin roof had been blown almost all the way off, but we managed to bend it back enough so that it covered the portion still standing. We threw out the burned clothes and mats, the nuns swept the floor, and when the work was done I went out to the edge of the field and sat by myself.

I looked out over the bay toward the base, sitting quietly. Surveying the surroundings with new eyes, I began to see what had happened. Like a movie in slow motion, the facts of the fire fell into place, and with the impact of a mortar shell my stupidity exploded before me. I began to cry, pounding the ground next to me with my fist. The orphanage was sitting about two or three miles directly off the end of the air base runway, an obvious dumping ground for loose bombs or an improperly hung napalm cannister, jettisoned by the vibration of takeoff! My God, why hadn't I seen it before? The monsoons were here, the wind direction had changed, and aircraft had begun to take off and land through our beautiful sunsets every night. That was why no one was living in the barn. With shelter in such demand—refugees living in the streets and cardboard boxes—how was it that a solid building in such beautiful surroundings remained empty? Now I knew. Now I knew that the sunken area which I thought was an old well was really a bomb crater. The whole place was pocked with them. No one lived on the hill—no houses remained! Everyone knew it was a death trap, and I had planted them right on the bull's-eye. I was so impatient to get rid of them, and then so involved with my own enjoyment playing with them, I had been totally blind to the now so obvious earmarks of past tragedies!

I was so furious with myself that I couldn't face the nuns or the children. I knew now what Sister Hoa meant last night. The Americans had struck again. I ran to the truck and drove away, unable to look at the charred hillside reflected in the rearview mirror.

Dear Brian,

I miss you . . . let me say that first. I thought I learned to love, but unfortunately once again, too late. The little girl you saved and I were just getting to know each other. But instead of holding her tight and telling her I loved her, I let her jump rope under a napalm bomb. We buried her, Brian, next to six others. Love sucks, Brian.

—— 12 ——

Saigon

I couldn't sleep no matter how long I lay sweating on my cot. At work I hooked up one pallet after another like a zombie. Everything was confused, mixed up in my head, blurred by fatigue and anger. I saw clear images of the children playing in the open meadow, watching me trying to jump rope, then a second later their bodies, twisted and gnarled, were covered with sheets. I cried, terrifying anger running through me. I wished them back to life, asked God to forgive me, tried to think of what I was going to say to the nuns, then broke down again when I remembered Sister Hoa, taking my hands, touching me for the first time, and praying so hard I could feel her powerful faith in God rushing from her hands into mine. I couldn't get it straight in my head. It was my fault. It was the war. It was inevitable. It was irreversible. Self-recriminations of selfishness and guilt twisted around what I had done and thought was good for the children. I still felt a deep sadness for the dead children. This time I had no lesson from the past to fall back on. My parents had never taught me how to deal with death by stupidity.

Two days after the fire I walked up the hill, my arms loaded with food. As usual, Trong ran down to greet me. Some of the children stood outside the dormitory, their faces washed clean now but their clothes and hands still stained with soot. The shell of the barn stood out grotesquely, a huge blackened skeleton, still reeking of smoke and napalm. Through the open wall of the dorm I could see blankets and clothes neatly stacked, sleeping areas reestablished, and a cooking area set up in the rear doorway. They had put it all

115

back in some sort of order, clean and as neat as possible . . . almost life as usual at the orphanage on the hill. The children, at first surprised to see me again after my abrupt departure, waved to me as they jumped rope, their laughter ringing out across the green fields.

Sister Hoa looked up from the pad where she was showing Tu how to write his numbers. I thought of the poor American Red Cross worker on the base, tearing her storeroom apart, looking for the fifty pads of construction paper she had asked me to put on the shelf.

Sister Hoa watched me approach, not smiling but emanating warmth from her eyes. She got up, said a few quick words to Sister Tuan, who was teaching the class, then walked a good distance out into the field. She knew we would have to talk, that I would have many questions, and so she chose the field where I had said I felt so comfortable.

"We have been worried about you," she said cheerfully. I sat down facing the orphanage, trying to get my thoughts in order. She waited a patient moment, then sat down next to me, folding the skirt of her soiled habit beneath her.

"You must not blame yourself, Paul."

"I've been trying for two days, Sister, to figure it out. I just can't get it straight about why . . ."

"There is no answer, Paul," she said, interrupting me.

"Oh, that's a great help, Sister. That makes me feel a lot better," I said, raising my voice. "Why don't I just line them up against the building. You and Sister Tuan, too, and I'll just shoot you all and end the misery this country has in store for you."

"You are speaking like one of the children," she said impatiently. "You know what is happening in this country, it is not new to us. Our country has been at war for over thirty years." Her words stopped me. I would be leaving soon and I realized I was just now becoming aware of the pain and suffering inflicted on the innocent—especially the children—by both the Americans and the Vietcong. The closest I had been to the war was in triage and the hospital, and there the wounded and dead were grown men—or adolescents at least—and many had chosen to be where they were. The nuns and the children had no choice.

"I cannot make the pain any easier for you than it is for ne," she said, her voice softening again, "but I do not ques-ion my God or His will no matter . . ."

"Bullshit!" I screamed, surprising myself and Sister Hoa, oo. "Then you're saying it was His will that I put you and he children in this death trap!" Her eyebrows raised, and :olor flooded her pale face.

"Then let us *both* go to the church, to the confessional, and :ell the priest that we murdered seven children by doing what we thought was right and best for them." Her voice had risen and her breathing began to quicken. "I cannot allow myself to grieve because there are others who are living. My time and thoughts are on their next meal and our next home. I do not have the luxury of contemplating *why*. I simply trust my God!"

"And what will your God do when I leave in two months? Send you another?" I asked, getting to my feet.

"Perhaps. If it is His will. No matter what, we will go on. And when I die, Sister Tuan will continue our work, and an-other, and another. There will always be children, and there will always be those sent to care for them. Just like me . . . Just like you," she said, reaching out for help in getting up.

"You still believe God sent me into that church in Phan Rang. I don't buy that, Sister," I said, pulling her to her feet. "You kind of forced me into helping, if I remember cor-rectly."

"No, Paul," she said calmly. "You were not forced by anyone. You were called the very first time you saw the chil-dren. It was in your face and in your eyes. You were called by Him. By something inside."

The strange look that came over her face whenever she re-ferred to my presence as being ordained by God unnerved me. How could she know, if I did not? And what if she was right?

"Will you help us find another home?" she asked after a few moments.

"Well, you can't stay here, Sister. But where else should we look? Cam Ranh City is packed and we're already . . ."

"We will be all right here until you can take us to Saigon

. . . In Saigon there are many orphanages, well-established ones. I know of one where my friend works . . ."

I stood looking at her, unable to believe her request. Saigon was more than two hundred miles from Cam Ranh Bay. "Please, Sister. I think you know that is quite impossible."

"You'll think of a way. I know you will," she said and started back to the dormitory. I grabbed her arm gently, stopping her.

"Let's finish this now, Sister . . . I am going home in two months. I extended my tour to be here with you and the kids and for no other reason. I have done all I can and am truly sorry about what has happened. But I am finished getting involved in things I know nothing about. I will help you find a new home, even if it is in Saigon, and then I am through." I walked away, giving her no chance to try and change my mind.

Finding a place large enough for the nuns and remaining orphans would be like looking for the proverbial needle in the haystack, but I looked anyway. Getting them to Saigon would most certainly put my ass back on the court-martial firing line, but as I drove up and down the teeming, desperate, refugee-swollen streets of Cam Ranh City, Saigon quickly became their only chance. I couldn't just leave them in another barn or church in some village. Sister Hoa would settle for anything with a roof, but the children deserved more. I would succeed at my intention to change the odds in favor of the children by getting them to Saigon, no matter what. Maybe that would complete my unwritten contract with them.

Getting a vehicle for the Saigon trip was no problem—except when the motor-pool dispatcher handed me the keys to the only vehicle available—and it turned out to be a three-quarter-ton ambulance. Loading the children, nuns, their possessions, one puppy, and two chickens wasn't a problem either. But driving two hundred twenty miles on a wide open highway, through not so friendly territory, in an ambulance, replete with large Red Cross markings on four sides of the truck, would be terrifying. In previous wars the Red Cross meant safe passage, agreed upon by international law. But in

ietnam the rules had been altered. "If it moves, shoot it!"
as the enemy's motto.

We moved with a convoy for almost three hours, like a
aby duck following its mother, until the trucks turned into
he army base at Phan Thiet. After a potty break behind
ome banana bushes, we spent the next fifty miles choking on
iesel smoke emitted from a herd of armored personnel carri-
rs we latched onto. It was a great relief when they turned off
he road without warning and, tearing the shit out of some
oor old papasan's rice paddy, seemed to head for a firefight
everal miles off the highway. Miraculously, or maybe be-
ause the nuns chanted the rosary so many times I began to
hink Jesus was riding shotgun for me, we reached the out-
kirts of Saigon without incident.

Sister Hoa stuck her head into the cab and began directing
he toward a district called Gia Dinh, about five miles outside
he city proper. Saigon was enormous, the largest city I had
ver been in besides New York, and in the distance I could
ee skyscrapers, towers, and even billboards. My spirits
fted as I imagined there would be no problem finding them
new home in the sprawling suburbs. But the deeper we got
nto Gia Dinh, the lower my spirits dropped. We passed
nile-long caravans of motley-looking refugees, riding with
heir belongings in oxcarts, wagons, old trucks, and on bicy-
les. It was like passing a line of campers waiting to enter a
ark. These people were definitely not on vacation. Sister
Hoa saw me shaking my head and patted me gently on the
houlder. "Don't worry, Paul, we will find a place."

Wrong again. It was no better than Cam Ranh, Phan
Rang, or any other city I had passed while on convoy. The
only difference here was the people seemed more desperate.
Their faces registered their worst fear—starvation in a city of
apparent wealth and prosperity. No room, no food, no
vater, and a war forcing them into a literal death march. We
rawled for almost ten miles, passing people and water buf-
alo collapsed in horrible heaps, then pushed roughly to the
ide of the road so the march could continue. Like Cam
Ranh and Phan Rang, every conceivable space was occupied
by squatters—sidewalks, gutters, alleyways, graveyards, and
garbage dumps, where wild mangy dogs fought with children

for fish heads. I stared straight ahead to avoid the thousand frail hands outstretched and the matching sunken eyes, the pleading voices, "God Bless all American Soldiers, please help us." Where had I heard that line before?

Sister Hoa directed me to the orphanage where another nun from her order was working and went in to talk to her. could have told her the answer she would receive, just by the number of children sleeping outside the gate. There were no parents or grandparents watching them as they skittered across the street, playing with a deflated soccer ball. Horns honked, people screamed, and they just jumped out of the way as if they were playing a suicide game of Let's see who can keep from being squashed the longest. Sister Hoa returned a moment later, crestfallen. There was no room. Her friend had taken a group of children and fled the city.

Gia Dinh province was loaded with orphanages, run by religious groups from all over the world, and every one was loaded—packed to capacity with swollen tummies, diseases I had never seen before, and dead children wrapped in bamboo mats waiting to be taken away. Children so deformed that they were unsavable, and thus unfed, waited for death. Not even God, dressed in the habits of overworked nuns, seemed able to control this tragic backwash.

After three hours of searching I pulled over near a small market, bought the children some rolls and ice-cold Cokes, and took Sister Hoa aside so we could talk quietly.

"I know what you are going to say, Paul," she said before I could speak.

"No you don't, Sister. I'm not angry or anything, just sad about what I saw at that last orphanage."

"When they have no chance to grow up and defend themselves, it is more kind to let them die."

"I know that, Sister," I said, sensing her concern that I understand.

"Then you must believe that to let them die is to free them from suffering. In our country survival escapes even the healthy; the sickly child has no chance." Tears of anguish, held back by her fear of seeming weak, glassed her eyes. If only she could be saying the same thing to an audience of complacent or unknowing Americans, I thought. But I imagined the facts would be as hard for them to understand as it was for me—and I had a ringside seat.

Trong came running toward us as if being chased, followed by Sister Tuan, who was yelling in excited Vietnamese. They had found a place for them to stay, next to where I had parked the ambulance. It turned out to be a holding station, run by the Saigon police, or the White Mice, as Trong called them. Guarded by an elderly policeman, the building held fourteen children, whose parents were in jail, awaiting trial, or dead.

Sister Tuan began negotiations with the officer, and by her insistent chatter I could tell things were not going well. He had told her first that they could stay in the building as long as they watched over the other children. Now he was changing that story slightly, and I imagined it was because he had seen their tall American escort. Sister Tuan walked toward me slowly, getting her English together.

"He say we can stay. No problem. Lots of room . . . But we must pay a . . ."

"Bribe," Sister Hoa said angrily, then headed for the policeman with fire in her eyes.

"Sister, don't get him mad. This is the only open place we've found all day," I yelled after her.

"Do not worry. I want to tell him about how angry God can get," she called back to me.

"How much, Sister Tuan?"

"Uh. He say we pay him fifty dollar American," she said, embarrassed at her countryman's greed.

"Sister, I've got . . ." I pulled a soggy wad of Military Payment Certificates out of my pocket, ". . . forty-one dollars and fifty cents. That's it. And that leaves me no money for my trip back to Cam Ranh." I followed her back to where Sister Hoa was berating the policeman, seemingly with no effect.

"He is Buddhist," Sister Hoa said, wiping perspiration from her forehead. Sister Tuan began talking again, then turned back to us.

"He say okay, no money. You go PX buy him one Sony radio."

I thought I heard the word Sony in his greedy chatter. The

policeman was smiling at me with a stupid grin that I wanted to knock off his face. "Forget that idea, Sister. A Sony radio is more than fifty dollars. What else does he want?"

She chattered away for another few minutes, and when the man finished I heard Sister Hoa say something in a deep whispering voice. The man, Sister Tuan, and Trong, who had just joined the group, looked at Sister Hoa with shocked faces.

"What's wrong? What did you say, Sister?"

"Nothing really. I just told him something about his ancestors."

"Paul," Sister Tuan said to get my attention, "he say you give him twenty dollar and two carton Salem cigarette each month."

"It's a deal. Tell him, Sister," I said, giving the crooked cop a twenty-dollar bill. "Tell him we'll give him the cigarettes later." As she turned back to the policeman, I scooted Trong away and joined Sister Hoa, who was looking through the building. The two-story structure was white stucco and in terrible repair. There were four large rooms upstairs, two large rooms and several office-size rooms downstairs. Cooking fires had scorched the walls in almost all the downstairs rooms, and fingerprints, human waste, garbage, and scurrying rats completed the grizzly scene. The water tank outside was leaking and had only a few inches of water in it, and the walls surrounding the courtyard were falling apart. It was a mess. I couldn't imagine how they could clean the place up and make it livable. The nuns were already pointing and discussing what they would do as the children ran from room to room, leaving Trong and Thom to unload the ambulance. Standing in the middle of the courtyard, looking at the dilapidated but sturdy building, I found myself more anxious to get away.

Sister Tuan was walking on air, excited about their new home. "Paul, this good place. We can make numba-one orphanage here. You see when you come back." Sister Hoa joined us now.

"Sisters, the first thing you must do is find someone, another G.I., to bring the policeman his cigarettes. I will not be coming back. I did like I said I would and found you a new home. I'm finished." Thom approached now and took my hand. Sister Hoa's face turned stern, and she asked Sister Tuan to excuse us. She tried to push Thom away, but my little friend held tight.

"You put us in the barn and it burned down, from bombs dropped by your planes. That was not your fault. You bring us here . . ."

"Wait a minute, Sister," I said, standing up and facing her. "I'm not gonna let you twist it all around again. You have all the words. You throw them at me, saying I'm not blaming you, but every time you speak I end up feeling guilty. No more, Sister. I'm sure you will find another G.I. who will help you . . . I'm leaving now." Her mouth dropped open. I had never been so direct or so sure of my words until just then. Determined, I started to walk toward the truck . . . but what I really wanted to do was turn back and hug her. She followed me slowly.

"Paul, if you go now you cannot come back to play. That time has passed, and now we must start over. With your help or without it we will go on. If you commit yourself and your love to us, you will find a way to return . . . We will continue to pray for you. Good-bye," and with that she entered the building. She had done it again, and Thom tugging at my hand did not help any. When I got to the door of the ambulance, I bent down and hugged Thom close. Over her shoulder I caught sight of Sister Hoa, who, when she saw me, ducked back into the shadows. She was probably holding back all the children with her, knowing that Thom's good-bye would be one I could not forget. Thom made her sign for "I love you," and I returned it, hugging her again. I looked into her deep black eyes one more time, then carefully mouthing the words said, "I will be back, okay, to see you." Her eyes brightened, "and maybe I'll . . ." I decided not to tell her of my thoughts about taking her home to the States. "Maybe I'll even say hello to Sister Hoa when I get back, but don't you tell her." She shook her head from side to side no. "You keep all the children happy, okay?" and again she shook her head Yes. I hugged her, and this time I saw both nuns and several children duck out of sight when they saw me.

As I pulled away, Thom waved, lifting her hand and moving her fingers slightly, then turned and walked toward the building. I stopped a few yards down the street to look back and, sure enough, the entire orphan group—the nuns running ahead of the others—surrounded Thom, probably asking her what I had said. She folded her arms across her chest and shook her head no.

— 13 —

Purgatory

Cam Ranh Bay became a purgatory for me, its heat, my job and boredom, my enemies. There was nothing to look forward to except my future date with the kids and the nuns and going home.

One night, feeling particularly lonely, I joined three men from my company on a trip to the local whorehouse village, situated next to the base and composed solely of bars and massage parlors. The special village had sprung up since the arrival of the American forces, catering to them and checked regularly by the army medical staff. When the Military Policeman passed us on through its gates, I laughed and said to my companions, "Now, that's what I call army control—regulating the sexual practices of its fighting men!"

It was the first time I had been near a whorehouse since the fiasco with Brian in Phan Rang. Crowded with bars and black market stands, the whole village was only three or four narrow sandy streets. From every doorway country, rock, the Beatles, and blues blasted from colorful jukeboxes. I followed my three friends into the Southern Comfort Bar, passing a group of gaudily made up girls who were checking each other's hair for lice. A real unattractive thought—and I was going to run my fingers through her hair?

My ex-shift leader and owner of the Southern Comfort had left Vietnam, but anyone from his old company got free booze, compliments of the new owner. After countless shots of Southern Comfort and many beers, I stumbled into the back room with a girl I thought looked like Raquel Welch with slanted eyes and immediately passed out. The next thing I remembered was waking up on a hard wood bec naked—and still very drunk. The cubicle, like my walle was empty. My clothes were piled on the floor. My God, thought, I slept through it! I finally lost my virginity, and slept through it!

I pulled on my clothes and wandered clumsily through maze of hallways and doors that entered into little cubicle like the one I had just left. Heavy breathing, giggles, and woman's voice, "Sure, but that cost you plenty more," fol lowed me out into the main bar. I sat alone, waiting for th room to stop spinning so I could walk back to the base. At th table next to me, four marines were telling tall tales about th "gooks" they had shot, stabbed, married, or mangled. could only understand parts of their conversation, floatin between passing out and throwing up. But when one of th guys started talking about children, I moved closer to listen

"The kid rips my watch right off my wrist so's I chase hin right through the village in my jeep. I tore the shit outta th market, then catch him runnin' down the road." The gu' talking pretended he was driving.

"Did ya get him?" one of the others asked.

"Are you kiddin'? I ran the shitty little fucker over . . squashed him flat. But, you know what?" He was grinnin, stupidly. "My Timex made it!" They all broke into drunke laughter.

I went crazy. I jumped up, stumbling over my feet, anc screamed, "What did the kid look like? Was his nam Trong?" Like a volcanic eruption, all my anger, grief, an frustration—the orphanage fire, Brian, the wounded an dead soldiers—spewed from me. I got off one good shot, m fist smashing into his nose with a sickening crunch. Ten sec onds later it was over. The huge marine stood up ver slowly, a small trickle of blood seeping from his flaring nos trils. He lined me up with the beaded-curtain doorway anc hit me square in the face with what felt like a brick.

I woke up in an alley, vomiting beer and blood, tangled i the beaded curtain from the whorehouse doorway. My fac felt like I had just undergone plastic surgery with a hammer My nose was clogged with blood and sand and my whol body ached like I had been dropped from a helicopter. As

arted to retch again, someone turned me over and gave me
handkerchief. Stubbs was kneeling next to me, shaking his
ead.

"Jesus, Hensler, who'd you tangle with, some of those
creamin' eagles guys?"

"Worse . . . A three-hundred-pound marine," I said,
iping my face. "I thought you went home? . . . Oh God,
y face."

"They gave me the whole Med-Cap program to run, plus
y 3rd Class rating, so I stayed. Come on, I'll get your face
hanged for you," he said, helping me to my feet.

"What? Jesus . . . I'm gonna puke again."

"Not on me," he said and sat me back down. "Hensler,
ou're a real study in bravery."

"I think I'm dying" was all I could answer.

Stubbs took me back to the navy base, where he and a
riend packed my face in ice. My nose was not broken, but
he bruises on my cheek and under my eyes would be with
ne for some time. We talked through the night, the tables
ow reversed, with me recovering from my first real drunk
nd Stubbs listening. We both sat in the porch of his bar-
acks, blubbering like babies as I recounted the fire and bur-
al of the children.

"Why don't you come over to the Med-Cap unit? We've
ot people from the marines and army," Stubbs said.

"Hey . . . I've seen all the marines I can handle . . . I've
sked for three transfers to the Hospital Company and gotten
hree denials."

"Let's change that."

"Yeah, Stubbs, and the war ended last week."

"No bullshit, Paul, by the time you pack your duff, I'll
ave my CO transfer you to the Med-Cap unit. You can live
ight here at the base."

"Are you serious, or am I still drunk?"

"Count on it. You can take over the chopper missions,"
e said, shaking my hand.

Two days later I received permission from my Command-
ng Officer to report for Temporary Duty to the 24th Evacuation Hospital in Cam Ranh. After sixteen months in

Vietnam I was no longer a volunteer. I organized the m[e]
and equipment for two airborne Med-Cap teams that wou[l]
cover the area between Cam Ranh and Da Lat, about six[ty]
miles west of the base.

I was in heaven. My situation now supported my ability [to]
care for others without ever being called a candy strip[er]
again. Working in triage was just as painful as it had been [in]
Phan Rang, the wounds as traumatic and horrific; and thr[ee]
Med-Cap missions a day, two hours at each hamlet, was ba[ck]
breaking work, but it gave me a great sense of self-worth. [I]
was finally a respected member of the *team*, and I was happ[y.]

The only problem with my new assignment was that ever[y]
time I bounced a child on my knee—right before filling h[is]
tiny brown fanny with antibiotics—I thought of the orpha[ns]
. . . I missed them.

It was a week past my promised date of rent paymen[t]
when I caught a Dustoff chopper to Saigon. I told the guys [at]
the hospital I was taking my four-day in-country leave [to]
Nha Trang, a beautiful military-run beach resort north [of]
Cam Ranh. Stubbs knew exactly where I was going, thoug[h]
and gave me one hundred dollars he said he found in th[e]
sand. "How the hell did you find five twenty-dollar bills i[n]
the middle of this desert?" I asked. "Never mind! Just tak[e]
the kids out for an ice cream," he answered.

We flew through the smoggy haze of dusk, over Saigo[n]
the relentless golden sun shimmering as it slipped below th[e]
horizon. Saigon was massive, filling the doorways of th[e]
chopper, running out and away from its center of high rises[,]
cathedrals, and protected government buildings. Cars, bic[y]
cles, motorcycles, and millions of black-haired ants clogge[d]
the streets and sidewalks, moving, surging toward thei[r]
homes or markets, searching for shelter or the solace of te[a]
with a neighbor. Children waved and pigeons scattered as w[e]
roared over the rooftops; most paid no attention to the Amer[-]
ican presence in and around their city.

How the hell would I find eighteen children and two nun[s]
in a city whose population had swollen to over five million[?]

1. Saigon, Vietnam, April, 1969. My first day on duty as a Forensic Pathology Technician.

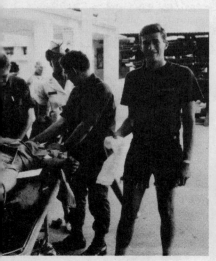

2. Called to duty in Triage (Emergency Room) of the Third Field Hospital in Saigon on my day off. Triage means deciding the degree of treatments needed by the wounded. Many times making a decision like that tore us apart.

In 1980, I was screenwriter and co-producer of the Sanrio Communications, Inc., film *Don't Cry, It's Only Thunder*, the story of my "adventures" with homeless children while I was in Vietnam. This was my first chance to tell people about what had become my life's work—helping the homeless and orphaned children of Southeast Asia.

3. Susan Saint James, who placed Dr. Cross, and Dennis Christopher, who played me under the name of Brian Anderson, seated next to refugee child actress Mai Thi Linh and one of the extras, also a refugee. Mai Thi Linh and her mother had been in the Fabella Refugee Camp in the Philippines for almost two years when she was cast to play Dinh Thi Thom. *Roger LeClaire, Sanrio Communications, Inc.*

4. Rehearsing a scene with Dennis Christopher and Mai Thi Linh. All these extras are themselves refugees of the upheavals in Southeast Asia. *Roger LeClaire, Sanrio Communications, Inc.*

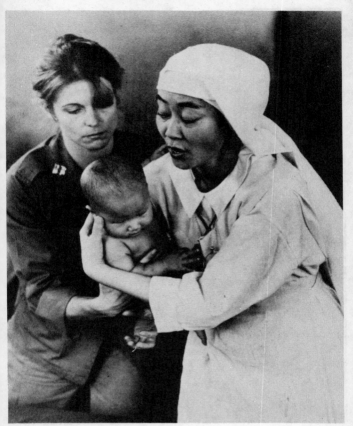

5. Susan Saint James and Chinese actress Lisa Lu, who played Sister Marie. The baby in Lisa Lu's arms is another of the many refugees who worked in the film. *Roger LeClaire, Sanrio Communications, Inc.*

6. Dennis Christopher and Hai Trong, who played Cao Van Tron, Brian Anderson's sidekick. Hai is another of the refugee children involved in *Don't Cry, It's Only Thunder*. *Roger LeClaire, Sanrio Communications, Inc.*

After I returned to the United States in 1970, I thought my life would be in a monastery as a priest. I was so wrong. My real life is helping the refugees, both children and adults, of the war-ravaged countries of Southeast Asia.

7. These five Vietnamese children were found in the Camp Pendleton Refugee Camp in California, unaccompanied by their parents or relatives. Once they were identified as unaccompanied minors, they were processed for foster homes in Southern California where they are today. *Author photo*

8. This little boy is one of the thousands born in the refugee camps in the Philippines, automatically making him an American citizen. *Author photo*

9. Keeping clean is the most important thing, next to food and medicine, in the horrendously overcrowded refugee camps. Here I am trying to teach the children how to use special shampoos for killing lice, in Refugee Camp #7, Kuala Lumpur, Malaysia. *Dirk Halstead, Time Magazine*

10. The only way to communicate with all the refugees is to constantly walk around the camps and when I do, I always wind up carrying the children, trying to give them some comfort. Here I am with an orphaned child as I listen to the requests for medicine for a sick member of a refugee family in Malaysia. *Dirk Halstead, Time Magazine*

11. Tuberculosis can spread rapidly in the dank climate of a Malaysian refugee camp. The best thing to do is to walk around the camp calling the refugees to the tents for the T. B. screening procedures. *Dirk Halstead, Time Magazine*

12. In the camps, parents hide their sick children for fear that they will not be able to come to the United States. Part of my work is to look for these sick children so they and their parents can be treated before they can travel. Even though they may be ill, the refugees try to fool you because being rescheduled for another departure date means one more unbearable day, week or month in the hellishly crowded refugee camps. *Dirk Halstead, Time Magazine*

13. You try not to become emotionally involved but it sneaks up on you. Here are Penatinah, Sompasong, and Palenia Sengsouvoung, my favorite refugee children. These three Laotians and their parents are one of the four families I have adopted, and they all now live together in Los Angeles. *Sanrio Communications, Inc.*

14. I took the Sengsouvoung family all around Southern California, including their first trip to Disneyland. The children particularly liked "It's a Small World." *Michael Neese, Neese Productions*

15. One of the many overcrowded barracks buildings of the Sikiu Refugee Center, Nakornratchaisma, Thailand, 1983. My work goes on. *Author photo*

16. Daily life takes on a rhythm of its own, even in a place as temporary as a refugee camp. These boys are grinding grain for their meals. *Author photo*

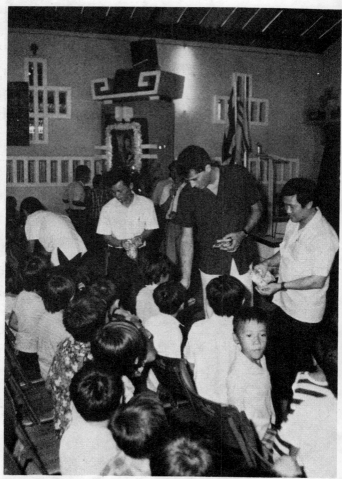

17. Kids love simple things. That's me distributing crayons and candy to 200 unaccompanied minors in the Center. Most of these children having living parents in Vietnam who forced them to leave the country because of the Communist government there.
Author photo

18. These boys are waiting in the boys' dormitory of the Unaccompanied Children Center for the Thai Government to decide if they can be sent to foster homes in the United States and Canada.
Author photo

19. The Catholic Chapel at the Sikiu Refugee Center. It is presided over by a Thai priest, Father Peter Prayoon Namwong who carefully watches over these Vietnamese children and has built them a school, the chapel, the Children's Center and the dormitories. *Author photo*

20. The Children's Mass in the Catholic Chapel. Listening to 500 children make "a joyful noise unto the Lord" is an incredible experience. *Author photo*

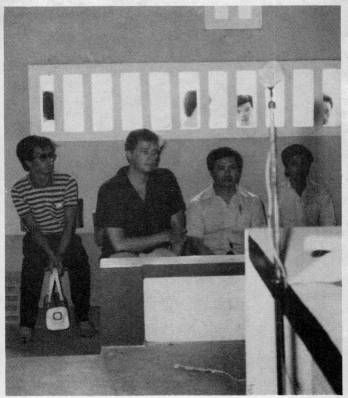

21. The Thai military police made me sit over to one side during the Children's Mass, so they could keep an eye on me. As soon as they left, I joined the children. *Author photo*

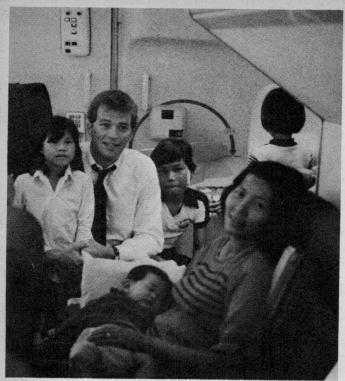

22. Coming home on the Pan Am jumbo jet from my latest trip to Thailand, bringing refugees to a new life, May, 1983. The entire crew, from the flight attendants to the pilot, fell in love with these children. *Eva Parker*

maybe even more now that the fighting has increased in the orth,'' the crew chief yelled over the turbine's whine.

The only clue I had was that they were in Gia Dinh, a ensely populated area about five miles from Central Sai- on. The taxi driver tried several times to take the long way, s meter ticking into profit, but with my few words of Viet- amese I intimidated him into believing I knew where I was oing. After twenty minutes of circling the same buildings, I und it but told the driver to go to the closest market so I uld buy some food.

After retrieving and pocketing the I.D. cards from three ambretta drivers, a document without which they would utomatically be thrown in jail, I was positive the Lambret- s, loaded with one hundred dollars' worth of food, would ot get lost on the way to the orphanage. The convoy pulled to the orphanage courtyard, like MacArthur returning to e Philippines. As usual, jump rope was in progress, along ith tag, who can throw their slipper closest to the wall, and enny toss. Sister Tuan and Thom were sweeping—until ey saw me unravel my legs from the cab of the Lambretta. hey flew across the courtyard, Sister Tuan's habit billowing ke a sail. Thom wrapped her arms around my legs, squeez- g them tightly. Sister Tuan stopped a few feet from me, uddenly shy.

''I know you come back!'' she said.

''Thom, did you tell them I was coming back?'' I asked, miling, and she shook her head no. The children and a few ew faces gathered around.

''She no tell . . . I just know you!''

''Where's Trong and Sister Hoa?''

''Trong go to the street everyday . . . Sister Hoa go beg at arket.''

We started to carry the baskets of food into the room they ad designated as a kitchen.

''I brought the cigarettes. I hope the policeman didn't give ou any trouble?''

''No he say O.K., one more day, then one more day, then ne more day.'' She shook her head at their luck with the reedy cop. ''Maybe he no come back now.''

The kitchen was only one poor example of their efforts to

transform the building into an orphanage. There were two
pots, no soap, grease and soot everywhere, and only the floor
to prepare their meals on.

"Why won't he come back, Sister?"

"I do not know. But everywhere in Saigon people scared.
They say on street Vietcong coming, make trouble."

"Come on, Sister. There's too many Americans here," I
said, taking the basket of chickens from Thom. "Yes, we see
many American, but they no have guns. Only walk around,
go to house . . . over there," she said, too embarrassed to
say whorehouse in front of the children. "They fat, no can
fight. Maybe they be careful now."

"What?"

"I don't know how to splain."

"Explain, Sister."

"O.K., I don't know how to say. I just hear people talk."

"They're just pulling your leg, Sister. This city is too
big." She looked at me incredulously.

"What you mean 'pulling my legs,' " she asked and I
wasn't really sure how to explain. "It's like a joke. When
I'm joking you, I'm pulling your leg." She cocked her head,
still not understanding.

"Never mind, Sister. Tell me where I can find some paint
or whitewash. I'm gonna make this place sparkle."

"Sure. You go China Town. Come I tell driver where to
go," she said, leading me toward the Lambretta drivers, who
were still waiting to get paid.

When Thom and I returned with fifteen gallons of local
whitewash, Trong was waiting. His face and clothes were
filthy, and he looked thin and wild, like an alley cat finally let
loose from his cage.

"Well, Trong. How's my partner?"

"My friend see you at market, tell me you come back.
How long you stay?" His face seemed more serious than I remembered.

"Till Sunday. You gonna help us paint this place?"

"Sure. We all can do."

"O.K., Joe. Let's go," I said, pulling off my fatigue shirt.

What a mistake the "all can do" was. After whitewashing
the kitchen, kids' dorm, the nuns' room, and their ceilings,

here was more whitewash on the children than the walls. But alabaster-white gleamed from the walls, reflecting the bright sunlight that poured in through the long narrow windows.

Sister Hoa returned from her begging trip, carrying only a few heads of Chinese lettuce and two small fish. She dropped the food in shock when she saw the newly painted kitchen full of food and walked over to where Thom, Sister Tuan, and I were washing paint off the squiggling, laughing children.

She stood over us, her hands folded in front of her, looking like she was about to give a lecture.

"Stand up," she said sternly, pretending to be angry. Sister Tuan shot to her feet, trying to wipe the whitewash off her face. "Not you, Sister. Him," she said, pointing to me. I rose slowly.

"And what's wrong with you, Sister?" I asked, taking a step toward her, smiling.

"Nothing. I just like to say, welcome back," and a big smile crossed her face. I spread my arms as if to hug her, but she backed away quickly.

"No, No, No . . . You finish here. Thom and I will begin dinner." She put out her hand for Thom.

Sister Hoa was happy again. She knew I would leave soon, for the last time, but right now she would take great joy in the new paint, a few days of food, and the happiness the children found in being with their tall American friend.

"You must make every moment good for them now," she said while watching me cement over the holes in the courtyard wall, "memories they can use again and again." When I looked up at her, there were tears in her eyes. "Do they know I'm not coming back, Sister?" She looked over at the children who were making big square pies with my cement. She pointed, smiling warmly, and we both laughed.

"You didn't answer me, Sister," I said, moving closer so that the children wouldn't hear us.

"No," she said, wiping her eyes with her narrow white apron. "If I tell them you will not return, what will they have to hope for? They will know the truth in a month or two, and maybe by then Sister Tuan and I will be able to give them new dreams."

I wanted to hug her again, even though my hands were

cement-covered, but Trong, yelling and chasing the children, stopped me.

"Paul, you tell girl go play in kitchen . . . We man, working."

"O.K., O.K. . . . tough guy," I said, smudging cement on his cheek. "I'll keep them away."

He shoveled the cement cakes back into our mixing pan and began to refill my bucket. "Paul, how 'bout you tell me why I fix bathroom. You know, it smell numba ten," he said, wrinkling his nose.

"Because your nose is smaller than mine," I said. Sister Hoa shot her apron up, covering her mouth.

Trong thought for a long moment, looking at my serious face, then said, "O.K., sure," and with a smile went back to his unpleasant task.

"Sister, I wanted to ask you about Thom while she's not around. How long would it take for me to get the papers so I could take her back to the States?"

Sister Hoa shook her head slowly. "It is quite impossible. The government papers are one part and take many months, but Paul, she has no papers from her family. What will you tell the officials, you found this little girl on the street?" She could see my face drop. "I am sorry. If you had more time, perhaps."

"Thanks, Sister."

Saturday we continued cleaning and repairing, but Sunday we played games—every game in the book. I even taught Trong how to lose gracefully now and then, to keep the younger boys from crying. Water fights, coconut ball (similar to football but no punting allowed), and their favorite—jump rope.

Monday morning at 4 A.M. I woke Thom and led her out into the courtyard. The nuns were waiting for me in the kitchen, sipping tea and offering me some potent instant coffee. I sat down facing Thom.

"I have to go home, Thom. Home to America," I said, taking her by the shoulders. Her eyes widened, and she broke into tears, the first time I had ever seen her cry. She pulled away from my grasp and stood up. "Wait, Thom, please. I want to tell you something," I said, grabbing her wrist. She jerked away from me and ran toward the children's room.

Sister Tuan stood quietly, fighting back tears. She didn't say anything, just stared at me.

"God bless you, Paul . . . For all you have done. God bless you," Sister Hoa said, with no tears, no arguments. Sister Tuan suddenly grabbed my hands and squeezed them tight. "You good man. Never forget us and children. O.K.?" The tears spilled down her face now. Sister Hoa took her hands from mine and said, "It is time for you to go now. Safe journey, and I will give Trong your message."

As we left the kitchen I could see Thom watching me through the slatted window, her beautiful eyes staring impassively. I lifted my hand and wiggled my fingers, like she did all the time. She didn't move.

I picked up my handbag and walked out the orphanage gates for the last time. Unless Thom runs after me so we can say, "I love you," I will not look back, I thought. Six blocks later I was still walking alone through the quiet alleys of Gia Dinh.

At seven thirty I caught a chopper heading to Phan Rang and would have to get another hop to Cam Ranh from there. I didn't even look out the doors as we climbed up over Saigon and headed east. I could feel the first heat of the rising sun glaring through the windshield and just closed my eyes to dream. Twenty-five days and a wake up, and I would be home. Home to New Jersey where I would see the family I had remembered and thought about so much recently. I could see their faces, smiling, ready to tell me in great detail what they had been doing for the past year and a half. But would they ever believe my stories, I wondered. My stories about thirteen beautiful children and seven who were killed. Would they allow me to describe the triage area, the fire, Brian's last words, the soldier I had baptized. No, I thought. They would only want to hear about coconut football, water under the puppy, the great Hamm's caper, or any story that would make them laugh. The others they would not understand.

After a ten-minute stop in Phan Rang, my old alma mater, the crew chief yelled for me to stay on board. We were going to pick up a couple of WIA (wounded in action) and take them to my Evac Hospital in Cam Ranh.

"You can give me a hand with them," he yelled as we lifted straight up, and I nodded sure. The chopper then dropped its nose to pick up ground speed and finally, with a stomach-turning twist, climbed up to a safe altitude. The crew chief fumbled with both his first-aid kit and a mean-looking M-60 machine gun slung in the left door. He saw me watching him prepare a bottle of IV solution, then load a belt of ammo into the machine gun. He shrugged his shoulders. "You gotta kill some to save some," he yelled. "This war sucks that way."

We dropped into a jungle clearing where I could see green smoke marking the landing zone. I grabbed onto the edge of the seat, waiting for my first taste of enemy lead to rip through the chopper. We were on the ground for one minute, just long enough for the patrol to load two men with multiple gunshot wounds of the legs and chest and the platoon medic, wrapped in a green poncho. Dead. As I pushed his body forward so we could work on the wounded, I remembered the corpsman in Phan Rang saying that the medics were always the first to get it. "The Cong would wound the point. He'd yell, 'Medic,' Doc would run to help him, and zap, no more Doc. Demoralized the hell out of the rest."

We were about fifteen feet off the ground when I heard a loud crack and saw a flash of light that lit the entire cabin like a strobe. The chopper shuddered, and the next thing I knew I was lying in mud, intense pain shooting through my legs.

I couldn't think or stop the screaming I heard inside my head. I sat up and could see the chopper lying on its side, its rotors bent and twisted. Flames began to appear from the doorway, but no one else was moving. Suddenly the copilot climbed out, struggling to pull someone else out, then gave up and ran toward me.

"Run! Come on man, run!"

"Something's wrong with my legs!" I screamed, and he ran back, grabbed my fatigue shirt, and jerked me backward away from the burning Huey. We got about seventy-five feet away when the main fuel tank blew with a deafening explosion. Suddenly the air was full of razor-sharp pieces of metal, nuts, bolts, and parts of bodies. The copilot stumbled and fell across my legs, and the second before I passed out I saw blood gush from his throat.

I could hear voices, the wind, someone crying in pain, maybe myself, but I couldn't wake up. Hours passed. I heard female voices, laughter, saw a bright light, and when I finally woke up I was in the Evac Hospital in Cam Ranh Bay.

Morphine confused the information Stubbs was trying to feed me. The copilot was O.K. My left leg was broken, my right ankle had a hairline fracture, and I was going home. "What?" I asked, trying to focus on Stubbs's friendly face.

"They're evacin' you to Japan tomorrow."

Once again I either passed out from happiness or traveled off on my morphine high.

The following morning I was sore but awake and excited. The hospital staff I knew stopped at my bed to say good-bye and handed me several letters to mail for them when I got to Japan.

At noon, an Air Force C-141 jet carried us up and out of Vietnam, and a cheer rang out when the pilot said over the intercom, "Gentlemen . . . you're on your way home." The aircraft was loaded with wounded men, strapped to stretchers against its inner bulkheads and made comfortable by two beautiful air force flight nurses. As we began to climb, I saw in my mind's eye the burned-out "orphanage on the hill" below us at the end of the runway. I thought I could hear the children singing . . . saw them laughing and winking their eyes at me. I could see Trong grinning and giving me his peace sign. I was glad I had a chance to say good-bye to them in Saigon and sure that if Sister Hoa knew I had fallen out of the sky on my way back from that first and last visit, she would say, "Yes, Paul. It was His will that you leave Vietnam as soon as you said good-bye to us. Your work was done."

PART II

PART II

— 14 —

Escape to Nowhere

After an overnight stay and quick medical check in Japan we were reloaded and flew on to Travis Air Force Base in California. There we took on fuel and dropped off a few of the wounded who were from the West Coast before we were on our way again. Five more torturous hours on an uncomfortable stretcher and we landed at Edwards Air Force Base in New Jersey. I could just see my parents running out to greet the flight. Wrong! Instead we were taken by ambulance to Walston Army Hospital, where everybody's family, except mine, ran up and down the hallways searching for wounded sons and brothers. I was told my medical evacuation from Vietnam had happened so quickly, arranged by my friends in Cam Ranh, that my original company commander had not been informed, and so my parents had not been officially notified of my arrival. As the sobs of joy rang down the hallway, I kept remembering the soldier I had baptized in Phan Rang and thought the parents running by my stretcher so lucky. After an hour of happy greeting I was ready for my own reunion with my family the following day.

My parents and two sisters rushed to the hospital the moment they received the phone call, my mother crying all the way, according to my sister Judy. But by the time they found the right ward and bed number, I was not at all ready to receive visitors. The worst jet lag, painful constipation, nervous anticipation, and Percodan for the pain in my leg left me brain-damaged. My eyes would not stay open, and when they did, my mother just kept saying, "Hi." I kept saying, "Hi. I'm okay. Shit, my leg hurts," and "How's everyone?"

139

After getting my body back to normal, my records straight, the cast off my ankle, and a new cast on my leg, I was allowed to go home for a month's leave.

When my father turned into the driveway at 18 Osprey Lane and pulled up to the big house where we had all done so much growing, it was a beautiful warm summer day like hundreds I remembered. My brothers helped me into my clean and sweet-smelling room, neatly arranged and decorated with flowers by my sisters. It was a grand family reunion . . . greetings by my relatives, reminiscing and laughing with my brothers and sisters, huge dinners, and, as I thought, requests for *only* the funny stories from my eighteen months in Vietnam.

For the first two weeks my mind and time were spent on my family. But after the stories from both sides had run out and the joy of my return had run its course, I watched my family's lives move quickly back to their normal routines. My mother wanted to keep me home forever, my father forgot I was there, my brothers had to play basketball, and my sisters had boys to chase or dolls to care for.

By the end of the month I was ready to return to the hospital and get my life back into some sort of forward motion. I loved my family and the attention shown me, but I felt alienated, not by any of their actions, but by my own feelings of inner boredom and loneliness. The shock of suddenly being immersed in a luxurious atmosphere after the gut-level intensity of survival in Nam was too great and too quick. I felt as if my mind and heart were still there, not having been officially released from that part of the Vietnam experience.

I was admitted to the Medical Holding Company, where I would wait for my left leg to heal, and was confined to a wheelchair or crutches until then. After a month of television for six hours a day, visits by well-intentioned Red Cross grandmas, and the most incredible boredom of life, I was ready for combat duty. The day my cast came off for the last time, I volunteered for any duty the company could give me. I was assigned, because of my hospital work in Nam, to the Laboratory Section at the Army Induction Center at Fort Dix. The blood lab set up a chair so I wouldn't have to stand, and I began my duty of drawing blood from one thousand new pimply-faced inductees a day. I sat there and watched

the new meat for Vietnam stream by—smiling, crying, faint-
ing at the sight of their own blood—and what would they do,
I thought, when they saw one of their buddies or perhaps
their own legs blown around backward?

Four months after my return from Vietnam I completed
my physical therapy, said good-bye to my crutches, was officially assigned to the Hospital Medical Company, but was
still absolutely, positively, no one. I felt empty and alone on
an army base with thousands of men around me. I was doing
my job and doing it well, and who cared? The only place and
time in my entire life where I felt needed and wanted came
rushing out of my memories the day I found a letter waiting
for me from Sister Hoa.

She had written the letter in her fine, French-schooled
script, to tell me of the orphanage's situation: the city was
swollen with refugees from the villages and towns around
Saigon due to a drastic increase in the fighting; for almost
two weeks fighting had been raging in the streets of Saigon
between the South and North Vietnamese troops, with fires
and bombs destroying many buildings and homes. Food was
scarce because all the markets had been abandoned and the
city water had been shut off for almost ten days. People were
starving and dying on the streets, and they were now only
able to feed the children rice once a day. She apologized for
not being able to send me better news but felt that I would
understand the truth. She asked if there was any way I could
help, maybe send some green money, always exchangeable.
She ended the letter by saying, "We are now forty children.
Sister Tuan, Trong, and I send you our prayers and ask that
you remember us in yours." At the very bottom of the letter
were two lines written by Thom in Vietnamese. Sister Hoa
had written the translation right below them: "I am sorry. I
love you, Uncle Paul-san. Ding Thi Thom."

I read the letter over and over. It shocked me, not so much
because of its depressing news but because the reality of the
orphanage reached out from it, like a ghost from the past,
and right when I had been thinking about them as if they
were only a happy memory. The letter brought to life the re-
alization of how much happiness I had shared with them.
Vietnam had provided the backdrop for the most important
and intense experiences of my life—the highest with the chil-

dren and the lowest working with the wounded. The losses had been painful, and I never wished to repeat them, but greater still had been the reward of feeling I was needed, really loved, and accomplishing something beyond rote duty. There in Vietnam, I started growing up. Here in Fort Dix, I was just another soldier doing time.

That letter, which I folded carefully and carried with me for the next year, started me back toward Vietnam. I decided to request Lab Technician's School, so I could increase my monthly salary, finally be something other than a volunteer, and be guaranteed a noncombat assignment when I returned. The next step was the hardest. I sat down with the Medical Company's reenlistment officer, signed on for another three years in the army—the first of which would be in Vietnam—was promoted to Specialist 4th Class, and picked up my tax-free reenlistment bonus of ten thousand dollars. Now that will buy a few weeks' worth of groceries, I thought. As I began tech school, I started to send Sister Hoa small amounts of money through the mail and even found a group of women who initiated a drive to send care packages to the orphanage.

All during my eighteen weeks of lab school in Texas and my eight weeks of on-the-job training at Fort Dix, I dreamed of returning to Vietnam, just as I had dreamed of returning to New Jersey almost a year ago. My family and friends thought I needed immediate psychiatric counseling, and I couldn't make them believe or understand why I was happy about returning. "I'll write it all down some day," I told my mother. "I can't explain it now."

"Just remember I love you, now and always," she said as she waved good-bye to me from the porch of 18 Osprey Lane. "And I love you," I yelled back to her as my father drove us out of the driveway.

On September 28, 1969, I left the United States Army Replacement Station, Fort Lewis, Washington, for Bien Hoa, Vietnam.

— 15 —

The Little White Lie

As our chartered Pan Am jet turned on its final leg into Bien Hoa Air Base, a fresh new private sitting to my right was staring out the window. "Man, look at that. I can see gooks running around all over the place down there," he said, then looked over to me. I decided not to say anything about his use of the word gook, but he knew it all. "What's the matter, Specialist, you afraid of the 'Nam.' Man, I heard Nam ain't shit . . ." He stopped after spotting the ribbons over my left pocket. "Sorry, man, you already been to the 'Nam,' " he said apologetically. "That's right, Private. Start getting scared," I said. "And by the way, all those little gooks down there are Americans. That's the 101st Airborne Base camp." He shot a quick look back out the window. "No shit. Airborne all the way, man, but those dudes is crazy," he said.

After three days of processing, I was assigned to the 9th Medical Laboratory in Long Binh. Two days in a barracks building with four hundred smelly feet, farting sleepers, and more radios than people in Japan. My name is called, the orders clerk hands me ten copies of my assignment orders, points out the door, and says, "It's right there. The big tin building across the way. That's the 9th Med Lab."

But I was still fifty miles from Saigon . . .

The 9th Med Lab processed blood specimens and other body fluids for hospitals all over Vietnam. They operated out of a neat little air-conditioned building and it looked like real easy duty. While I was waiting to meet the First Sergeant, I just happened to look across his desk and saw a list of the personnel requirements for the different areas of the company.

In the middle of the list was a request for a forensic pathology technician for the United States Army Mortuary, Tan Son Nhut Air Base, Saigon. I had no idea what a forensic pathology technician was or did, but I immediately made myself one. When the First Sergeant introduced himself to me, welcomed me to the company, and asked what I had done at Walston Army Hospital in New Jersey, the first words out of my mouth were "Mostly forensic pathology, First Sergeant. Some hematology and blood bank but mostly forensic."

"You're kidding," he said without smiling, and I started to sweat. What if my orders say, "This man has not done any forensic pathology work ever."

"I been looking for a replacement for one of our men at the mortuary for almost three months now," he said, slapping his hand down on his knee.

"That's pretty lucky, huh?" I said, with water now soaking the armpits of my fatigues. For two days I sweated in fear of the First Sergeant finding out I had told a little white lie. I was too afraid to even ask anyone from the company what a forensic pathology technician did. The following day I found out in explicit detail and wished I hadn't lied.

A supply truck dropped me off at the front gates of the Army Mortuary and sped away. The driver said he couldn't stand the smell that hung over the place. I carried my duffel bag to the portable truck-mounted offices of the Forensic Pathology Division and knocked on the door. Maj. Harris Williams greeted me with a handshake and ushered me into the air-conditioned office.

"This is our office," he said, sitting down behind his desk in the cramped little room that had two more desks and one extra chair. "Have a seat. Larry will be back in a second." He went back to the papers in front of him. That was my introduction to my new Commanding Officer. Thirteen words. This guy will be a breeze to work for if he is always this quiet, I thought. And how many people in the whole army are in a company where it's you and one officer. The next 365 days will be a piece of cake. I'll do my job and spend the rest of the time at the orphanage. I looked around the office and at Major Williams. He was a tall serious-faced doctor who looked to be about fifty years old. He was immaculately dressed in clean starched fatigues, spit-shined boots, and

ore his graying hair in a close-cut flat top. Total army by
ae book. I looked down at my sweaty wrinkled fatigues and
:uffed boots. As I was trying to wipe some of the dust off the
æ of my boot the door swung open and Specialist 5th Class
arry James entered. Larry was a neatly dressed black man
bout thirty-five, and although he seemed strictly military,
e was relaxed and cordial.

"Welcome, and let me say, you are a sight for sore eyes. I
as beginning to think they'd never find a replacement for
ae," he said, smiling from cheek to cheek.

"Larry. Why don't you give Hensler a quick tour and
aen we'll get lunch," Major Williams said without missing
line of the text he was reading.

"Yes, sir . . ."

We started the tour by walking around the end of a
arehouse-type building, two to three hundred feet long, and
ntered the administrative offices. Larry introduced me to the
rmy clerks and a young lieutenant, who was the Mortuary
Records Officer. We then passed a series of mess hall refrigera-
ors which were connected to the other mortuary buildings by
overed walkways. Next was a tour of the parking lot where
arry pointed out the incinerator where I would burn speci-
aens after an autopsy. "That is if the embalmers don't want to
ut the innards back in the body," Larry said, leading me into
he main mortuary building. AUTOPSYS? . . . INNARDS? . . .
ACK IN THE BODY? . . . Stacked around the incinerator in piles
igher than a truck were thousands of long metal shipping con-
ainers, and later I would find out the grisly reasons for their
bundant existence.

"Now, this here is the registration and identification sec-
ion, where the bodies are received from all over Nam." We
valked into a large, brightly lit room. The immediately
aauseating smell of blood, feces, and decaying flesh hit my
ace like the marine's fist. I had just walked into my worst
aightmare. "These guys identify and process the dead. Then
hey either send the body to us for autopsy or into the next
oom for embalming," Larry said, then started to introduce
ne to the three men in green surgical scrub tops. I tried not
o see the four tables, a bloodied, mangled body on each. The
echnicians were checking the dead men's teeth against their
nilitary dental charts and matching intact faces with photo-

graphs. I looked down; there was blood on the floor. I reached out to shake a hand but the rubber gloves were covered with blood. This cannot be happening to me. "After they are positively identified, so that the right body goes back to the right family, their wounds are checked. If it is determined that a dead soldier's wounds are either self-inflicted or from a close range, as in homicide, they can request an autopsy, and that's where we come in." Larry droned on. I was watching his lips move and could hear what he was saying, but I was trying to keep my feet from running out the back door. I wonder what would happen now if I told them I lied. Long Binh prison was only three miles from the 9th Med Lab Headquarters.

After Registration and Identification, we entered another huge, cavernous room. Along each wall were six embalming tables, a naked body on each of them. "This is the embalming room, where our four civilian embalmers prepare the bodies for shipment," Larry said and again introduced me to four Americans, who waved. At the head of each table I could see a glass-topped pump filled with a pink fluid that ran through tubing and into the dead soldiers' necks and groins.

"Is there a bathroom around here, Larry?" I asked.

"Sure. You're not gonna blow your breakfast, are ya?" he said, slapping me on the back.

"No. Just gotta pee."

"It's right next to our room, come on," he said, leading me out a doorway at the end of the room.

I ran into the locker room and stopped when I saw three Vietnamese janitors squatting on the floor eating. They smiled up at me, then went back to their lunch of bony fish and rice. How could they eat with dead bodies only fifty feet away? I went into the toilet stall and leaned against the wall. What had I done? How could I have been so stupid? I was shaking and beyond losing my breakfast, angry I had lied my way into hell.

"Let's go, Hensler," Larry called from the hallway.

Before showing me the actual autopsy room, Larry took me back outside to the refrigerator section. "These are the reefers where bodies waiting to be autopsied or embalmed re kept. Some of these reefers hold bodies waiting for identification, so make sure when you come in here to get a body or autopsy you check the tags.''

We entered a dark smelly icebox where body bags were packed like lumber against the walls, and above them more were suspended on racks. ''Like I said, make sure you check the tag on both the body and bag before you start work on them. When the fighting picks up, this place gets pretty crowded.''

We entered another reefer that had nothing to do with autopsy and contained the remnants of bodies, six bones and a handgun, a torso with no legs or arms. I was sure Larry was trying to show me around so I knew what and where everything was—but maybe he was also trying to see if I could take it, I thought. I looked across the stretchers with their tiny mounds of evidence stacked on them. They gave the room a strange feeling of eerie loneliness, a sadness as desolate as the empty space on the stretchers surrounding the pitiful remainders of human life. I looked at Larry, slamming through the refrigerators, chattering to me matter-of-factly, as if we were butchers touring a meat-packing house.

The final stop on the morgue tour was our autopsy room. It was a simple, white-tiled room with four white enamel autopsy tables, butted up against a drain that ran the length of the room. A large gray storage cabinet for our tools, a couple of garbage cans, and a hose to wash down the room completed the furnishings. Through a large wooden door was the X-ray room where every body was X-rayed, head, chest, and abdomen, before being autopsied. ''Don't worry, I'll show you how to operate the machinery. That's the easy part. It's taking the brain out with no scalpel cuts that Williams is really tough about. Come on, let's eat,'' he said, slapping his hands together enthusiastically, and I almost collapsed in a heap on the floor.

Lunch was the farthest thing from my mind, but I was happy to get away from this morning's horror show. As Larry drove our jeep the short distance from the mortuary to the air base gates, Major Williams lectured me on the virtues of being stationed in Saigon . . . its beauty, its art galleries, antique stores, restaurants, all giving it a cosmopolitan air. ''It has everything you need and can be a lot of fun, but re-

member curfew: 10 P.M. And watch out for the bar girls
There's a strain of syphilis running around that is resistant to
all conventional types of antibiotics.'' He was almost fatherly
as he dispensed his advice. The cool breeze popping the canvas top of our jeep was no relief for my sweating palms. The
orphans were going to be a lot more important to me than I
ever dreamed, I thought, and then smiled. I can do it, no
matter what. The nuns and children will just have to help me
out for a change.

We arrived at the 3rd Field Hospital where we would eat
all our meals and report for any medical problems. As we
were waved into the parking lot by a Military Policeman, I
knew this hospital was very different from any one I had seen
in Vietnam. All the others had been makeshift buildings,
tents, or quonset huts with rough living quarters for their
personnel. But 3rd Field, with its substantial and attractive
whitewashed cement buildings and high protective walls
around it seemed more like an embassy. One facet of the hospital layout was immediately familiar to me, though. The triage area. Theirs faced the parking lot and sat on a large
cement pad with a tin roof shading it. Modern stretcher
stands, rows of fancy new equipment, sterilized surgical
trays, and piles of inventoried medical supplies waited on
one side of the pad. It was the only outward feature of this
white elephant of a hospital that connected it to the war that
raged on many miles away.

The mess hall was like a small-town stateside coffee shop,
but I was more impressed with the hospital staff who sat
around eating. Doctors in Class A khakis wearing lab coats,
nurses in white uniforms, cap, and shoes, and the enlisted
personnel in starched fatigues. Saigon was definitely fat city,
I thought, as we sat down at one of the tables. Through the
screened wall an old Vietnamese papasan was tending a
small garden of ferns and orchids, his wrinkled hands snip-
ping dead leaves, admiring the delicate flowers. As I watched
him, my apprehensiveness about my new assignment less-
ened. When I found the children again and had them and
this oasis to retreat to from the mortuary, life would be easy.
Still, I had only taken a bowl of lime jello from the food line,
and I couldn't eat it.

There were no autopsies waiting for us when we returned,

so Major Williams told Larry to drive me to my quarters, where I could take the afternoon to get settled.

Plantation Road was one of the major city streets that ran from the center of Saigon out to China Town and the suburbs. My new quarters were just one in a series of apartment buildings along Plantation that had been taken over by the military and were conveniently located in the center of the poor man's whorehouse district. My building, about fifty yards off the road, looked like a college dormitory, except for the sophisticated labyrinth of squatters and refugee shacks that ran up to it on three sides.

I signed for my room and was issued two sheets, a blanket, and pillowcase. "Give your maid ten bucks a month and she'll do your laundry, iron your fatigues, and spit-shine your boots. You gotta buy her the soap, starch, and shoe polish, though," the army sergeant said, as Larry and I started up the stairs. My room—two beds, a cold-water stall shower, two skinny lockers, and a seatless toilet—was on the sixth floor, and this building had no elevator.

"Where do you stay, Larry?" I asked.

"Eighth floor, but I haven't slept here for months."

"Nobody checks on us? Williams doesn't . . ."

"Look . . . I'm going to tell you the easy way to do Saigon," he said, sitting on the bed across from me. "Williams is a good man. He'll never hassle you as long as you're on time, in uniform—a clean starched uniform," he said pointing to my pants. "Do your job and keep your mouth shut. What you do on your time off is your business as long as you stay out of trouble. Just stick by that and you'll have an easy tour."

"How the hell can doing autopsies all day be an easy tour? How do you do it?" I asked.

"Hensler, they sent you down here to replace me because you have autopsy experience. So you know what it's like. Right?"

"Yeah . . . But . . . I've only done a couple of babies and one old man. Easy stuff," I said, beginning to sweat with fear.

"It ain't no different here. These dudes are gone. Dead bodies forever. Our only job is to find out the reason or cause of death. That's all there is to it. Do your work and get the hell away from that place . . .

"I don't know what else to tell you except jump in one of those three-wheeled cyclos you saw out front. Say China Town or Tu Do Street for French food. Meet a pretty lady, shack up, and cruise. That's how it's done here . . . I gotta go . . . I'll pick you up out front in the morning. Seven. Okay?"

"Yeah . . . Thanks."

I took a quick shower and lay down on my bed, smoking a cigarette. My mind reviewed the day's events, recoiling from the terrifying image of bodies stacked in a refrigerator, a pile of bones on a stretcher, and radios blaring rock and roll while embalmers worked over the dead. I tried to picture my reunion at the orphanage, but my thoughts kept returning to the mortuary. I could see Major Williams standing over some boy's body, pointing, "There you go, Specialist Hensler. Show us what you can do."

I wondered if Thom and Trong had changed . . . it had been almost a year since I left. In Vietnam a year was like ten. A lot could have happened, they could be dead, the orphanage gone.

Something touched my foot. There was a woman standing at the end of my bed. "I'm sorry, Sister," I yelled as I sat up.

"Joe . . . my name Bic, I wash for you," the pretty young woman said. It was my maid. My watch said 6:55 A.M. and I shot out of my bed. The woman giggled and turned her back. I was standing stark naked trying to get my bearings.

— 16 —

Autopsy Number One

At six fifty-nine I raced out of the building still pulling on my clothes. I wasn't going to be late my first morning of a new assignment, even if I looked like I slept in my uniform all night. We drove toward 3rd Field Hospital for breakfast, Larry pointing out the better whorehouses in this part of town, a couple of the cleaner restaurants, and maybe by mistake a series of alleyways that ran from the street into dark winding dungeons, where he said one could get the best price for black market goods.

"Everyone survives on the black market around here, officers and enlisted men," he said when I asked him how dangerous trading in Saigon was. "I don't mean to say that people like Williams do it with intent. It's just that most of the time when you can't find what you want on the base, you can find it down one of those alleys. Most of the stuff never makes it to the military supply houses," he said as we crept through the morning rush hour traffic and came to a stop at a traffic signal. Larry pulled a handkerchief out of his pocket and covered his face. "What's wrong?" I asked. "You'll see when this light turns green." I looked out around the jeep and saw that we were surrounded by Vietnamese riding Honda motorcycles. Thousands of 50-cc Hondas, their banana seats packed with entire families. Dad on his way to work and three children in neat little uniforms on their way to school. When the light finally changed, we were totally engulfed in white blue oil smoke from the motorcycles, and I started to cough.

"Rush hour in this city is worse than Manhattan," Larry said as we turned into the hospital parking lot.

"I'll be picking you up at your quarters for the next few days until you find your way around the city. Then you'll have to get here on your own. We meet here every morning for breakfast at seven, and Williams is in the jeep ready to go at seven thirty. Whatever you do, don't keep him waiting. And Paul, we drive him, like chauffeurs—when he wants to go someplace, we drive. The jeep is parked here at night, and he keeps the key . . . You got all that?'' Larry asked. "Yeah. No problem,'' I answered.

Twenty minutes after gulping down real scrambled eggs, toast, hash browns, coffee, and a doughnut, the best breakfast I had ever tasted in Vietnam, Larry and I were dragging a body out of the reefers. We pushed the gurney into the X-ray room and I began my first day in hell on earth.

After putting on a surgical scrub top and rubber gloves, we approached the green body bag on the gurney.

"Everybody that is to be autopsied is X-rayed first to see if there are any metal fragments, bullets, or foreign objects in an area we might not be able to see. We are also looking for broken bones in homicides, suicides, drug overdoses, and anyone found dead without an apparent cause,'' Larry said, turning to the body bag and pulling the full-length zipper open. "This guy will be easy.'' He opened the bag. My eyes nearly blew out of their sockets. The bag contained the badly burned remains of a human. Its arms and legs, like the children from the orphanage fire, had contracted back to the fetal position. The man still wore his helmet, a name and a skull and crossbones painted above the sun visor.

I took a step backward when the smell of barbecued flesh hit my nostrils. "This guy crash-landed. Why do we have to autopsy him?'' I asked, gulping for fresh air.

"Oh yeah . . . We also autopsy every pilot killed in Nam. This guy was a helicopter pilot, something we see almost every day. The cause of death is not what you see. I mean it's not because he was turned into a crispy critter by jet fuel,'' he said, dragging the body onto the table with a sickening thud. "The military wants to know what made him crash. Was he shot down, blown out of the air, mechanical failure, on drugs while he was flying, had a heart attack, and so on. In other words, they want to know why this guy buried millions of dollars worth of taxpayers' money into the Vietnamese countryside, going six hundred miles an hour,'' Larry said, adjusting the X-ray cone over the pilot's head. 'Come on back here behind the screen, unless you don't mind frying your balls.''

Somehow my breakfast remained in place, mostly because of Larry's endless speech about autopsy procedures, some of which was interesting but most of it brutal and bizarre. It wasn't until he pulled a long-handled pair of tree-trimming shears out of the tool cabinet and began snapping through the dead man's ribs that I started toward the door.

''I drank too much coffee, gotta pee,'' I said, feeling the muscles in my stomach begin to spasm.

''You only had one cup,'' Larry said, snapping through another rib.

''Okay, I'm gonna puke, sorry.''

''Hurry back, Williams will be in soon.'' Snap went another rib, and I ran to the drain and lost my breakfast.

''Put some cold water on your face quick, and don't feel like an asshole. The same thing happened to me. Only it was a guy whose chest was full of maggots that got me,'' he said, and I barfed again.

''Okay? You feel better?''

''Oh God, I'm dying.''

''You can't . : . Let's keep going,'' Larry said, and kept talking.

''First off, you fix the specimen bottles, blood tubes, plastic bags for the larger toxicology specimens, and make sure everything is labeled with the dead man's name and autopsy number. Every case we do is logged into our main book and given the next autopsy number in the book. All those numbers have to match or Williams will have a stroke. On almost every case, we do toxicology. That means we send brain, liver, kidney, as organ specimens where a foreign chemical will collect and can be identified. Then you take blood, urine, and gastric contents, for the same reason. If the guy was on drugs, it will show up in one of the six,'' Larry said, picking up a handful of rusty tools and placing them on the table next to the body.

''Do we do the toxicology?'' I asked, pulling on a fresh pair of rubber gloves.

''No. We freeze the specimens in the icebox freezer in our

office, then ship them packed in dry ice to the 406th Med Lab in Japan. I'll show you all that stuff later. Never—and I repeat for your own good—never open a body until Williams has seen it—or tells you to. There's a lot of evidence needed in some of these cases that you may screw up.''

"At the moment you don't have to worry about me playing with these guys unless I have to,'' I said.

"In two weeks doing autopsies will be like driving a truck,'' he said smiling at me.

"Bad comparison. I used to be a truck driver!'' I said, now feeling a little better.

"This guy we can open because even if there was external evidence we couldn't find it for all the burned tissue.''

Larry picked up a large scalpel and cut through the skin that remained. Within seconds his deft hands had the chest and abdomen opened, exposing the entire array of internal organs. He cut away the breastplate and threw it five feet into the drain, where it landed with a wet thud and caused my knees to begin shaking again. It was all so automatic or mechanical, throwing body parts around, banging the body on and off tables and gurneys. And yet I realized that I would probably have to become as dispassionate toward the inert flesh and bones in front of me, if only to keep myself from ever becoming autopsy number two.

Major Williams walked around the table, a diagram of the human body on a clipboard in his hands. With marks and pencil shading he indicated degree of burns, broken bones, approximate height and weight.

"Okay, Larry,'' he said, relighting the stub of a cigar that hung from his lips.

"Okay, Hensler, move over here and watch closely,'' Larry said, snapping into a teacher-student attitude with Williams watching us.

"Yes, Specialist!'' I shot back. Two can play at this game.

Again, like a practiced surgeon, Larry's hands manipulated the scalpel down through the windpipe right above the vocal cords, then straight down the spinal column, cutting the entire block of internal organs out in one piece. After placing a cutting board at the end of the table, Larry deposited the entire mass on the board so Major Williams could begin his pathological dissection and examination.

"Thanks, Larry. Let's take a look at the brain," Major Williams said as he began to cut into the heart.

"Yes, sir."

"Hensler, why don't you cut the helmet off while I pre-are some tissue bags," Larry said and turned away from me.

It's over, I thought. I'll probably slip, cut this guy's head ff, faint, and wake up in prison. I picked up the electric tryker saw that Larry had placed on the table during the etup lecture. It was the same saw used to cut casts off broken ones with a vibrating rather than spinning blade, but where he hell do I start? I picked up the saw and flipped the switch. Nothing.

"The plug's over there," Major Williams said without ooking up from his work.

"Thank you, sir," I said. Now he knows, too.

I pushed the plug into the wall socket and the vibrating aw jumped to life, bouncing and grinding against the namel table with a bone-chilling sound. Both Major Williams and Larry jumped, and I jerked the plug back out of he socket. Be cool, I thought. That can happen to anybody, nd for one brief moment I thought maybe cracking rocks in he hot Vietnamese sun would be easier.

After four minutes of grinding, jamming, and an acrid moke that filled the air from the fiberglass helmet, Larry ook the saw from me.

"Sometimes these helmets are tricky," he said and then lmost whispering, "especially when you try to cut through he metal SNAPS."

"Sorry. I've never done helmets before," I said, trying to ide my embarrassment.

That afternoon I did my first solo autopsy, with Larry elping me along the way. It was a fairly simple one as far as lead bodies go. A 250-pound, career army sergeant, who te, drank, and smoked, all in excess. He was eating lunch at he base Noncommissioned Officers' Club, turned blue, fell ff his chair, and died, before anyone could determine what was wrong with him. We found a large piece of steak lodged n his throat. He had simply choked to death while eating his second sirloin for lunch.

After two hours of cleanup and paperwork, we dropped

Major Williams off at the hospital and said good-night. I at
a quick dinner, then wandered out to the American guard a
the hospital gate. He had no idea where Gia Dinh was ex
actly but knew that the area was off limits for all U.S. person
nel. I asked several other people and got the same answer.

It was already dark, so I decided to wait until the next da
so I could find a toy store and look for the orphanage in day
light. Standing on the curb, watching the Saigon evenin
begin, I felt both happiness and fear about my reunio
with Thom and Trong. If for some reason they were gone o
dead . . .

——— 17 ———

From Bodies to Babies

Another taste of the horror that would be mine to deal with once Larry left waited for us the following morning.

> The body is that of a well-nourished, well-developed twenty-eight-year-old white male. Preliminary examination shows extensive and traumatic blast injuries to the face, chest, abdomen, groin, arms, and legs, with almost total expulsion of the internal organs . . .

This twenty-five to twenty-eight-year-old 2nd Lieutenant had only been in Nam for two months. He ran his platoon into the ground with suicidal raids on known enemy strongholds, barracks, and weapons inspections before and after long missions and generally right out of the book, ridiculous bullshit. The men showed their appreciation and affection for their new leader by rolling a hand grenade under his bed while he was dreaming of his promotion to General!

Right before lunch I washed the last of the autopsy tools, rinsed the blood off the table and floor, and with no autopsies waiting was given the afternoon off.

Larry dropped me off in downtown Saigon and noticing my high spirits said, "You already got yourself a lady, huh? You work fast, Hensler!"

"Yeah . . . She's got kids. You should see them!" I said and walked away before he could answer.

Larry had dropped me on Tu Do Street, the only downtown street name I knew. I couldn't believe I was in a combat zone. A warm breeze blew past me, shuffling papers and leaves in circles at my feet. I could have been standing on any city street in the world, where life moved forward, business was conducted, and shoppers stopped to check the new fashions in carefully decorated windows.

I passed beautiful old department stores, their windows and shelves not so full as the days of French Saigon but still stocked with the imports of the Far East. Antique shops with gilted Buddhas, rare jade, and the beautiful rosewood furniture of China. Art galleries, ice cream parlors, small cafés, and grand hotels, all visited by the immaculately, carefully dressed rich of Saigon. American civilians passed and nodded, their arms laden with ceramic temple dogs, pottery, and the spoils of some ancient shrine, trampled by war.

Where were the refugees, I thought, and their desperate architecture of tin and cardboard. The alleyways here were open and held only chauffeur-driven Citroëns and Mercedes Benzes. That was the difference, I decided, the people I passed, the vendors with neat little stands, the chauffeurs, and their fat prosperous passengers were comfortable because of the war. They were safe in the huge city, protected by wealth and friends in high places. The rest of the country was up for grabs.

Three blocks west of Tu Do the street life returned to normal for me. The first block was a fragrant treat for the eyes and nose. A flower market filled the streets in front of pastel-colored government buildings and wrapped itself around beautiful small cafés. The second block was composed of black market stands crowding the sidewalks, with only narrow passageways for easy access to the fancier whorehouses of Saigon. The third block contained the Pearlon market, surrounded by the squalid conditions I had seen so many times before. Here was where the war reached out: from the eyes of women begging for food; from the cry of a South Vietnamese soldier, dragging himself along the curb—his legs mangled; from the sight of a child whose stomach was swollen with worms; and from the thousand faces that simply stared at me from dark doorways or from under a torn blanket. They all seemed to be waiting for something . . . maybe God or Buddha, to save or take them away.

As I walked through the Pearlon market buying cheap plastic toys for the children, I felt surrounded by intense human life. If the war ended tomorrow it would go on, as if this energy emanating from the desperate and the rich had been here always and would continue forever. We Americans would only see it, or like myself feel it, but never learn its source.

I hired a "cyclo," the strange three-wheeled taxi of Saigon, and told the driver, "Gia Dinh." I climbed into the seat that was set on an axle in front of the driver, piling the bags of toys next to me. The moment the motorcycle moved forward, I felt like I was riding on the front bumper of a car. No matter what we hit, I would be the first to know it. I kept seeing myself impaled on the rear bumper of a truck or wrapped neatly around a tree, as we careened through town, heading toward the outlying districts.

The driver kept yelling, "Gia Dinh," and pointing to street after street, but I saw nothing I remembered. We asked for orphanages and were sent to schoolyards. I described the nuns and found myself stopped at a church, then a Buddhist temple, then another church. Finally after an hour of breathing the exhaust of a million small motorcycles, the driver grabbed my shoulder and said, "O.K. . . . I know!" He had finally figured out my description of Sister Hoa, surrounded by many children, and drove directly to an orphanage only two blocks away. He stopped the cyclo and pulled me by the arm to the gate of an orphanage whose courtyard was packed with children.

"No, Papasan. This is not the one." I turned to get back in the cyclo and saw our building. The gate was hidden now by new squatters' huts and a soft drink stand, but I had found it. Papasan smiled and patted me on the shoulder, followed by the outstretched palm.

The gate was locked. Three or four children saw me and approached cautiously. They were tiny, very thin, and sickly-looking. I didn't recognize any of them or the ten children playing in the courtyard beyond. These were not the children from our orphanage on the hill. My heart sank. They're gone, I thought, as I looked across the faces. Probably back to Song Pha.

A small boy stumbled out of the doorway, followed by an angry girl who kept slapping at his back. He was the American-Asian boy from Cam Ranh. I motioned for the children to open the gate, waving some of the toys at them, and although they were tempted, no one touched the latch. I felt someone tug at my shirt and turned. Trong backed away and scrutinized me, his eyes raking up and down my six-foot-four frame.

"What you want, Joe?" he asked. He didn't recognize me. He hadn't grown much and still wore his dirty little shorts and shirt. There was something different about him, though—a hard edge seemed to have sculpted away the soft lines of his beautiful face, and his eyes were cold and steely as he swept them up and stopped on my face.

"Where's my watch, Trong?" I yelled with a smile. His first reaction was to run, slapping one foot to the left. A second later a glimmer of recognition ignited his face. He smiled his wide crooked-tooth grin! Now he was the same Trong I remembered.

"What take you so long come back . . . Paul?" It looked like his face would break, he was smiling so hard. He yelled to the children to open the gate, then ran ahead of me screaming, "Paul come back! Paul come back!"

In a flash I was surrounded by faces both familiar and new. They hugged my legs—now that I had been declared a friend—while some of the older children from Cam Ranh stood back and stared in disbelief.

Sister Tuan stuck her hand out of the kitchen door and almost fainted. Sister Hoa pushed past her and, upon seeing me, covered her mouth with her hands.

My heart was pounding through my chest. So many dreams of seeing them all again were coming true. Visions of the children's happy faces, Trong's crooked-tooth smile and Thom, who ran across the courtyard and flew into my arms. She buried her face in my neck and pulled me close. I could feel her trembling and gently stroked her back. Through her fine black hair wisping across my face, I could see the nuns walking toward us.

I set Thom down, but she would not let go of my hand.

"You look so . . . so different. Maybe older," Sister Hoa said, and Sister Tuan added, "But you still have baby face!" Although they were smiling they both looked tired and worn. Their habits were soiled and fraying at the hems.

Suddenly Sister Hoa looked back at the building, then

turned back to me. "It is good to see you but I am very busy. Please wait awhile. I would like to talk to you."

"Sure, Sister. I'll be here for the next year," I said, and the faces around me smiled even wider.

"Good," she said and walked quickly back to the kitchen. Sister Tuan noticed me watching Sister Hoa and moved closer. "No sweat. She not angry . . . Just many baby sick now. We have many new children, too much work."

"How many are here now, Sister?" I asked, looking across at the new faces.

"Maybe thirty-five or forty . . ." She looked down at her feet, tired and clearly concerned about something. Her face was still lovely, the bone structure more noticeable because of a new thinness in her cheeks. Her eyes, which used to dance merrily without provocation, were still bright but now held a subdued sadness. She looked older . . . not physically—she was seventeen or eighteen—but her demeanor had lost its childishness.

"Things very bad for us," she continued. "No money, no food sometime for five day, nobody to help us," she said, looking back up at my face. Suddenly her face brightened, like Trong when he finally realized who I was. "You stay?"

"Yes . . ." I answered.

"Then now we be O.K."

Sister Tuan led me around to show me the more serious problems. Everywhere we went the children followed, Trong telling the new additions who I was and, by his gesturing, the story of the great Hamm's caper.

Inside, the building looked like a combat zone. Dirty little handprints bordered the bottom half of the wall. The bathrooms were unoperative, the floor covered with foul-smelling sewage. Screens that had been so hard to find and the slatted glass windows I had repaired were blown out by an explosion during the recent street fighting. Flies buzzed around several sick-looking children, landing on their gaunt faces.

"After you go, many Vietcong come to Saigon, make trouble. The house there," she said, pointing to an old two-story villa next to the orphanage that was now just a burned-out shell, "something big hit house, like bomb. Every window here break out and—one boy die." The unpleasant memory stopped her for a moment, but then the tour continued.

"Has the policeman bothered you?" I asked as we entered the kitchen.

"Only two time. He say get out, but Sister Hoa stand outside like this," she spread her arms out like Christ on the Cross, "and she say 'no can do,' no one can make us go, so the policeman say O.K. Now we no see him many months."

One wall of the kitchen was blackened by more than just cooking smoke. Trong jumped out in front of us to tell the tale.

"You know Sister," he pointed at Sister Tuan, "she cook and then big tank outside, from the Vietcong, so she throw the pot. The oil and fire go up and up and we think we die. But girl very stupid, she put water . . ." Sister Tuan let out after Trong, chasing him into the courtyard. "I save us, throw sand, not water like Sister," he yelled from a safe distance. Sister Tuan picked up a small stone and threw it at Trong's feet, purposefully missing him.

We entered one of the smaller rooms the nuns now called the nursery. Sister Hoa was cleaning the bottom of a baby with severe diarrhea. Eight more of the younger children were sleeping or crying, some lying in their own feces, their stomachs distended with worms or malnutrition. There was no laughter now, as Sister Hoa looked at me then back to the baby.

"Sister, please finish for me . . . ," Sister Hoa said. "Please, Paul, I would like to speak to you for a moment."

"Sure, Sister," I said, following her out the door. She stopped suddenly, looking through the children, then spotted Trong. "Trong, take those rags out to the garbage." Without argument he and Thom began to pick up the feces-covered rags.

About halfway across the courtyard Sister Hoa stopped and, composing her words carefully, turned facing me.

"Are you going to stay?" she asked, holding her unwashed hands behind her back. The dark circles under her eyes spoke of worried sleepless nights, tending children she could not save.

Not quiet understanding her question, I said, "I'm back for another full year, Sister."

"I know you are back in Vietnam, but did you come here to play and visit with the children or did you come back to help us and make our orphanage good?" She was looking at me sternly, demanding that I answer honestly.

"I came back to Vietnam because I missed you all. Because your letter said you were in trouble, and there was nothing for me at home . . ."

"That is not a reason to come back," she interrupted.

"I'm not saying I was bored at home, Sister . . . It's just that I knew there were more important, more fulfilling things I could do here."

"That *is* a good reason to come back." She looked at me for a few minutes and then smiled, her face flooding with a sunniness that took ten years off her age. "You must promise to commit yourself to helping us regularly—not as a whim or something to do when you want to play. It is hard for us to count on you, depend on you . . . love you, and then be let down. It is a responsibility, not a game," she said, her arched brows accentuating the importance of her words.

I stumbled around for words. "Well, Sister, I can't promise that I'll be here everyday, because I still have my army job. All I can say is, I'll come as often as I can and we'll change this place back into a number-one orphanage. O.K.?"

"Good. That is good . . . We must first get rice, the special banana and medicine for the sick ones. Then food so my children will be strong again."

"Wait, Sister," I said, pulling out my wallet and retrieving two hundred-dollar bills, hidden from the military customs officers. "You keep this in a safe place. It is for food or an emergency in case I am not here." She took the money from me.

"O.K. I will hold it for you, as Trong has kept your watch. When you need it, ask . . . I must get back to the children," she said and walked away.

I looked around the courtyard and at the building. It would take me months and probably the remainder of my reenlistment bonus just to make it work. Well, this is where I wanted to be, I thought. I came back to it. She had given me the chance to back out, but memories of more good times than bad, Thom running toward me now, and the children

zooming around the courtyard with their plastic planes confirmed my decision to return.

The market run, to beat all market runs, began with a
cyclo race through the streets of Gia Dinh. Thom and I in
one cyclo, Sister Tuan and an angry Trong, because he
wanted to ride with his partner, in the other. The drivers
seemed to be having more fun than we, as they went up over
curbs, played chicken down narrow alleys, and terrified us
with turns that almost flung us into the street.

The large market nearest the orphanage was still recovering from recent street fighting, many of its stalls vacant or
taken over by squatters and their families. I yelled to the
drivers, ''Pearlon,'' and we sped away.

When Sister Tuan saw the huge ten-block marketplace,
her face went white. I gave them each forty dollars MPC,
and taking Thom with me, we split up. It was apparent they
had not been to a real market for a long time. They raced
from stall to stall, eyes wide with the variety of choice before
them, grabbing vegetables, fruit, bottles of fish and soy
sauce, cooking oil, rice, spices, and even sweet rice cakes for
our special meal tonight. They moved in what seemed a pa-
thetic frenzy to stockpile the food before it disappeared, perhaps like recent fantasies their imaginations must have
hungrily created.

Thom and I picked out bolts of flowered cotton fabric for
baby clothes and yards of plain white material for diapers.
Thom unrolled a bolt of soft white muslin, looked up at me,
and folded her hands as if praying. She wanted us to buy the
material so the nuns could make new habits. ''Yes,'' I
nodded, and she added it to our collection. As the stall keeper
was adding up my bill, I spotted a beautiful blue presewn top
that looked to be Thom's size. The old lady tried to get her to
try it on for size, but she refused over and over. When I
pointed to different colors, she continued to shake her head
no.

Forty minutes later the four of us began to gather the
goods at the south entrance of the market. The pile got
higher and higher with each successive trip Sister Tuan and
Trong made. We would need a truck, I told Trong, and
that's exactly what we got, a medium-sized truck half filled

with caged pigs and chickens. The entire ride back we held our noses and covered our eyes, as we were bombarded by the smell of pig manure and flying feathers.

The driver of the cackling smelly truck pulled up as close to the orphanage gates as he could get. Trong looked strangely nervous, as if he were feeling sick, and jumped from the truck, almost knocking Sister Hoa over as he ran for the dormitory.

The children were quickly connected into a chain line, their eyes bulging as item after item passed before them.

"Is Trong O.K., Sister?" But before she could answer, Thom grabbed my arm and put her finger to her smiling lips, meaning for me to be quiet.

"Never mind about Trong," Sister Hoa said smiling, "we must clean the kitchen before we put this food in." She continued to help the children stack the goods outside the kitchen wall.

I paid the driver, whose look darted from me, to the children, to the money, then back to me. The children's eyes were working on him, as they had on me at the church in Phan Rang. He started to get back in the truck, stopped, then ran back, shoved the money and two of his hens into my arms. With a smile and a courteous bow he was gone.

Laughter preceded me back through the gates, but I couldn't understand why. Trong popped out of the dormitory door carrying two hens he had stolen from the old farmer. We approached each other laughing, the orphanage's two victorious men.

"God will get you some day, Trong."

"No sweat . . . Sister Hoa say all go to heaven with you!" he said, tossing the squawking chickens at me. The children broke into hysterics when I dropped the two chickens in my hands and tried to catch the others.

We scrubbed the kitchen from top to bottom, with only one quick water fight started by Trong. Next were the children, naked in line, waiting for the sweet satiny luxury of a soapy bath. As I washed child after child, I checked the sores and skin rashes. The babies were the worst, with terrible sores from head to toe and severe skin irritations from urine and bacteria-laden feces. A new diet would be the first step.

Getting tubes of antibotic ointments from 3rd Field's supply room the next.

The nuns spread bamboo mats on the courtyard cement and set the food in a large circle, picnic style. The children gathered around quietly, checking and looking to each other for reactions. Never in my life had I seen such eyes, beaming with the anticipated taste of the chicken, rice, and vegetables. Thom, Sister Hoa, and I each carried a baby to the mat and sat with them on our laps. Sister Tuan led the children in grace, then began handing each child a steaming bowl of rice. They politely waited for Sister Hoa to nod her head, and manipulating their chopsticks—like perfect ladies and gentlemen—they began sampling the pots of chicken and broth. None of them ripped into the food or stuffed their mouths, and if a child seemed to be scooping too abundantly or too quickly, the Sisters just called their name, and they slowed down.

I pushed small pieces of the starchy plantain banana into the mouth of the baby on my lap. His tiny eyes began to water, his face turned red, and before I could move him my pants leg was covered with soft, pungent stool. When I picked the baby up to check his bottom, the children to my left and right moved quickly away, all except for Thom, who put a washcloth over the mess. The nuns admonished the giggling children, then went back to their meal.

"This has got to change, Sister," I said, setting the baby back down.

"Welcome back . . . give him more banana," she said with a smile.

— 18 —

The List

After eating an early breakfast, I wandered around the triage area looking to see if there were any antibiotic ointments or creams on the main counter. Several people walked down the hallway, and each time I leaned against one of the posts like I was waiting for a bus. Without opening any drawers or lifting the plastic that covered the medical supplies, I could see there weren't any antibiotics. Plan B.

I entered the emergency room and walked up to the line marked SICK CALL. A fat and slightly effeminate medic shuffled papers behind the counter.

"Name?"

"Paul Hensler."

"Serial number?"

"RA 11755055."

"We don't use the RA or US numbers anymore. Do you know your Social Security number?"

"Yeah, sure. 146-40-6720."

"What unit are you with?" he asked and for the first time looked up at me.

"Ninth Med Lab. US Army Mortuary," I said, and the medic's face flushed. He moved another few inches away from me trying to be subtle, afraid of germs perhaps or the possibility of a residual smell or odor on my fatigues.

"What?" he asked, his eyes blinking.

"Ninth Med Lab. US Army Mortuary. Out at the air base . . . How long will this take?"

"What's wrong with you, besides having to work in that cheerful place?" he said.

"Diarrhea. I just need a bottle of Kaopectate or something."

"I'll bet. But you still have to see the doctor. About fifteen minutes."

I looked at my watch. "O.K."

"Have a seat. I'll call you in a few minutes," he said, watching me sit down. Then, clicking his tongue in pity or disbelief, he disappeared behind the curtained-off treatment area.

About ten minutes later an attractive nurse, about thirty years old, opened the curtains, pointed out the pharmacy to a marine with a bandaged hand, and looked out to the waiting room.

"Spec 4, Hensler," she called in a soft voice.

"Yes, ma'am," I said, getting to my feet. She walked back behind the curtains and I followed.

"Up on the table, please."

I sat on the edge of the table. "Are you . . ."

"I'm not the doctor. I'm a nurse," she said interrupting me. "The doctor will be right with you."

She put a thermometer in my mouth, then began to take my pulse. Her eyes lifted from her watch to me, and she smiled. None of the nurses at the hospital in New Jersey were this beautiful, I thought. She let go of my wrist, read the thermometer, wrote the results on my chart, and with another wide smile left. I liked Saigon for another reason now.

Suddenly I spotted several tubes and jars on the treatment counter. Listening carefully for footsteps, I pocketed two of everything on the counter and quickly walked out to the front desk. My concerned medic was still looking for some papers.

"Excuse me," I said, scaring him.

"That was quick," he said.

"I can't wait or I'll be late for duty."

"Those guys out there will wait for you. They're not going any place . . ." he said with a smile. "Sorry . . . Just wait a second and I'll get you some Kaopectate . . . Anybody who can work in that place all day and needs Kaopectate instead of a Quaalude has my total respect," he said very seriously. "How many you need?"

"Four bottles, if you can spare them." His eyes bulged.

"You got it."

The newness of my job at the mortuary wore off quickly. In any new army assignment there is always a period of interest in learning the job, becoming proficient, so that one can stop feeling like a student and become a member of the team. It reminded me of my first experiences at the hospital in Phan Rang, where, for the longest period of time, I felt like an observer, no matter how valuable Brian told me my help was. But unlike any other job in my past, doing autopsies was like getting deeper and deeper into a mystery novel from which horrible secrets began to appear, daring you to read on or put the book down. If this were a job in civilian life, I would have quit after day one and gone on welfare.

Major Williams plowed through the work load, saying very little about life and much about this case and that case. Larry was helpful when we were swamped but was moving closer to his departure date and began spending more time tying up unfinished paperwork and preparing to go home. And like the mystery novel, this job held many secrets that, as I feared, became worse and more frightening. But unlike a book, I couldn't put it down . . . I started another letter to my family, composing it carefully in my head, and once again I couldn't finish it:

Dear Mom, Dad, and Family,
My new job is really something. Every morning I have a nice breakfast at the 3rd Field Hospital here in Saigon, then I walk through a room where there are lots of dead people who look like the sophomore basketball team from Rumson High.

An index card on the bulletin board outside the air base PX provided me with an answer to my transportation problem. "For Sale, HONDA 350 Chopper. Excellent Condition." Freedom! Major Williams gave me permission to buy the motorcycle so I could get back and forth from my quarters to work and the hospital, thus guaranteeing I would never be late because of traffic. I wanted the motorcycle so I could get to the various markets, work at the orphanage, and make it back to my quarters by curfew. And then even the curfew problem was answered one afternoon.

I insisted on a planning meeting with the nuns to counter

the daily and scattered requests for two items at the marke
or the endless "This is broken" or "We need a new . . ."
The repairs alone would take me the next six months, an
that's if I spent every nonduty minute at the orphanage.

"Sister Tuan, the only way I could do all this and get a
least an hour's sleep per night is if I sleep in the kitchen."

"No need to sleep in kitchen," she said, motioning to
Thom. "Thom have place for you. You go with her."

Thom was excited and smiling broadly as she took me by
the hand and led me upstairs. A rat darted across the narrow
balcony outside the second-floor rooms, then disappeared
into one of the many holes in the wall. A half-hung screen
door sagged on its hinges and squeaked loudly as Thom
pulled it open and pulled me into the small room. There was
a sink, toilet, and shower in a narrow closet at one end of the
room, and a neatly made bed, clean sheets, and a blanket in
the opposite corner. She had set a candle in a tin can on a
crate next to the bed. A small ashtray and a pack of Salems,
which she didn't like me to smoke, were neatly arranged nex
to it. The biggest shock was finding one of my old fatigu
shirts, starched, ironed, and folded neatly on the bed. Thom
pushed me backward until I was sitting on the edge of the
bed, then made me fold my hands, one on top of the other on
my lap. She then walked to a small wooden sleeping platform
against the far wall under the only window. She sat down
folded her hands like mine, and closed her eyes as if asleep.
was sitting on my bed and she on hers, her playful charade
was telling me.

"Come over here, Thom," I said, curling my long finger
back toward myself slowly. She jumped to her feet and ran to
the bed. "So you think I'm gonna stay in this room, in this
nuthouse orphanage?" I said with a serious face that did no
fool her. She nodded her head yes, exaggerating the up and
down movement of her beautiful face. "Well . . . you're
right . . . I'm gonna stay here and tickle . . ." I began to
tickle her under the arms, "you into silliness," wrestling her
into a heap on the floor. Oh God, I wished she would cry out
with laughter. I wished I could unlock her tongue so she
could scream or cry or tell of the horror that held her in silence.

I sent Thom off to keep the young ones occupied so I could

ntinue my meeting. The nuns were hiding in the kitchen, a off-limits area for the children, so we would not be continally disturbed by "Sister, Trong hit me with a rock." And very time I couldn't help but laugh with memories of, Mom, Paul hit me with a dirt bomb."

"Whose idea was it to fix a room for me?" I asked Sister Hoa.

"Thom," Sister Tuan interjected. "She keep room for ou almost a year. Since you go America." I was stunned nto silence. The nuns continued writing on the fix-it list with stubby little pencil, obviously not thinking it strange or out f the ordinary that Thom had kept a neatly made bed in her oom for almost a year, waiting for someone she could not ave known would return. I hadn't even known myself until ne letter from Sister Hoa.

"Sister, how could she have been so sure that I was coming back?" I asked. Sister Tuan looked at me, surprised that had questioned her statement about Thom.

"I no can explain to you. Thom special girl. She know nings. Maybe no can speak but she know things with this," he pointed to her heart.

Several times since meeting the orphan group, I had experienced this curious blend of superstition, Buddhist dogma, nd Catholicism that they used in their perception or explanation of a specific incident. The possibility that Thom had imply made up a bed for me, as a childish expression of hope nd faith that I would return, did not enter Sister Tuan's nind. She accepted the act as an omen and, when I did return, a proof of Thom's special knowledge. Instead of erceiving her inability to speak as a sign of weakness, a andicap to her survival, Sister Tuan said it gave her extra owers. And, of course, Thom's unselfish and loving manner with the children added fodder to this belief. No wonder hey hadn't acted surprised to see me!

When the nuns finished the list, they shoved it across the able toward me and waited. Fix the screens and windows, nake tables and chairs for the feeding area, fix the bathroom, build potty seats for the little children, fix the holes in he dormitory walls so the rats will stay out, make new sleeping platforms for the children, fix the stove and sink in the citchen, make cribs for the babies, fix the holes in the outside

wall so the children will stay in, fix the leak in the water tank,
paint the walls in the dormitory (and the Sisters' room),
build a blackboard for school, and if there is some free time
please build a swing for the children in the courtyard.

That was just the fix-it and make-it list. From her habit
pocket Sister Hoa pulled the shopping list. "We do not need
all this now, just as soon as possible," she said with a smile,
then set about plucking a chicken nervously.

"Rice, canned milk, mosquito coils, mosquito netting for
the babies, medicines, sheets, diapers, clothes for the children, pots (one large one for rice), cooking spoons, new
bowls for the new children." I looked up from the list but
both nuns were now plucking the same chicken, afraid of
looking right at me. "We'll talk about new children later,
Sisters. Now where was I . . . new slippers, hair-cutting
scissors, soap for bathing, soap for washing laundry, pans for
washing laundry, string for hanging up clothes, sewing machine, and the regular foods for the children . . . So they can
get strong again." Having finished the list I looked up again,
and now there were feathers floating all over the kitchen. The
two nuns were so nervous that they were still pulling at the
naked chicken.

"Sisters, I think you've pulled all the feathers off that
chicken," I said.

Both of them looked down in shock. Sister Hoa quickly
flung the bird across the room into a large pan. "What do
you think, Mr. Paul? You can do?" Sister Tuan asked in a
low voice.

"Sure, Sister, as soon as I find a magic wand. This list will
take me months to finish."

"Well, you will be with us for a long time to come, and I
am sure you will . . ."

"Don't say it, Sister," I said, interrupting her. "I'll do
what I can, but first, here are the new rules. First, no running back and forth to the market every day. We will buy the
meat when you need it or the chickens, but rice, milk, and
those kinds of things we will get every Saturday. Second,
three meals a day for the children when we can get the food,
but no meals in between. Every time we go shopping the children eat, and then they say they're not hungry at dinner.
Third, no more children unless you ask me first. I don't have

an endless supply of money and the children we have now already keep you busy enough. Fourth . . ."

"But, Mr. Paul, what if a child is left at the gate like the one we found this morning?" Sister Tuan said. Sister Hoa looked at the younger nun with fire in her eyes.

"Don't open the gate, Sister . . ." Both nuns looked at me in disbelief. "I'm sorry, but if everyone finds out that we will take any child that is left out front, we'll have two hundred kids here in a month."

"O.K., Paul. You do what you can and we will help you. But it will be very hard for us to turn away a child who might die on the street, who is defenseless against rats and dogs," Sister Hoa said with a serious face that once again went to work on me.

"No matter what I say, Sister, you two will keep taking children. Just remember, they'll be no better in here than they were on the street if we can't feed them," I said, getting up.

"We find a way, Mr. Paul. No sweat," Sister Tuan said, and again Sister Hoa nudged her under the table.

On my way back to pick up a few things from my quarters, I stopped at the large black market area I had seen behind the Pearlon market. They had everything under the sun from new cameras to complete stereo systems. Film, beer, whiskey, American cigarettes, cases of condoms, jewelry, and the largest shop I passed even had complete surgical trays neatly layed out in its window. I entered the shop and felt like I was in Sears back home.

"We numba-one store in Saigon. We take anything you bring and give top price. You got any green money?" the wiry old man asked from behind an enormous display of U.S.-made tools.

"No, but I might have some other things."

"Greenback get best trade here, but I take anything you bring. You come to only my shop I give better price. You go to other place I give bad price, O.K.?" he said with a wide smile.

"You got a deal, Papasan. But you cheat me and I'll take care of your shop," I said, puffing out my chest for emphasis. It never failed for me. The Vietnamese had never seen people as tall as the Americans and either crossed the street so they wouldn't have to pass me or made funny gestures with their hands indicating how much taller I was than themselves.

The old man looked around, then outside the door to make sure no one was around. "Joe, I got numba-one Thai stick and very best grass. You no can get this good in Saigon. I trade with you something, you sell grass at base making big profit, O.K.?" he said, opening a cigar box that was full of neatly wrapped Thai sticks, a type of very potent marijuana from Thailand and, from what I heard around the base, a real good high.

"O.K., Papasan, I'll be back."

The entrance to the I.D. section of the morgue was lined with body bags. Jokes flew back and forth between the men trying to keep up with the workload. "Do you know why there are fences around cemeteries? . . . Because people are just dying to get in." Other men talked about their families, a local girlfriend, and the damage done to the human body by war.

There were three autopsies waiting for me, two helicopter pilots and a suicide. One of the I.D. men saw me looking at the dead men's charts. "Hensler, I wonder if these guys think about their families right before they pull the trigger. I mean total military disgrace is pretty hard on these dudes' parents," he said, prying open the mouth of a thin black soldier.

"What the hell do they care about military disgrace. They're blowin' their brains out all over this country because of the military."

"That's not what I mean. This guy's records are being processed right now for a court-martial charging him with destruction of government property. That means no burial in uniform, no burial in a military cemetery, and no ten-thousand-dollar insurance policy for the family," he said, finishing the dental identification of the man. "One quick pull of the trigger and his nightmare is over. He's ready for you guys."

"This war really sucks, man," I said, pulling the body onto a gurney.

"You got that right! . . . Next!"

The supply room at the mortuary turned out to be my first target for black market goods and materials needed at the orphanage. Bar soap, cases of toilet paper, paper towels, rubber gloves (something I would need tomorrow when I tried to unplug the toilets), toilet brushes which would be excellent for washing pots, and cases of specimen jars that would be good for the black market and food storage at the orphanage. Everything I looked at around the mortuary or in the PX and its adjacent warehouses was either useful at the orphanage or tradable on the black market.

I took my time cleaning up after two messy autopsies so that Major Williams would leave before me. Allowing him enough time to get at least halfway back to his quarters, I snuck a large cardboard box out the storeroom window and strapped it to the back of my motorcycle. The Vietnamese janitors didn't even look up as they washed out one bloody body bag after another. There were two ways of getting off the air force base. The main gate was staffed with both U.S. and Vietnamese Military Policemen and sometimes tough to get by with four cases of beer on the back of the motorcycles. The other way was out the Vietnamese Air Force gate. A much longer trip, but for a couple of U.S. dollars I could drive a tank out the back gate and sell it on the black market.

One afternoon I spotted a new case of twenty-five gauge needles under the plastic triage equipment cover. I had plenty of syringes from the mortuary storeroom but the old man was always asking me for needles. He said the local hospitals paid handsomely for them and would give me top trade. The problem was that there were always a few people walking down the long covered hallway near the triage area. I got the plastic cover off and waited for the right moment to put the needles in my large side pocket . . . The minute my hand touched the box a siren blared out from above me, and a second later people appeared from doorways all around the triage area. I was finished, I thought. Caught red-handed, but no one seemed to notice me. The siren sounded again, and the crew began preparing the equipment for incoming wounded. Leaving the needles right where I found them, I began to back away.

"You here to help?" A soft female voice asked from behind me. I turned around and found myself standing face to face with the nurse I had met in the emergency room.

"If you need me, sure," I said. "Just tell me what you want me to do."

"You're a tech, right?" she asked, putting a stethoscope around her neck.

"Yes. I worked in triage in both Cam Ranh and Phan Rang."

"Good. Then you can start some IVs, O.K.?"

"Sure. I mean, yes ma'am," I said, searching for her name tag.

"Out here in triage we call each other by their first names. Inside it's Lieutenant . . . The name is Marie . . . Marie Donaldson," she said with a warm smile.

"In the morgue I'm Specialist 4th Class Paul Hensler. But out here I guess it's . . ." A Dustoff chopper roared over the hospital only fifty feet above the rooftops, drowning out our conversation. After a second chopper rattled over, I began again. "The name's Paul." We shook hands, and I felt like I was holding the soft fanny of one of our children. I had forgotten what a woman's skin felt like, except for the time Sister Hoa and I prayed together in the field, but her hands were tough and calloused from tireless work. Marie's hand felt like my mother's. Always soft and gentle when she would rub a bump or massage a sore back.

Marie was beautiful, I decided, as I watched her talk with one of the hospital doctors. She wasn't pretty. Or even cute. Neither of those descriptions fit her. She wore no makeup or pungent perfumes. No heavy eye coloring smeared above her bright green eyes. Plain, beautiful clean skin and her infectious smile reminded me of every girl I had ever been attracted to.

An ambulance roared through the rear gate, backed up to the triage area, and its driver and two medics began to unload the wounded. The 3rd Field triage team was the best I had ever worked with. Maybe it was because they actually received fewer patients than the field hospitals, but this team was sharp and very quick. Marie had me start four IVs, and as I worked I could see her watching me. Checking me out perhaps, or maybe just being friendly. I smiled back, but before me lay bad memories as I stared down into the shattered face of a young soldier. Death would free him soon from a life that would be too horrible to describe. The doctor examined his head and, upon discovering brain tissue seeping from a large circular wound at the back of his skull, stopped us from any further procedures.

"Have him put behind the screen, Marie," the doctor said and moved on to the next patient.

"Paul. Get me a sheet from the counter, please," Marie asked, as she removed the intravenous needle I had inserted in his arm.

"What's the screen?" I asked.

She covered his naked body up to the neck with the clean sheet, which immediately began to stain red from his other wounds. "You see that small room over there in front of the ambulances? We call that the waiting room or behind the screen. When we get a case like this, where there is no way to surgically repair the damage to the brain, we leave him in the waiting room until he dies."

"Until he dies? How can the doc be so sure surgery wouldn't help him? I've seen . . ."

"These doctors and I have seen hundreds of brain cases. Take him into an operating room and the anesthesia will kill him. Put him on a plane to Japan and he'll be dead before they take off . . . This way he lies quietly, without pain, until the brain activity quits and maybe a few minutes later the heart just stops . . . I guarantee you it's not easy for us, Paul, but there are others who need the doctor's time, who have a real chance of surviving," she said, motioning to a couple of stretcher bearers.

When the triage area was quiet again, no screaming for morphine or prayers over the dead, Marie asked me to join her for coffee in the mess hall. She checked the soldier in the waiting room once more, and because she did not order the medics to move him, I guessed that he was still alive. She passed the Vietnamese janitors who were picking up the bloody bandages, ripped fatigues, and a severed hand, its wedding band still attached, and we walked the short distance to the mess hall.

"You're a good tech, Paul. I still have trouble hitting the veins on guys with no blood pressure," she said. Her eyes were friendly, darkly lashed, and set deeply under thick brown eyebrows that matched her wavy hair.

"A medic I knew taught me how to use the brachial artery pressure to find the smaller veins."

"He trained you well . . . So what then are you doing out at the mortuary, besides the most gruesome work in Nam?" she asked, sipping her coffee.

"Forensic pathology is one of the lab sections, and I wanted to be in Saigon . . . It's not that bad."

"You said you worked in Cam Ranh and Phan Rang. This year, or is this another tour?"

"My second tour . . . Insane, right?"

"Not insane but surely a questionable decision . . . Did you come back for a specific reason? Like a beautiful young mamasan?" she asked, her smile trying to soothe the prying question. I was surprised by her remark. But to her and many others, I imagined, there were very few reasons why anyone would return to a war zone!

"No . . ." I thought about Thom and the nuns. "Well, in a way, I guess I did," I said proudly.

She looked down at her watch and quickly finished her coffee. "Gotta get back to the ward. Thanks again for your help, and anytime you see us going crazy out there, jump in. A good pair of hands are always welcomed," she said and rose to her feet, smoothing out the wrinkles in her white skirt.

"I'll do that. Thanks, Mar . . . ah . . . Lieutenant," I said, watching her move to the door. On her way she stopped to talk to one of the doctors. I think I blew it again. She had asked the question that could have meant let's get together if there is no one else in your life at the moment. And I had answered stupidly. How the hell would she know my girlfriends were two nuns and a ten-year-old. What a dreamer you are, Hensler, I thought, as I watched Marie talking, her hand resting on the doctor's shoulder. She is a lieutenant and you're a lowly little enlisted man. The Uniform Code of Military Justice, or some other ridiculous rule book, specifically states that enlisted men and officers are not allowed to fraternize, date, kiss, or even talk except for "Yes, sir/ma'am," and "No, sir/ma'am." Marie walked back to my table and bent down to speak. I wasn't sure whether she was going to kiss me or spit at me and leaned back slightly in my chair.

"If you ever find yourself without your mamasan some evening, let me know and we'll have dinner," she said in a whisper, and a second later was out of the mess hall's screen door.

What about tonight, I was ready to yell, but remembered that I had promised the nuns I would tackle the last and most unpleasant job on the repair list, the plugged toilets.

Every night after the children were put down to sleep, I would begin the never-ending repairs. And each night either Trong or Thom would be there to help me. The minute Trong saw me coming out of my room wearing hip boots, he knew what was on the list and became suspiciously unable to keep his eyes open.

"O.K., Trong. You get some sleep. A girl will help me. Thom will help me," I said, knowing how much he hated girls. But not even that worked tonight. He had no boots, and the thought of wading around in the cesspool that was our bathroom sent him to the sleeping mats early.

Thom waited at the door as I waded through the black, putrid water, stirring up a smell that could kill a lair of skunks. We tied rags over our faces that helped little, and with a hanger wire I began removing the rags that had been dropped down the toilets. The water finally slurped down the drains of the strange toilets, a hole in the floor with cement foot pads on either side, and Thom and I began scrubbing with army issue cleanser. At 3 A.M. we finished and left the bathroom, its white tile floor and walls sparkling in the kerosene light.

In a steady succession of sleepless nights, and somehow without waking the children, Thom, Trong, the nuns, and I transformed the orphanage into a clean safe home for children. I continued to see new faces from time to time, but we were doing all right for the moment, so I remained silent. Three out of four of the new faces were Amerasian. Mixtures of Black, Caucasian, Latino, and even a few I could not identify. As always, the new children clung to the nuns and Thom but in a few days were in the play groups and mixing with the other children.

One bright Sunday morning the nuns asked me to babysit so they could go to mass and I said yes. This was the first time I would be alone with what looked to be fifty to sixty children and I assumed meant an easy time of watching the babies in the nursery and keeping the others from raiding the kitchen.

The first ten minutes were quiet as the little ones finished their bathroom visits, watched and wiped by Thom. I checked the nursery, changed two wet diapers, and plugged a few bottles back into crying mouths. Trong returned from the market with the long roll of wrapping paper I had sent him for, and we began to set our surprise for the nuns in motion. Trong interpreted my instructions for me; each child would dip his hands in a pan of poster paint that I had stolen and very carefully make a set of fingerprints on the paper, below which he would write his name. Then we would very carefully go right to the water tank, wash our hands, and then hang the long, fingerprinted paper over the eating area. Trong began to laugh in the middle of the instructions, and I had the strangest feeling that maybe I was making the biggest mistake of my orphanage career. I should have listened to myself. It started innocently enough. The children lined up in front of the pan that held the color they wanted, red, blue, yellow, or green, dipped their hands into the paint, and then started to fight. One wanted green, but the line was too long. The next couldn't get to the paper and slapped the child in front of him. Trong was in total hysterics as Thom and I tried valiantly to stop the disaster. I picked up two little girls who had paint all over their faces and carried them to the water tank. The paint would not come off. The surface paint did, but their skin was now stained in rainbow colors. I ran back into the melee of slapping hands and flying paint but could not stop them. Now they were stepping into the paint and putting footprints and handprints on the paper, walls, tiled floor, and somehow one of them even managed to put a footprint on the seat of my pants. If you can't fight them, join them, I thought, as I soaked my hand in red paint and silenced the laughing but still untouched Trong with a handprint on the side of his face. He was furious and screamed that this game was for children and not for men like us, then marched out of the courtyard wiping the red paint off his face.

When the nuns returned from church, Sister Tuan began

to laugh the moment she entered the gate, but Sister Hoa, like Trong, was furious.

"This will not do. Why could you not write their numbers or something? Look at this mess," she bellowed, and I chased her into the kitchen with blue hands.

"Sister, they made a surprise for you. Come on. They had a great time, and I'll clean up the mess," I said, leading her back out into the feeding area.

The children unrolled the long soggy paper that looked like the worst of some Impressionist's work, but she saw how proud they were.

"What this supposed to be?" Sister Tuan asked, cocking her head to the left and right.

"Sister, it's the children's fingerprints, and other body prints, and they all signed their names." "How nice," Sister Hoa said, looking at me with a placatory smile. "Now, children, you help Mr. Paul clean up this mess, and Sister and I will fix you all a treat." They all cheered and began tearing around the feeding area with dripping rags, smearing the paint even more. It would be another long night spent with cleanser and a rag, but it was worth it. I had not heard nor had I seen the children laugh this hard since jump rope in Phan Rang.

At dinner that evening I looked across the faces, old and new, that were gathered around the feeding area. The numbers of mixed blood had increased, but that was to be expected in a city that had as many whores as there were G.I.s. The most surprising thing I noticed as I traded winks with several of them was that in the few months since my return the children looked one hundred percent healthier. The sunken cheeks and swollen tummies were almost gone. There was a new sparkle in their eyes now—or maybe it was because of the tray of rice cakes that Sister Hoa was placing on the mat in front of them. Even the nuns were more relaxed, and with a fixed schedule and only two meals a day they now had time to begin lessons again. It was all coming together, and for the very first time. An organized, unauthorized shelter for orphans, kept in operation with stolen goods, two overfaithed Catholic nuns, and one skinny, confused, but very happy G.I.

I made time each evening to sit with the children before

they fell asleep. It was a lonely time for them. The day's activities done, no more games to play, only quiet moments to think and remember before sleep won them over. I began telling them stories of America, my family, and the many fun times I shared with my brothers and sisters. Trong would translate the stories for the children, accentuating the funny parts with forced laughter and wild hand gestures. At first they would not tell me anything about themselves or their past. Too many painful memories, perhaps, or too shy in front of their little peers. Trong would point to one of the children and begin his own interpretation of the child's past from what they had told him or he had overheard. He always made the story funny by giving each main character an animal personality. I was awed by his sensitivity, his ability to create just the right animal characters and events to tell the story, which was in fact a case history on each of them. If the child was a boy, he was always a brave animal, like a tiger or a sly, smart fox.

"This boy was a tiger-boy, very wise, very tricky. He sit in the tree and wait for Vietcong. Then jump on them and eat them. He get everyone to run when VC come, make them hide rice and VC get hungry, go away. If they come in night he make a growl and VC run, not take his family."

Trong would go on and on about the incredible feats of the child, jumping over the children on the floor, forcing them to huddle closer to me in fear of the brave tiger. Then he would end each story quickly with "Then mother and father die, or go away, so he cry for one day then come here, now he O.K."

The children would applaud quietly, so the nuns would not throw me out for keeping them awake, and then wait for the next story. When Trong told about the girls, he was much less eloquent. To him girls were just plain dumb. To him they were like lazy cats or a flighty chattering bird that could not hold still. The girls' stories ended with him being chased out of the dorm by several of the flighty birds, including Thom.

One night, as I watched a little boy adding to Trong's tale of bravery, I realized that none of the children ever spoke of fantasy. Their stories were true, real incidents from their short lives, hard for me to imagine, and, I believed, impossible for any American child to survive. When a dream was included as part of a story, the dream was to wake up and find their mother or father asleep next to them in the orphanage. Their only fantasies, I was beginning to learn, were about surviving. There was no time for fairy tales of Peter Pan, because the only people who flew in their minds were bomber pilots and a sister who had just stepped on a land mine. Mother Goose would be eaten and the Old Woman Who Lived in a Shoe was a common sight. Little Archie lived near the presidential palace and cared little about poor children, and G.I. Joe killed their pet dog. No fantasy. No dreams about growing up to be a doctor, lawyer, or Indian chief. Nothing was imaginable beyond tomorrow. They could only deal with the reality that had made them orphans. Fairy tales never held the answers to their thousand questions.

When the eyes began to close, story time ended. I set a low-burning kerosene lamp next to my chair in the doorway and waited for them to fall asleep. They liked me there, not only because it made them feel safe, but also because they never knew if their favorite monster would crawl into the room and tickle them to tears or start one of our famous pillow fights. Many times I never had to leave my chair. Just by clearing my throat or trying my impression of one of Trong's animals, the whole dormitory would burst into titters and giggles. That's also when Sister Hoa would throw me out.

By the time I finished chores and took a shower, most of the children were asleep. Thom and I would step quietly through the room, covering up legs or taking off their sandals. They were so beautiful when they slept, all their tiny, frail little figures huddled together on the mats. Once asleep they had no cares or troubles, only silence and peace for a few short hours. When I saw one of them smiling in his sleep, I could only hope he was enjoying times when great happiness was given and stored to be cherished for many a night to come. Dreams were all they had right now, the only gift I could really give them. A moment of happiness, a funny story, a new game, water fights, fingerpainting, jump rope, or just being hugged by the nuns and myself. Small moments to be used in their dreams, over and over again, tonight, tomorrow, forever.

Other children stirred or called out in their sleep, an unavoidable nightmare dragging them back to a place from where I could not help them escape. They would blindly reach out for the child next to them, small arm over small shoulder, and quiet sleep would return. If they were at home where Mom, Dad, and all the kids slept on the same bed, sleep would be much easier with their parents on each side of them, protecting them from villains, bad dreams, and even the Vietcong. Mom, Dad, a family, their homes all having been long forgotten, the child next to them on the mat had to suffice.

I wished almost every time I walked by the crowded mats that I could transport them all in their sleep to a soft bed in an American home. They would sleep soundly, a teddy bear under one arm, wrapped in soft, flowered pajamas, and buried under a thick, warm quilt. A soft voice would call them to breakfast of thick buttermilk pancakes, golden butter, sweet brown maple syrup, and mother watching, waiting to make another batch when the first call for seconds was heard.

Maybe someday there would be a way to get them out of this mess. But how, I thought. Yes, we were now well organized and happy, but neither I nor the nuns had any paperwork on these children. No birth certificates or letters from parents who could not care for them anymore, saying they were legal orphans. We were also not like some of the other orphanages, which were funded or run by a wealthy church or government organization. Our orphanage was an unauthorized institution for the unwanted children of whores. A cold chill ran through me as I looked around the room. At first I was scared by the immensity of what I and two Catholic nuns were doing. We were totally responsible for the lives of the fifty to sixty children lying at my feet. A second later I was proud and happy. It was right in every way to help those who were helpless. To give them everything I had. To make them laugh, share with them what I was given, what I knew . . . and if the nuns were right, and God really brought me here, that was O.K., too.

As I stood in the middle of the dormitory, my extended family breathing, sleeping, dreaming around me, I felt a wonderful strength. It didn't matter anymore how it all started. They were my family and my responsibility for now.

Dear God:

It all seems right, and somehow I get the feeling you're deeply involved. But then why am I so scared? Don't let me down, please.

— 19 —

Life and Death

Week after week it went on in the morgue. An autopsy on a Vietnamese woman shot to death by her jealous American lover, two more from a bar fight that ended with an explosion. Neat, one-shot suicides and fumbled suicides where they had accidentally taken others with them. Aircraft pilots seemed to be bent on burying themselves in the Vietnamese countryside, and then there were the helicopter pilots, so burned and twisted that their X-rays looked like jigsaw puzzles.

When I finished one autopsy, another waited, and I couldn't escape. I stepped outside to smoke a cigarette, and green, bloody body bags were spread out before me. I walked out to the airstrip side of the mortuary to sit in the sun, and bodies fresh from the battlefields were being unloaded from a helicopter. I said, "Hi" to one of the technicians, and he answered back, "Hey, Hensler. Did you see the guy that got blown away while he was sucking his thumb?" Several of the guys from administration were cooking steaks for dinner in the parking lot. One of them threw me a beer that was being kept on ice in the top half of a shipping coffin. I couldn't drink it.

I delivered the last of the day's autopsies to the embalming room. The Beatles' song "Magical Mystery Tour" blared from a tape cassette player, and I stood in the middle of the huge room, alone except for the bodies of seven brave men who had died in combat. Unlike the man I was pushing into the room, dead from a self-inflicted gunshot wound to the head, the bodies around me were valiant young men and boys, gone in a flash of angry gun powder—killed in a coun-

they knew little about, leaving behind them a piece of
ld soaked with their blood—weeping families, and new ba-
es never seen. The suicide case I had just completed was
e same in every way, I decided. The only difference was
at he had saved both sides a single round of ammunition.
One of the men from Graves Registration, the mortuary
tion that shipped home the personal belongings of the
ad, found me crying in the embalming room, staring down
the head of a boy who looked like my brother Mark.
at's all there was on the table, a head and the right shoul-
r. His face untouched, the stubby new beard unshaven, his
rk, black-brown hair, wet and neatly combed back, but the
st of his body blown clean away. I didn't know why I was
ying. I had seen less than that shipped home to a devas-
ted mother. Fatigue, maybe, or the unending questions
at had been flying around in my head recently. We sat out-
de for the longest time, smoked a couple of joints, but still
uldn't answer each other's questions. I had asked Major
illiams a couple of times about the war, how he felt or what
all meant, and was told it was our duty, ours was not to rea-
n why, ours was to do or . . . My friend said he had only
eard the same or similar answers, but what else should we
xpect from career military men?

I bought two small cassette players and sent one home to
y parents. If I couldn't write them maybe I could talk for
a hour, then send them the tape. I never got through the
rst ten minutes. How the hell would they understand what I
uldn't describe.

Hi Everybody,
    This is my first tape from Vietnam and from my new
job in a morgue. I'm starting on side A. Guess what, Mom
and Dad, number three son is hooked on drugs. Nothing
serious, grass, Thai Stick, and the only thing that gets me
through a week of dead faces, Dexedrine. Sorry, but there
is no other way at the moment . . .

The best thing about Dexedrine, or Bennies, as some of
he men called them, was that they were cheap and almost
ndetectable. It gave me the strength and ability to work in-
essantly, without fatigue, without getting hungry, and al-

ways kept my mind one step ahead of the task at hand. Whi
disemboweling a floater (a body that is bloated twice its no
mal size after floating in water), I was at the same time mal
ing a mental list of the materials needed to build a swing fo
the orphanage. While listening to Major Williams yell at m
for being half an hour late for work, my mind was rehearsin
how I would ask Marie out to dinner. I was totally hooked o
Dex after only ten days, and frightened, but moving too fa
to worry about it.

Before I ever gathered the nerve to ask Marie out, I ende
up begging her to help with a serious orphanage problem. I
the middle of the night, several of the children developed se
vere stomachaches and diarrhea. It was not the first time th
children were struck with loose bowels; too much soap in th
dishwater, bad cooking oil, too much grease or rotten mea
kept the nuns and myself busy many nights, nursing sor
tummies and washing soiled bottoms. But this night
seemed to be spreading through the orphanage like wildfire
All fifty children and Sister Tuan. At about 4 A.M. the symp
toms spread to vomiting and high fevers, and I knew we wer
in serious trouble.

I searched the hospital but couldn't find Marie, nor coul
I get past the American guard at the entrance to the nurses
quarters. I left a note with another nurse in the emergenc
room that she should meet me at the mess hall at noon an
headed for my motorcycle. As I passed the long row of ambu
lances I heard someone moaning and walked toward th
noise cautiously. More than once I had stopped to help upor
hearing what I thought was someone in trouble, only to fine
one of the ambulance drivers with a whore in the back, teach
ing her about love. This time I found Alan Jarvis, one of th
hospital drivers, lying face down in the dirt.

"Hey, Jarvis. What the hell's wrong with you?" I asked
turning him over. His face looked like he had run into a cin
der block wall.

"Nothin'," he said carefully feeling his nose. "Oh shit
He broke my fuckin' nose."

"I think you're right. But who . . . ?"

"One of the dudes from supply. I was supposed to get him
something, an' cause he paid me already he was a little pissec

off," he said, pinching his nostrils to stop the blood from running down his face.

"You'd better get that nose checked, man, before you bleed to death . . . So why couldn't you get him the dope?" I said, shocking Jarvis, but everybody in the hospital company knew he was the local connection. "Your source dried up?"

"No. I'm restricted to the company area for driving a bunch of whores to a party in the CO's jeep . . . I gotta go, man," he said and began to walk away.

"Hang on, Jarvis . . . I've got a source. I'll get you the stuff, you sell it." He stopped and turned back to me. "Sixty-forty, or I'll let that guy continue his plastic surgery on your face," I said and moved closer to him. "Deal?" I asked, putting on my motorcycle helmet.

"Deal," he said, still holding his nose.

"You get caught, you'd better forget my name. Tell anyone we're doing business and you won't have to worry about whether your nose will ever be straight again cause I'll rip it off," I said, then walked away. It was fun being macho once in a while. Especially considering Jarvis was only about five foot three and looked like a gopher.

All morning I rushed through the dissections, cutting and weighing organs mechanically, but all the time worrying about the children. I had heard just a few weeks earlier how plague, or cholera, or some other exotic Asian disease had wiped out half the population of a home for street boys in China Town . . . I cursed the Dexedrine that was coursing through me, making me flash on the little burned figures in Cam Ranh, then seeing the courtyard of the new orphanage crowded with sheet-covered bodies.

"Shit!" I shouted for no apparent reason and scared Major Williams who was standing right next to me.

"You cut yourself, Hensler?" he asked.

"No, sir, I . . . This brain is just too soft to get out in one piece, sir."

"Don't you masticate another one, Specialist. Larry never had a problem with the brain," he said, looking over his glasses at me. For the one-millionth time he compared me to Larry James, and I was right on the verge of telling him that Larry was not quite the sweetheart he thought he was.

"Sorry, sir, but this guy's been floating in the Mekong River for three weeks and . . ."

"I know all about the case, Hensler," he said, interrupting me. "Just don't screw it up. I need good sections for histopathology."

"Yes, sir," I said, watching the brain matter fall apart in my hands.

Marie was waiting for me in the mess hall, even though I was thirty minutes late. She smiled brightly as she watched me cross over to her table.

"Specialist Hensler requests permission to sit at your table, Lieutenant Donaldson?" I said, embarrassing Marie who looked around to see if anyone had heard me. "I'm sorry. My CO and I are starting to get on each other's nerves . . . May I sit down?"

"Please," she said, pushing my chair out from the table. "You look pretty beat. Is it bad out there?"

"Not bad . . . Yeah, it sucks . . . Sorry again. I can't seem to get it straight today."

"You want to talk about it?" she asked, then lifted my hand which was bleeding. "That's a bad cut! Did you do it in the morgue?"

"Yeah, I guess so, but it's O.K. . . . I didn't ask you to meet me so I could talk about autopsies. I need help. A favor. You're the only one I know, or can trust, and I can't really explain it now. But would you come with me after work tonight to see some sick friends?"

She was surprised by my request. She hesitated and then asked, "Have you gotten some girl in trouble, Paul? I mean, there's not much I can do medically for . . ."

"Wrong. You'll have to trust me. It's a complicated situation, and the easiest thing is for you to see it. I helped you in triage, now please help me . . . O.K.?"

Her eyes looked at me hard, and finally she smiled. "Sure. Do you want me to bring a medical kit?"

"Whatever you will need to stop diarrhea, high fevers, and vomiting . . . I gotta go . . . thanks, Marie," I said, backing away from the table.

"How many people have diarrhea, vomiting, and high fevers? I mean how much . . . ?"

"Fifty . . . and wear fatigues," I said, interrupting her, en slipping out the door.

At seven thirty that evening she was waiting for me outside e nurses' quarters. I pulled right up in front of her on the otorcycle.

"Need a lift, Lieutenant?" I said, taking off my helmet and anding it to her.

"I'm not sure why, but I'm actually looking forward to is mysterious escapade. You want to tell me about the fifty eople with diarrhea?" she said, climbing onto the seat be-nd me.

"You'll meet them soon enough, Lieutenant!" I yelled as I vved the engine and pulled out into the traffic.

"The name's Marie . . ." she said, wrapping her arms ound my waist.

I could feel Marie's body press into my back, her breasts ke two soft cushions on each side of my spine, nervously queezing me tighter as we flew through the traffic, weaving and out between the cyclos, motorbikes, and an occasional Mercedes. What a feeling I had, Marie's hands against my elly, a little rush of Dex warming me all over, or maybe it as the beautiful woman pressed into my back, holding me ght like I had never been held before.

"Where the hell are we going? . . . Hanoi?" she yelled bove the wind and the roar of the Honda's engine.

"We're almost there. Hold on."

"Any tighter and I'll be sitting in front of you . . . Paul, lease tell me who the sick people are."

"Orphans," I shouted, smiling as I thought of the chil-ren.

"What?" she leaned closer to my shoulder so she could ear better.

"I'm taking you to my orphanage. Most of the kids have een sick all night."

"Your orphanage? . . . You're not kidding me, are ou?"

"Nope . . . We're here," I said honking the horn. Thom, ho was always waiting for me at this time of day, quickly ulled the metal gate open for us.

After setting the kickstand, I jumped off the motorcycle

and scooped Thom up into my arms, happy that she looke[d]
better. Marie was still in a state of shock as she walked ove[r]
to us.

"Remember the little lady I said I came back to Vietnam
for? . . . Well, this is her. This is Thom. My number-one
girl." Thom smiled shyly at Marie and locked her arm[s]
around my neck.

"You weren't kidding! But what are you doing runnin[g]
an orphanage? I mean, how do you do it? . . . and wor[k]
at . . . ?" she asked, her green eyes wide with astonish-
ment.

"I don't run it alone. I help two nuns. But I'll give you a[ll]
the details later. Let's see how the kids are doing," I said
starting across the courtyard.

Sister Tuan flew out the nursery door holding a baby i[n]
front of her and stopped midstep when she saw Marie. Befor[e]
she could move again, the baby's loose bowels and full blad-
der let fly at the same time. It wasn't until she heard the bab[y]
grunting in pain that she held him out over the dirt of th[e]
playground.

"Sister, this is Marie. She's a nurse from the Army Hospital."

"Hello, Miss Marie."

"Hi, Sister, here let me see the baby," she said, as sh[e]
lifted the child out of Sister Tuan's hands carefully.

"How are the others?" I asked.

"Big kids better now, but babies more sick. No can eat
only sleep and . . . you see," she said pointing to the baby'[s]
dirty bottom.

"Is there some place I can examine this child, Paul?"

"Yes," Sister Tuan said, getting to her feet. "Come t[o]
nursery. Sister Hoa wait for you, Paul."

I held the nursery door open and followed them into th[e]
room that smelled of vomit and human waste.

Sister Hoa was holding our youngest baby in her arms, [a]
half-black, half-Vietnamese child left at our gate only tw[o]
days ago. The baby lay motionless in her arms as she tried t[o]
cool the forehead of one of the ten or twelve children spread
out on the floor.

"Sister Hoa, this is Marie Donaldson from the hospital
She's . . ."

"Please, Miss Donal . . ." she said, getting to her feet quickly. "This baby is the sickest of them all."

I took the baby Marie was holding as Sister Hoa handed her the other. Marie looked at Sister Hoa in surprise, not expecting such eloquent English from a Vietnamese woman. Marie only had the baby in her arms for a second, checked his pulse, then looked from me to the tired nuns.

"Sister, this baby is dead," Marie said softly. Sister Hoa leaned against the table and lowered her head. Sensing the pain that her words had brought to everyone in the room, Marie continued quickly, "When did the diarrhea start, Sisters?"

"About midnight," Sister Hoa said as she gently wrapped the dead baby in a soiled sheet.

"Leave him there, Sister. I'll take him out later," I said, stopping her from picking up the little body.

"And when did the vomiting start?" Marie continued.

"An hour or so after they woke with sick stomachs."

"What is it, Marie? Dysentery or cholera or something?" I asked.

"No. I think it's food poisoning, but it's hard to tell. All we can do is treat the symptoms and try to stop them from dehydrating, because food poisoning looks like a lot of things."

"I know what you are saying, Miss Marie. I have been giving them lots of liquid and . . ." Sister Hoa said, pointing to the children on the floor.

"That's no good, Sister," Marie said, stopping her. "Fluids will go right through them, continuing their vomiting and diarrhea. We need to start IVs on the ones who are the most dehydrated and try to stop the diarrhea on the others."

"IVs? What you mean?" Sister Tuan asked.

"Never mind, Sister, we will take care of these. Please, go tend to the other children," Sister Hoa said softly.

"Yes, Sister," she answered and started for the door. I always felt bad for Sister Tuan when she was summarily dismissed from one conversation or another.

"Sister Tuan, Thom will be your nurse. O.K.," I said, giving Thom a little shove. Thom looked up at me with a smile, then took Sister Tuan's hand as they left the room.

"Paul, I need four or five bottles of five-percent dextrose

in water and a handful of scalp vein needles,'' Marie said as she inserted a rectal thermometer in another little baby.

"I'll have to get them from the hospital. You know anyone who is on duty now that would give them to me?"

"No. I mean yes, I know a couple of people in the ER, but they won't give you five bottles of IV solutions,'' she said, looking up at me.

"Well, I sure don't know of a local hospital supply shop in the neighborhood . . . You stay here and I'll get them like I get everything else you see around you.''

"Do not worry, Miss Marie, our friend always gets what we need,'' Sister Hoa said, tapping me lightly on the shoulder.

"Paul, I . . . I guess triage would be the easiest place, I mean . . .'' Marie said, looking at me, then up at the shelf of medical supplies on the wall.

"As Sister Hoa said, don't worry, I haven't been caught yet,'' I said, opening the door. "Sister Hoa, why don't you take a rest? You've been up all night.''

"And you also. You have been looking tired, Paul. When you get back we will make you some coffee. Go now, we will watch over the children,'' Sister Hoa said, giving me a gentle push out the door. Marie was speechless. Everything so far was just too unbelievable.

The triage area was loaded with wounded and the medical team attending them when I arrived. There was no way to wander into the middle of an emergency situation and walk off with five bottles of IV solution under my arm.

Jarvis walked me to the supply room to see if a friend of his could help me out, but it was closed. He wrote down the name of another friend who worked in the main supply depot at the air base and said, "You can't miss this guy. He's the biggest, strongest, meanest black dude in Vietnam. Remember the day you found me in the dirt? He's the guy who put me there, so don't mention my name, cause I still owe him ten bucks,'' Jarvis said, handing me the note. "He's been askin' me to hook him up with someone who can dish out doses of penicillin. I ain't a medic and I hate needles, but you could do it.''

"Why doesn't he just come in to the clinic like everyone else?'' I asked.

"Cause Uncle Sam and the Hospital Commander can give you an Article 15 for gettin' syph. They says you're damaging government property every time your stick gets sick."

"Thanks, Jarvis, and I've been thinking about the money you owe me . . ."

"I'm gettin it together," he said, interrupting me. "Couple of the guys were a little short."

"I'll take what you owe me in meat and canned goods from the mess hall, anything you can get outta there that is edible."

Jarvis's eyes bulged. "You serious?"

"Dead serious."

"Dead serious? . . . You guys are sick. How can you make dead jokes and . . ."

"Forget that shit. Do I get food? Or do you end up in surgery?"

"All the food you want. No more sixty-forty split, right?"

"You got it," I said.

"And you'll get it. And check out this Moses dude. You get in good with that guy and you'll cruise in style," he said, feeling his nose at the thought of his last meeting with Moses.

"Tomorrow I'll need a couple of cases of milk powder. I'll pick it up at six thirty," I said and walked away.

"Meet me behind the ambulances," he yelled after me.

Jarvis's description of Moses was perfect. He was the largest man and definitely the meanest-looking black man I had ever seen. As he walked toward me, summoned by an equally mean-looking co-worker, he reminded me of Paul Bunyon and his ox, Babe. As he got closer, cracking his huge knuckles with resounding pops, I was ready to run. One punch from one of those fists and I could be guaranteed a new identity.

Moses turned out to be one of the nicest guys I had met in Vietnam. Tough in his dealings with the white man but illegally married to a Vietnamese woman with two kids. The penicillin he needed was for others who frequented the Soul Brother Bar he and his wife were running downtown. He loaned me a case of five-percent Dextrose in water, with my promise that I would come down to the bar on Saturday and take care of his friends who had picked up the clap or whatever else was running through the whorehouses.

I thanked him with a handshake that left my fingers numb, turned to walk out of the warehouse, and remembered the scalp vein needles.

"I forgot to get some scalp vein needles, Moses. Twenty-five gauge, if you've got 'em," I said with a smile.

"What the hell you doin'? Startin' your own hospital, man?"

"No . . . I've been helping with an orphanage in Gia Dinh. A couple of nuns run it most of the time and I help out at night."

"Is you sweet on gook kids and nuns, man? Is you a little soft or somethin'?" he said, shaking his head incredulously.

"I've known this group for almost two and a half years now. They're great. You oughta . . ."

"I think you better stop right there, little brother. Penguins and orphans ain't my thing, first of all. And second, I think I can figure out how you feed them. Maybe with shit like what you got in your hands, tradin' on the market, or with some gook hospital?"

"I've got ten kids with food poisoning. That's what this shit is for. And if you want penicillin for your friends, I've got that too. I'm not here to rip you off. I work in fair trade, just like every other asshole on this base. Just like you," I said and started to sweat again. I had no idea whether it was Dexedrine or pure stupidity that made me so brave, but all of a sudden I was scared.

"Understand me," Moses said, taking another step toward me. "I ain't tryin' to stop your action. No sir . . . But remember this, I run this action. And that means the supply room here, at the hospital, and any other supply room on this base. They are off limits to you. You trade with me, no one else, and we be great friends. I catch you stealing from me, and you'll be payin' an early visit to the base morgue . . . lyin' down . . . in one of them green body bags . . . O.K.?"

"Yeah. Thanks again," I said, almost ready to give him back the cases of IV fluids. The children needed it now, but I had a bad feeling about getting involved with penicillin for the black community.

In the past three weeks I had met seven people who in one way or another were going to provide what my depleted reenlistment bonus no longer could. Six of them were trouble, and I knew it. They had already twisted me into more lies than I thought possible, keeping one from the other, getting deeper and deeper, and all the while keeping the food, tradable goods, and drugs coming. Marie was the only one so far that had actually come to help, and I prayed we had won her over so she would return.

An hour after the IVs were in and running, the children started to feel a little better. Their fevers dropped rapidly, aided by the fluid and our ice baths, and their beautiful little faces began to get color and their smiles back. Kaopectate had stopped the diarrhea, so we gave all the little ones baths and applied powder and cream to their red and sore bottoms.

Marie sat on one of the children's stools, surrounded by children. They pulled gently at her silky hair. Thom and another girl even began to braid it and try different styles. As I had suspected, she had fallen in love with them . . . with their gentleness, unlike the street children she had encountered around the city. They watched every move she made, feeling her soft, smooth, hairless skin, watching her talk, as she explained what each instrument in her medical bag was used for. Trong felt about Marie as she did about the other girls and watched from a safe distance.

"How are you feeling, Trong?" I asked as I walked up to him.

"I strong, no sweat. How long she stay?" he asked, pointing at Marie.

"Why? You want her to leave now? She's the one who made you all feel better."

"We no like anyone but you. Sister Tuan think she better," he said, and I grabbed his arm when he turned to walk away.

"What? She's my friend, and maybe she will come back to help us. You don't like that idea?"

"No. I go black market with you, work with you. I no like her come back!" he said, pulled free from my grasp, and walked away. I couldn't believe it. He was jealous of Marie.

Thom brought me a cup of coffee and carried another one

for Marie. I followed her and sat down on a stool next to Marie.

"So. What do you think of our little orphanage?" I asked as we tapped our coffee mugs together in a toast.

"To the incredible Specialist Hensler," she said, then took a sip of the hot coffee. "You are really something else. I mean, I've never met a G.I. like you."

"And you are the first lieutenant, actually the first person, who has ever come to the orphanage here. You're a natural with kids."

"And you're a natural for the priesthood. Have you ever thought about it?" she asked, gently rubbing the back of the baby on her lap.

"No. Not recently. I don't think God and I agree on a lot of subjects . . ." I said, surprised that her question was so similar to the thinking of the nuns.

"Anyway, I'm impressed. How do you manage all this on a Spec 4's salary? You couldn't do it on my salary."

"I really don't have time to explain the whole story and get you back before curfew. So . . . How about let's have dinner some night, the lowly Spec 4 and Nurse Donaldson, and I promise to tell the whole story from start to finish," I said, helping her to her feet.

"Listen, Paul. I don't care how you do it or what you have to steal to keep it going. I think it is incredible, and yes, we'll have dinner, and yes, I want to hear the whole story, and yes, I want to come back. Maybe once a week or something, just to do a Med Cap. I can't help you on the black market, but I can get a little medicine from time to time . . . O.K.?"

"Great . . . You've got a deal, date, and our thanks. Oh, if you see a little boy walking around, staring at you with a scowl on his face, don't pay any attention to him. He's the leader of the he-man woman hater's club."

The children who were up and around waved to us as we drove out the gate. Thom diligently kept them from running out into the street and closed the gate after us.

About two blocks away from the orphanage I spotted Trong, walking alone, smoking a cigarette. I didn't know he smoked. I laughed as I remembered the many times my brothers and I had walked down the lane, smoking Marlboros like the grownups. If either of our parents came driv-

ng along, we would stomp out the cigarettes and pretend to
e looking up in the trees at a kite that had been lost years
efore.

I made a quick U-turn and then another, cruising right up
o the curb where Trong was walking. "Hey, mister," I
houted, scaring him. He threw the cigarette down quickly
nd nearly choked on the mouthful of smoke. "You like buy
umba-one American girl?" I yelled and then drove away.
He broke into hysterical laughter, still choking on smoke,
nd waved to me.

"What did you say to him?" Marie asked, leaning around
ne so I could hear her.

"Nothing. Hold on tight, the roads are real bad around
nere," I yelled back at her and then felt her press against me.

— 20 —

Death Begins to Win

Christmas Eve, 1969, produced one of the most spectacular sunsets I had ever seen. Every shade of deep red and orange filled the horizon, splitting the low clouds with shafts of brilliant gold. I raced toward the orphanage, a duffel bag stuffed with gifts strapped to the seat behind me. After a complicated week of cross-trades, penicillin injections, dope sales, and thievery, I had managed to get each child a toothbrush, toothpaste, a new pair of rubbery slippers, and either a small toy for the little guys or a notebook for the older children.

The head count required to find out how many gifts I needed produced the worst argument between myself and the nuns since the founding of the Saigon orphanage. On top of my anger that the population was now up to seventy-one, I had not slept in almost three days. Not because of work at the orphanage, but the Dexedrine, now mixed with hash, Percodan, and a Quaalude once in a while to calm me down, had left me strung out and feeling as if I were speeding toward a stage of moral and mental numbness. I could feel myself coming apart, seeing and remembering only pieces of the day's activities both at the morgue and the orphanage. I was starting to forget things, my hat, my wallet, what I had entered the PX for, and even what time I was supposed to be at work.

I sat up tall on my motorcycle seat and took another deep breath of air. Suddenly I realized that I had just passed the street the orphanage was on, and at that moment, promised myself, for Christmas 1969, to get off the drugs before I hurt myself or someone else.

My Dear Family,

This is still tape number one. It's almost Christmas. We here at the U.S. Army Mortuary can tell the day Christ was born is approaching, not because of a calendar, or Christmas wreaths on doors, but because the number of suicides throughout the country has increased. It's hard to explain, but just imagine that a lot of these guys only believe in God, the president, and their families . . . God won't answer their questions about whether it is right or wrong to kill! The president and his military leaders don't seem to want to end this stupid senseless war, and their families say it's dumb and they should be home for Christmas . . . I'm sending them home, Mom and Dad. In long metal shipping coffins . . . As for me, God and I aren't getting along. I don't know who the president is at the moment and I don't really care how you feel about the war. I'm in the middle of it and can't escape . . . Deck the halls with lots of bodies . . .

Thom let me in the gate and began dancing around my motorcycle, pointing at the gathering of children in the center of the courtyard. Sister Tuan and the children had spent the day decorating the skinny, pathetic-looking Christmas tree I had stolen from outside the air base basketball court. It was the children's first tree and they were proud of the stars and bells they had made from Styrofoam cups and aluminum foil.

I tried to sneak across the courtyard, holding the duffel bag behind me, but one sharp little pair of eyes spotted Uncle Paul-san, and the attack began. The children surrounded me, grabbing my legs, laughing and jumping up, trying to reach the bag. They knew I had something for them, maybe candy or some sweet rolls from Jarvis at the hospital. Suddenly my master bodyguard, Trong, clapped his hands together hard and barked at the chattering children. They quickly separated and watched Trong lead me safely up the stairs to my room.

"Sister Tuan, the tree looks great," I yelled down to her. She looked up quickly and then went back to placing the last of the ornaments on the tree. She had been very quiet the past couple of weeks, and I was afraid to ask her why.

When we arrived at the door to my room Trong tried to follow us inside but Thom put her hand on his chest, stopping him. His angry persistence didn't work as she gave him one last shove backward and slammed the door in his face. Thom touched my hand to get my attention, then made a circular motion with her finger to her temple, the Vietnamese sign for crazy. No one was allowed in my room, and Trong knew it but always tried. To him it was the inner sanctum of the orphanage, the one place he was denied privilege to, and it galled him that Thom, a girl, was the only one allowed to share the space with me. It was a sore spot between Trong and myself, and many times lately I had seen him look at me petulantly, as if I had let him down.

Thom had been ironing before my arrival and went back to it, her thin arms, strong as steel cord, pushing the heavy iron up and down the pants leg of my fatigues. Her strength never ceased to amaze me. Her tiny white teeth bit down on her bottom lip, and she glanced over at me as I tried to wrap the little gifts in newspaper. She was still my faithful shadow, vigilant overseer to all my needs. She washed and ironed my clothes, polished my boots, cleaned the room, and brought me coffee at regular intervals. Thom was also the only person at the orphanage who knew I took pills, and although she didn't know what they were for, she saw me taking them frequently and didn't like it. Everytime I pulled the Dexedrine bottle from its hiding place, she would move to my side and try to put the bottle back before I took one. I always smiled and said they were my vitamins, but I believe she knew I was lying. She never persisted, nor was her unwavering solicitousness overwhelming; perhaps it was the pantherlike quietness of her movements—or the aura of stability that surrounded her—which made her unselfishness so gracious and comfortable to receive.

I caught Thom looking up at me again and motioned for her to come and help me wrap the gifts. She flew across the room and wrapped her arms around my neck, shaking me with happiness. Not happiness because I was going to let her help me but, I believe, because she knew how excited the other children would be when they received their presents.

"Wait until you see what Santa Claus brought Thom," I said as I showed her how I was wrapping each set of gifts with

ewspaper and tying them up with red twine. She looked up
t me and smiled. I had two very special presents for Thom.
One she would receive tomorrow, and the second, adoption
apers that I had initiated at both the Military Assistance
Command Headquarters and with the Vietnamese Immigra-
ion Department downtown. The chances of my request
eing approved were slim, so I decided not to mention it to
nyone. But at least I had finally started what I had been
hinking about for almost two years.

There was a hard knock at the door. "No, Trong," I
elled. "You can't come in . . . so go away or I'll call the
MPs." Thom recognized the knock and opened the door for
Sister Tuan, who stood there with towels draped over one
rm and a bucket in her other hand.

"Paul, you want to help me wash kid? Sister Hoa too busy
now!"

"Children, Sister. Not kid. And yes, I'll be right down," I
aid smiling.

"O.K. children. I no like English. Why you no can speak
Vietnamese?"

"Why can't I speak Vietnamese? . . . Because Thom
won't teach me." Thom looked at me and smiled shyly. Sis-
er Tuan thought a long moment and finally realizing that I
was making a joke started to laugh.

Washing the children was another one of the daily chores I
really enjoyed but rarely had time to do. It gave me a few
minutes with every little boy in the orphanage, to tickle and
at the same time check for new sores, skin rashes, and any
signs of worms.

We sat on little stools next to the water tank, the boys lined
up naked in front of me and the girls in front of Sister Tuan.
After a good scrubbing with Phisohex surgical soap, the children would rinse themselves off in a second large pan of
water. Several times I looked past the child I was washing
and caught Sister Tuan staring at me.

"What are you staring at, Sister?" I asked.

"I like watch you with children. Your hands very big but
very soft with the babies." She was embarrassed that I had
caught her watching me.

"This is just like washing my brothers and sisters when
they were little."

"How many kid you have in the family . . . oh sorry . . children?" she asked, wrestling with the little girl in he arms.

"Ten. Six boys and four girls." As I said the words I real ized I had never told the nuns anything about myself. Tw years had slipped by us and they knew nothing about me no I about them. There simply wasn't time in the day anymore Too many kids to feed, diapers, baths, fix this and fix that And when everything was done the nuns could always b found on their knees in prayer, rosary beads clicking pas their tired fingers. I wondered as I looked at Sister Tua what they really prayed for. Peace maybe. Keep Paul comin back even though he's been acting a little strangely lately. O maybe their prayers were deeper and more powerful than I could imagine.

"Sister . . . You're very good with children, too. Do yo come from a big family like me?" Her smile disappeared and she let go of the little girl she was tickling.

"I no have family. These children be my family now," she said and continued with the next child.

Her soft black eyes, now wet with tears, looked back at me warmly. All of these people had such deep secret pain. Thom, Sister Tuan, Trong. Everytime I asked a question it seemed to set off a memory that upset them or shut them up in silence. It seemed years ago that we had jumped rope and played tag together with the kids. She was growing up . . . and so was I. I felt a twinge of sadness, remembering the old orphanage on the hill and our carefree romps in the fields. Here in Saigon it had become serious business. Like running a hotel. A full-time occupation that allowed little time for fun or laughter, not only for the nuns but for myself. The respon- sibility for feeding, clothing, and caring for seventy-one or seventy-five children overruled the homey atmosphere of a large family and forced the description of Institution upon us.

Little Kiet, a hyperactive boy, was last in line for his bath and just couldn't hold still, hopping around, singing to him- self, and splashing water all over me. Finally, I threw a cup of water in his face to calm him down and laughed as he jumped in fright. He immediately retaliated with another cup of water, but I ducked and both the plastic cup and water

hit Sister Tuan square in the face. When Kiet heard Sister
Tuan yelp in shock, he took off as if being chased by Trong,
his wet, muddy feet leaving a clear trail right to the dormitory door. I was laughing so hard I couldn't get my breath,
until Sister Tuan snapped me on the leg with the wet corner
of a washcloth.

"Sister, you have just declared war," I said, scooping a
bucket of water from the tank. The children fell silent,
smiling but unsure.

"No, Paul . . . I go to help Sister with dinner," she said,
backing away slowly, her arms outstretched as if they could
stop the water.

"You should've thought of that before."

Just as I raised my foot to take another step toward her,
one of the children sneaked up from behind and gave my
backside a shove. My foot slipped on the soapy cement, and
the bucket of water hit Sister Tuan, quickly soaking her thin
habit. With eyes flashing mischief and a grin transforming
her lovely maturing face into a adolescent's, she began to
chase me with a pan of soapy water. The courtyard filled
with laughing children, astonished by the two grown adults
throwing water at each other and soaking everything in
sight. As I hid behind one of the balcony posts I caught sight
of Sister Hoa watching us from the dormitory window, holding up two young children so they could see. The children in
the courtyard, finally unable to contain themselves any longer, joined the water war, throwing off clothes, racing for
buckets, cups, or anything that would hold water.

Suddenly the face of the last man I had autopsied today
filled my vision. He was a good-looking man with blue eyes,
and I saw myself washing the blood and brains out of his
hair. I stopped running in the middle of the courtyard,
frightened by the detail and realism of the flashback.

A gush of cold water hit me in the middle of the back and
stopped the mortuary flashback. When I turned around
Marie was standing there, an empty bucket in her hands.
She dropped the bucket and raised her arms in surrender.
"Peace. I surrender," she said, backing away from me
slowly.

"Oh, it was you. I thought it was Sister Tuan," I said,

taking a step toward her and raising the bucket of water in my hand.

"No, Paul. You'll ruin this dress. Please . . . ," she said, grabbing my arms so that I couldn't throw the water. I hadn't noticed, but she was wearing a loose, white summer dress that hung straight down from her shoulders.

"So how's the chief cook and baby washer?" she asked, giving me a quick kiss on the cheek. Over Marie's shoulder I saw Sister Tuan watching us and walk away quickly when Marie kissed me.

"He's fine, I mean I'm fine. What are you doing out here so late?" I asked, looking at my naked wrist for the watch that Trong still had.

"First of all I thought I'd come back and clear some of the kids out of the isolation room so they can attend the party to-morrow . . . and I was wondering if you'd like to escort this good little Catholic girl to midnight mass?"

"Where? On the base?" I asked, drying my face with a towel Thom had just handed me.

"Hi, Thom," Marie said, pulling the hair out of Thom's eyes. "I thought we could go to the Cathedral downtown. They've lifted the curfew for this weekend."

"Sure. That sounds great . . . I'll tell Sister Hoa to set up another rice bowl . . . O.K.?" Marie looked at me, then at the kitchen, and I knew what she was thinking. "I eat here every night, Marie, and just look at me."

"I am. And you look a lot thinner than when we first met, Paul. Have you been feeling O.K. . . . . Eating?"

"I'm fine," I said, interrupting her. "I gotta get out of these wet clothes. You go check on the kids. I'll change and then help you," I said and ran toward the stairs.

I met Marie in the holding room where she was giving two new children physicals. If they got Marie's seal of approval, they could then be set loose with the rest of the children. Every new admission was a potential walking time bomb and was put in the holding room until Marie could check him. Plague, cholera, smallpox, and tuberculosis, rampant in the refugee ghettos, could wipe out our population in a matter of days.

Our latest problem had been trying to save the infants who were left outside our gates. Most of them were the children of

hores, left only hours after birth, and many times after
idnight, so we would not find them until morning. One
orning on my way out the gate, I ran over the remains of
n infant that had been attacked by the wild street dogs. That
ight I built a dog house with a one-way door, so that once
side, the baby would be safe until morning. That plan was
o successful that after finding three babies inside one morn-
g I pulled the dog house off the street. The nuns put the dog
ouse out, I pull it in, new babies and all. And the war goes
n.

"Why are they all the same age?" Marie asked, while lis-
ning to the lungs of a new two-year-old. "They're either
fants or one and two years old?"

"Sister Hoa told me that after the age of three or four they
an work, or at least babysit a younger brother or sister. At
ight years old they can begin their military training. Below
at age they're just another mouth to feed," I said.

"Do you ever wonder what American children would do if
hey were made to work as soon as they could walk?" she
sked.

"I think they'd be better off for it. But an American child
nows nothing about survival. He wouldn't last a week on
he streets here."

"It's sick," Marie said, looking up at me.

"But unchangeable unless you know how to turn a mira-
le."

"You turn miracles every day here, Paul. This place is a
niracle."

"What? This place is an overcrowded way station for the
nfected children of this shitty city. A big building full of
appy kiddies, run by a stupid G.I., who everybody knows
vill take just one more kid . . . Marie, I'm running out of
vays to feed the kids we have, and I can't argue anymore
with the two holy ladies out there. It's all gonna fall down one
lay. Right on top of us."

"What's wrong with you, Paul? What's making you go
sour on the greatest thing I've ever seen an American soldier
lo? And why can't you take a little pat on the back once in a
while?"

"Because it all looks great, but I feel like there's something very wrong. It's not the nuns. It's me . . . Come on, dinner should be ready soon," I said and started toward the door.

"Wait, Paul," she said, taking my arm and turning me back to face her. "Are you in trouble . . . with, or . . . ?"

"Right . . . Heroin!"

"Don't bullshit me. Your dilated pupils aren't from too much sleep." She took my chin in her hand and kept me from turning my face away.

"Drop it, Marie. My problem is a lot worse than drugs . . . ," I said, pulling away from her gently and picking up the little girl at my feet. "Try working in that death house all day, doing autopsies on big, strong, handsome cowards. Or watching one kid after the other being wrapped in plastic, like a giant sandwich, ready for delivery to Mom and Dad . . . and then I come over here and try to smile for the kiddies. You can't imagine . . . I'm sorry. I really don't want to get into it now. O.K.?"

"Sure . . . But swear to me that you'll find me if you need help."

"No promises. Come on, I smell food."

"I hope you guys have a fork I can use. I haven't quite mastered the old chopsticks yet," she said, following me out the door.

"Thom will teach you in one easy lesson."

The nuns had prepared a Christmas Eve feast that easily beat any meal in the past. Chicken with peanuts, fresh vegetables, a large steaming pot of rice, and a sliced, canned American ham that sped the children through grace, their eyes devouring this rare addition to their menu.

"Watch this," I whispered to Marie, as the children finished their thankful prayer and calmly passed each other's rice bowls to Sister Hoa. Total order. No flying chopsticks or reaching across the table. They were perfect ladies and gentlemen, and Marie was impressed.

"This is incredible," Marie said, tasting the chicken. "It's delicious."

"You should see what the table looks like when my family eats. Ten kids, food flying around . . ."

A loud banging on the orphanage gate scared the entire feeding area into silence. Trong ran to the gate and was back at my side quickly, his face white with fear.

"Paul . . . MP want talk you," he said, looking from me back to the gate. I was terrified. I had stolen more army, air force, and marine equipment than I could remember and was sure that they had finally connected me to one of the crimes.

"Did they ask for my name, Trong?"

"Sure . . . They say, let me talk Paul Hans . . ."

"Marie, go in the nursery and wait. Sister Hoa, you and Trong go hide those boxes of army pants and cover those batteries," I said, getting to my feet. Marie ran for the nursery, Hoa and Trong for our secret black market supply room.

"Sister, make the children sing a song. No American would believe seventy Vietnamese orphans were this good with food in front of them. They'll know something is wrong."

"Seventy-five," Sister Tuan said, correcting me.

Seventy-five, I thought, as I walked toward the gate. Maybe if I surrendered and claimed insanity, they'd go easy on me.

Waiting for me on the street was a tall, black Military Policeman. He stood with his back to the gate, his right hand tapping impatiently on a holstered .45. In the MP jeep next to him was a young Vietnamese woman holding a child on her lap.

"I'm Hensler . . . what can I do for you?" I asked, pulling the gate open.

"Moses told me, asked me to bring you his two kids. His place caught fire this afternoon, and he's with his old lady at Cho-Rei Hospital."

I looked again but still only saw one baby in the jeep. "Is she all right?"

"Who?" the man asked, removing his shiny black MP helmet.

"His wife . . . Moses' wife?"

"She won't make it. Burned real bad. Moses said to tell you he'll come by and take care of things."

"Right! Where's the other child?"

"Here he comes," the man said pointing up the street. "Let's go, Nick."

A beautiful, well-dressed five-year-old who looked like Trong's double but with darker skin raced down the street and literally flew into the MP's arms. He was a beautiful child, with smooth, light skin and a head of soft black curls.

"This is Nick, and the baby's name is Alice. I gotta split . . . You take 'em, and run, cause Nick here ain't gonna be too happy about me leavin' without him," he said, taking his helmet off Nick's head.

"O.K., let me have him." The minute I said the words, Nick locked his arms around the man's neck. The Vietnamese woman handed me the baby, who was the same coloring as Nick but cuter, then gently pulled Nick away from the man.

"You take good care these kid," she said, tears falling down her face. I took Nick in my other arm and backed inside the gate, closing it with my foot.

When the MP and his lady pulled away, Nick let out a scream that I was sure could be heard at the air base.

No matter what Marie, I, or the children tried, and several even did headstands, falling comically against each other, Nick screamed, cried, kicked, and called for his daddy. His baby sister took to a bottle and was sound asleep an hour later. By eleven that evening I almost wished that the man had arrested me. Every time cute little Nick yelled "Daddy" or "Mommy," another one of the children started to cry. Now I had a dorm full of crying, sobbing children that Marie, Sister Tuan, Sister Hoa, and I tried valiantly to calm down.

Trong entered the dormitory with his hands over his ears and screamed at the top of his lungs, "Shut up. I get headache." Miraculously the room shot to silence. Even Nick, his eyes now watching Trong, who was pointing at the children and sputtering away in Vietnamese. Trong moved over to Nick, who cowered in Marie's arms, pointed a bony finger at him, and laughed. First softly, then louder. One after the other the children followed suit. Marie looked at me with a confused expression, and I held my hand up to keep her from saying anything. Trong was telling everyone the story of Nick, the brave gorilla, who saved his family from the burning house.

Nick's eyes were like black diamonds, sparkling as they followed every movement Trong made. His face changed from sadness to awe, then a smile, as Trong played out the story.

Marie understood no Vietnamese but could tell by the seventy-seven faces around her, and the way Nick's hands now played across the smooth skin of her arm, that Trong was working his magic.

Marie and I made one last run through the dormitory to check on the sleeping children. Sister Tuan had told them that Saint Nicholas was making a special stop at our orphanage tomorrow but would not come unless they were all good and went to sleep early. It worked. Every child in the building was out cold, including Trong, who slept with a thumb-sucking Nick wrapped around him.

When we came out of the dormitory we met Sister Tuan, still fingering her rosary from evening prayer and stepping lightly toward the nursery. I took her small hands in mine, the rosary still clasped in her palm.

"Sister, thanks so much for the great dinner and the water fight. Marie and I are going to midnight mass at the Cathedral. Would you or Sister Hoa like to go with us?" Her finely featured face was serene, so different from the mischievous grinning girl I had battled with buckets of water earlier in the day. It continued to amaze me how much she had changed. Yet there were flashes of the younger Tuan I knew, moments of childish laughter and enthusiastic friendliness. Sister Hoa, Trong, and Thom had remained the same personalities I had left when I went back to the States. Only Sister Tuan seemed different, more grown up, more serious, more a woman.

"No thank you, Paul." She pulled her hands from mine, a strange look veiling her eyes. "Sister and I go early today, before children get up."

"Then we'll say good-night, Sister, and Merry Christmas."

"The same I wish you," she answered and walked quietly into the nursery, her long skirts swishing on the concrete floor.

"Wait here a second, Marie. I forgot something."

"Sure. Say good-night to her for me, too," she said as I climbed the stairs to my room.

The candle by my bed was still burning, a beacon of vigilance lit by Thom who waited for me every night. Tonight she had fallen asleep, curled at the end of my bed, but not before wrapping the remainder of the presents for me. I brushed the hair from her face and kissed her lightly on the cheek, then stood for a long moment watching her sleep, her peaceful face round and soft, her long lashes lying against her cheeks like sprays of black silk thread.

There was no more beautiful child in all the world, I decided. I wondered how she would like her new name? Thom Hensler.

Marie was waiting by my motorcycle when I came back downstairs. She climbed on behind me and adjusted my helmet on her head.

"Paul, I think she's in love with you."

"What?" I said, turning as much as I could to face her.

"Sister Tuan is in love with you . . . look," she said, motioning with her head toward the orphanage building. Sister Tuan stood in the darkened doorway of the nursery and when she noticed us looking her way stepped back into the shadows.

"Come off it, Marie. She's a nun," I said, kicking the starter until the engine coughed to life.

"But she's still a woman under that habit, Paul." Marie sensed that she had said the wrong thing and tried to turn it around. "I mean, she cares for you a lot more than you realize, that's all."

"That's all I need now is to hear that. I think I know her a little better than you, Marie. So let's drop it, O.K.?" As I said the words I realized they were a lie and that Marie was right. That was the change I continued to see in Tuan. A first love for someone she knew she could never have.

The interior of the old Cathedral was crowded and warm. Hundreds of bodies moved against each other, trying to get as close to the altar as possible. Candles had been set in every available space in the sanctuary, on the floors, on the altar, and all around the side altars honoring Mary and Joseph. The burning wax filled the air with a familiar oily fragrance and cast a wavering golden glow on the interior of the old stone and brick building.

We moved carefully down the center aisle, trying not to

step on those who knelt on the hard tile floor in prayer, and stepped into a crowded pew, the family occupying the hard wooden seat making room for us. As we knelt down to pray, a small choir began chanting the first part of the "Hail Mary," and everyone in the church finished the prayer in song. It had been so long since I had been in a church or knelt before the crucifix which drew so many millions to the mystery of His death. My mind had been so clouded recently with religious contradictions and ambiguous teachings which had kept my faith in check, and I found myself distracted and unable to pray. I looked around to see if anyone else was having trouble with this man nailed to a cross. All I could see were lips moving rapidly in silent prayer. Wrinkled old faces and young ones, too, eyes closed, speaking to their God, and rosary beads moving through small brown hands. I looked over at Marie, whose prayers I could almost hear, her eyes locked on the crucifix above the altar. I tried to remember any one of the many prayers I had learned in Holy Cross school but found myself repeating over and over, "Thank you. Thank you. Thank you, Christ."

I felt my eyes fill with tears, and for one suspended moment the church seemed aglow with a brilliant light, illuminating the altar and crucifix like a searchlight. My body shuddered as if chilled but in fact was feverishly warm. I put my hand on Marie's, wishing to share all that I felt. Wanting to say thanks and how great a feeling this moment was. We looked at each other, our eyes silently speaking of real peace and this time together, Christmas Eve, 1969, never to be forgotten.

After mass we walked toward my motorcycle, the cool midnight air a welcome relief from the hot stuffy church. Thousands of happy people congregated outside the Cathedral doors, greeting neighbors and enjoying the freedom of no curfew. I felt like I had just seen a movie that had left me speechless, its message profound, and ringing in my ears. Marie stepped in front of me and took my hands in hers.

"What do you want for Christmas, Specialist Hensler?" she asked with a broad smile.

"A padlock for the orphanage gate, Santa."

"No, really. What would you like?"

"Peace, and a way to take Thom home with me . . . and what would you like for Christmas, Lieutenant Donaldson?"

She squeezed my hands, "For you to stay with me tonight . . . at my quarters. I don't want to be alone on Christmas Eve." Her face was soft, childlike with her appeal.

"I'd like that," I said, a little surprised at the surety of my answer. The truth was there was nothing I wanted more from Santa but was just too shy to ask.

All the way back to her quarters, over a wall and in through a window, my mind raced with a thousand little bits of information about sex. Scenes from old movies, couples on a beach, the surf roaring over them, Bogart grabbing a woman and smashing his face into hers as the music hit a spine-tingling crescendo, and the famous, let's do it in front of the fireplace scene. It always looked so simple. Grab the girl and squeeze until she screamed. But what about condoms—all of which I had sold on the black market—birth control, and anatomy. Getting it up had never been a problem for me, but where to put it once ready was still a deep, dark mystery. If only I hadn't fallen asleep in that whorehouse, all of this would be so simple.

"This is going to sound really stupid, Marie," I said, standing in the middle of her comfortable little room, the military furniture softened by flowered drapes and sheets. "But I've never slept with a woman before." If she was surprised she didn't show it, as she handed me a small water glass of brandy.

"How about sheep?" she said smiling.

"Nope, although I've heard they're pretty close."

"Men?" she said, still smiling.

"Nope!"

"The local girls don't interest you?" she said, wrapping her arm around my waist.

"There was this one night down in Cam Ranh Bay, but I was so drunk I could have slept with a cow or somebody's grandmother."

She spit brandy across the room and started to cough. "Sorry, you mean you did sleep with somebody's grandmother?"

"No . . . I wasn't that drunk. All I remember is going into the back room with a young lady where I proceeded to pass out on the bed. I woke up naked, but how the hell do you tell if anything happened? I mean, nothing looked or felt different," I said, now totally embarrassed.

"I'm sorry, Paul. I didn't mean to laugh at you," she said, stroking my cheek with her hand. "I guarantee that you won't fall asleep tonight." She kissed me on the lips softly and time stood still. "Merry Christmas, Paul," she said, wrapping her arms around me and drawing me close to her. My embarrassment and fear melted away as I kissed the gentle curve of her neck, the smell of clean hair and gardenias teasing my senses.

"Merry Christmas, Marie."

Dear Jesus,

It sure was nice seeing you again . . . I'll make you a deal. You answer our prayers, and I'll come back and see you more often. You've been silent far too long.

— 21 —

Christmas Day, 1969

I had spent four days trying to convince Jarvis to make four frozen turkeys disappear from the hospital mess hall. He argued that there were only enough turkeys to feed the hospital staff, but I knew him too well. He would make the mess hall disappear for the right amount of dope. On top of this he was almost two hundred dollars behind in payments, mostly from smoking more dope than he sold. His last words were that the peas and mashed potatoes were no problem, but stealing and delivering the birds would wipe out our debt.

He was waiting for me at 7 A.M. when I arrived at the orphanage. Nervously smoking a cigarette, he paced back and forth in front of his ambulance.

"Hensler!" he yelled, seeing me drive into the courtyard.

"Jarvis. What the hell are you doing here so early?"

"Your goddamned turkeys have gotten my ass in trouble again. The . . ."

"You got them, great," I said, walking toward the back of the ambulance.

"No . . . I came down to adopt a kid . . . Yes, I got them, and they're cooked but not from the hospital," he said, holding the back door of the ambulance open. "They caught me in the reefer and almost sent my ass to Long Binh . . . I had to hit up a guy over at the air base."

"I don't care where they came from, we had a deal," I said, lifting one of the golden brown turkeys off the floor of the ambulance.

Jarvis put his dirty hand on the breast of the turkey, stopping me. "Our deal didn't work out, Hensler. I had to pay

217

for these. Like I said, the peas and potatoes are on me but you gotta pay me for these fuckin' turkeys."

"Jesus, man, you are a real case. You owe me two hundred bucks and here you are laying this bullshit on me for more money."

"That's the way it is, bro."

Suddenly from behind us a voice boomed, scaring both of us.

"You white boys should be careful about how you use that bro shit."

We both turned around slowly and standing two feet away from our faces was Moses and the black MP, shiny helmet and all. Jarvis's face went ashen, and for one fleeting moment his eyes crossed.

"I knew it, Hensler. I knew I shoulda just told you . . . Aw fuckit!" he said, putting his wrists out, ready for the handcuffs. "Nothin' ever goes my way. I shoulda gone to Canada."

Moses looked at me and winked. "O.K., Hensler, how are you involved with this sorry excuse for a soldier?" Moses boomed, placing his hands on his hips.

"Well, you see, Sergeant, I was trying to throw a little party for some poor little orphans here," I said playing along with him and pointing at the dormitory door that was now filling with children. "They haven't eaten in about ten days, Sergeant, and I thought I'd ask my good friend Jarvis here to help with the food."

"Ten days?" Jarvis mumbled in disbelief.

"Where'd these military issue turkeys come from, Jarvis?" the MP asked, now catching on to Moses and me. "They looks like the ones I seen on base this morning!"

Jarvis was dying a thousand times in front of us. "I ah, you see this friend of mine, well . . . ," Jarvis said, now stammering and moving from foot to foot nervously.

"Wait, Picks," Moses said to the MP, "he's donating some food for thems that ain't got. I mean, I don't see any stolen turkeys in the back of this here ambulance . . . do you?" Moses said, almost unable to contain his laughter.

"Nope. Sure did think we caught the guy though."

"Listen, Jarvis, I thinks what you're doin' for these little uns is to be commended . . . Let's help you unload so you an get back to the hospital.'' And with Jarvis standing here, his mouth hanging open, Moses, Picks, and I began to carry the Christmas dinner to the kitchen.

Jarvis climbed in behind the wheel and was anxious to leave, when the three of us walked up to his window.

"Anybody gives you any shit about them turkeys, you let me know," Picks said, patting Jarvis on the arm.

Moses was next up to the window, "I think we could write up a commendation for your CO if you like."

"My CO. Ah, no. Let's just say this is my little gift to the poor little kiddies," he said, wiping the sweat from his forehead. "But thanks anyway."

"If you changes your mind let me know, cause Picks and I is at the hospital all the time. Wouldn't be no big thing."

"Yeah, thanks," Jarvis said, starting the engine. "I gotta get back now."

"I'll make this up to you somehow, man," I said, leaning into the window.

Jarvis smiled at us lamely and drove off.

There was no laughter once Jarvis was gone. Moses' reason for coming to the orphanage had nothing to do with Jarvis. His Vietnamese wife had died from her burns and he wanted me to take his two children as permanent residents.

"I don't know how you take care of the kids you got, but whatever you need from now on I'll get you. Picks here patrols the area around here so you're protected that way too."

"I'm sorry about your wife, but why don't you try and take the kids back to the States with you?" I asked.

"I got a wife and three kids in South Carolina. I don't think they'd take to the idea."

"They'll be O.K. here," I said.

"Where are they?" Moses asked, looking at the children crowding the doorways.

"Probably still asleep. Today's a sleep-in day. You wanna see him?"

"No, no. I . . ." Moses turned away from me, tears filling his eyes. Picks slapped him on the back and walked a few more steps with him.

Thom approached us now with three cups of coffee and carefully walked a safe distance around Moses. The Vietnamese feared and avoided the black soldiers from America. Black was the color of their ghosts—and evil spirits to the Buddhists. It had taken several arguments before I was able to persuade my two very Catholic nuns to allow our four or five black-Vietnamese children on the same sleeping platforms as the others. The nuns felt no hatred for the mixed bloods, but years of fear kept them from tempting the unknown.

"Thanks, sweetheart," Moses said to Thom as he sipped the hot coffee.

"That's Thom . . . and Thom, this is Moses and Picks." She made a quick bow at the waist and smiled up at me.

"Oh, Jesus. I almost forgot. Tomorrow is little Nick's birthday, and we brought a couple of things for him . . . and the other kids," he added.

They ran to the MP's jeep and Moses returned with a huge, slightly lopsided sheet cake. Picks carried a wrapped gift and three big containers of ice cream.

"We was gonna give him a party tomorrow, but all that's gone. You split this," he said, handing me the sheet cake that had the Military Assistance Command logo on its top and underneath said, MERRY CHRISTMAS GENERAL—but the general's name had been smeared over. "I hope there's enough for all of them? And these two gifts are for Nick," he said, handing them to Thom.

"Thom, please go put those in my room." She walked toward the stairs and was almost run over by the curious children.

"There's plenty of food, and thanks, but I can't give him the gifts. It wouldn't be fair to the others. You know what I mean?" I said, moving toward the kitchen.

Moses and Picks followed me inside and started to laugh when they saw several children gathered around the roasted turkeys, poking and prodding the dark brown meat of what they thought were giant chickens.

"All right, you guys, out," I yelled and the children scattered. Sister Tuan joined us, now carrying Moses' daughter, Alice. She went about preparing a bottle as if she were alone in the room. Moses looked heartbroken when he saw his daughter and left the kitchen quickly.

"Doesn't this look great, Sister," I asked, holding the edge of the sheet cake up.

"Sure," she said coldly and left the room. They knew I hadn't slept at the orphanage last night, and from Sister Tuan's not very subtle attitude I had the feeling I was in trouble again.

I invited Moses, Picks, and any of their friends to our Christmas party, but both declined. Moses promised to come by and bring other helpers as soon as it was easier for him to see his children. He also reminded me that I now had access to any supplies needed to maintain the orphanage.

As they drove away in the MP jeep I said a quiet thank-you for a such a quick answer to one of my prayers. A new supply of tradable goods, food, and friends would finally make it all right for the nuns to take a few more children.

Preparations for our party began right after breakfast, with baths, forty pounds of ice to keep the ice cream from turning to soup, a bucket brigade that cleaned the feeding-area floor, and an excitement among the children like I had never seen before.

Sister Hoa came out to the courtyard and sat down beside me. We had not really spoken since my last screaming match with them about taking in new children before talking to me.

"What are you doing, Paul?" she asked, looking at the list in my hands.

"Sister Tuan wrote all the names of the children down for me."

"Yes, but why?"

"Sister, we don't know anything about the children we have. We don't even know where they've come from, so I'm starting a list with their names, places of birth, and ages."

"And what will you do with it once it is completed?" she asked, pulling her glasses off her nose.

"Add the names of the new children to it." I looked at her and smiled. She was puzzled and thought carefully about her reply.

The smile I remembered from happier days in Cam Ranh crept across her face. "This is good news. Your new friends will help us?"

"Yes. But we have to be careful, Sister. A few more children will be easy now, because everything is O.K. If something were to go wrong with . . .''

"You must not think that way," she said, patting my arm. "We are being protected from above. He will provide for us as He always has." Her left hand opened slightly and I could see her rosary beads rolled in her palm. Time was moving too fast these days. One moment I was close to them and the next they were like strangers to me. What questions should I ask that will let her know I still care very much about the orphanage and her. Or what grand statements should I make to prove to her that I was growing up. That it was getting easier to understand the people of Vietnam and, specifically, her and Sister Tuan. My world was so small and untrained, troubled by the mortuary, death, and the shared responsibility for the children who played around us. Hers was wide and learned, practical, and powered by her faith and a special love for children.

"Why are you so quiet, Paul?"

"I was just thinking, Sister."

"You seem troubled lately. Sister Tuan and some of the children say you are not the same, Paul," she said, turning to face me.

"Everything's O.K., Sister. Just a lot of things on my mind."

"Maybe you can talk to your new lady friend."

"Marie? . . . Maybe."

"You can always talk to me." Our eyes met suddenly. She had never offered to listen before. Why was it so hard to accept her, talk to her, just as I would my mother, who was about the same age. She was the same, and yet she was Vietnamese, the word for a people very different from myself.

"Thanks, Sister. I'll remember that."

"Good . . . Now if you will help Sister Tuan with the food, I will go check on the child I found by the church this morning," she said and walked away without looking back. Her happiness about being able to take in a few more children added the light, girlish bounce to her walk that I had not seen for many months. She didn't want much. Only peace and enough room for one more.

Small bowls filled with rice, topped with two or three thin slices of turkey, sat before each child. Marie and I walked out

the kitchen with large bowls of peas, potatoes, and cab-
ge soup. It looked like a scene from the movie *Oliver,* with
venty-five expectant faces lining the tables, waiting for the
nal to dig in. When grace was finished with the sign of the
oss, Sister Hoa gave them the nod of her head to begin . . .
othing. They all waited for the child next to them to take
e first bite of this alien food. Big brown birds, cut up and
ving huge skeletons, had worked their imaginations over-
ne. They urged each other to taste the meat, whispering
eir dares quietly, but no one made a move until Thom
ood up, took her bowl, and with her chopsticks, lifted a
ece of turkey into her mouth. A wide smile crossed her
ce. That was all the children needed to see, and they all be-
n devouring their dinners. The potatoes did not go over
o well, but within five minutes the turkey, rice, peas, and
bbage soup were gone. Hands shot up in the air for sec-
ds and the adults ended up distributing their dinners to the
ungest. I couldn't have eaten anyway for the excitement I
t about their first Christmas party.

The cake and ice cream were carried to the table, cut up,
shed out, and gone in another ten minutes. In the middle
Nick's piece of cake I planted a small crooked candle and
him blow it out. When everyone asked why only Nick got
candle, I explained that because he had come on Christmas
ve it was good luck to let him blow out a candle. Puzzled
es stared at me, little shoulders shrugged, but an instant
ter they were back to licking their bowls. Trong was the
ly one who didn't fall for the story and stood with his arms
ded at his chest, shaking his head.

As Marie, Thom, and I washed the bowls, pots, and
ghty pairs of chopsticks, the children cleared the eating
ea of its tables and chairs. Trong came and escorted us to
ir special seats, and the rest of the children sat in a half-
oon around Sister Tuan. I had seen them practicing all
eek the special little show that was now beginning.

Sister Tuan cleared her throat and began to sing a song in
ietnamese. It was a haunting, lyrical melody, with intimate
anges in pitch. Her beautiful pure voice rang throughout
e courtyard like a bird, high and lilting, telling a story that
rought tears to the eyes of many of the children. Trong, two
f the older girls, and Thom, who was sitting on my lap,

seemed especially affected by the song. Maybe it was becau
they were older, I thought, and so the song had more mea
ing. Or perhaps it was a song about a peaceful Vietnam, an
I had just not realized they knew what peace was.

When Sister Tuan finished, the children applauded on an
on until Thom jumped from my lap and began setting th
children in three straight lines in front of us. Sister Tua
checked the lines, then turned facing us.

"Paul, the children make a song for you and our Amer
can friends. It is talking about the special love they give
you," she said and then moved to a position behind
where she could direct without being seen. She began singin
again, and the children started dancing, making carefull
practiced hand movements, all in perfect unison with eac
other and the music. They pointed their little fingers at the
hearts, then at us, and sang the chorus of the song with Siste
Tuan. I melted in my seat. I had heard some of them sing be
fore, but never sixty or seventy children all at once. The
truly sounded like a chorus of angels, and when I looked ove
at Marie I could see that they were having the same effect. A
they sang the last words of the song, they finished with a nea
bow at the waist, and their hands palmed together in a pray
ing gesture.

Marie and I both returned the gesture and then flew to
ward the children, hugging as many as would fit in our arms
Sister Hoa clapped her hands together and began to sin
"Jingle Bells," my cue to change into the Santa costum
The children joined her in the only American Christma
song they knew.

"Jinger bers, jinger bers, jinger all the day. Oh wha fun
is to go in a la la la la la sley," they sang, jumping around.
was close enough for Marie and I.

I came out of my room and walked to the railing above th
courtyard. "Ho, ho, ho, Merry Christmas, boys and girls."
The children froze in shocked silence. Marie and the nun
covered their mouths as I came stumbling down the stairs
The children obviously had no idea what to make of thi
Vietnamese version of Old Saint Nick, for I surely didn'
look like the pictures of Santa they had seen in the America
magazines. With flaming red silk pants, a mop head for
beard, and the customary Vietnamese conical hat, I proba

ly looked more like the devil than the benevolent old man
who brought gifts to good children. Some of the younger
ones seemed to have grave doubts about my intentions and
moved to a protected position behind Sister Hoa. Once again
the brave Trong didn't fall for it and laughed from a safe spot
behind a post.

Marie was holding her stomach, in pain from repressed
laughter, as she took my arm and led me to Santa's chair.

"Come on, Marie, you're gonna spoil it for them," I said
through the scratchy beard.

"I'm sorry, Santa, but your green underwear is showing."

"What? Where?" I asked, turning my head and ripping
the skin of my neck where the beard was taped on.

"Never mind," Marie said, spinning me back around,
"just sit down before anyone else notices." She tried to push
me down in the chair, but the belt holding up my pillow
stomach felt like it was going to cut me in half.

"Oh God. I can't . . . something's wrong," I groaned.
Marie gave me one more hard shove and I fell into the chair,
my silk pants ripping from the back to the crotch. "Santa's
little helper made his pants too tight . . . didn't she?" I said,
trying to get the pillow back down to its normal position. The
children could not control themselves any longer and burst
into laughter, no longer frightened of this ludicrous figure
Americans loved so much. I could hear Trong crying with
laughter above the rest and vowed to pay him back later.

Each child approached and was lifted onto my lap by Sister
Hoa. After bouncing them a bit on my knee, which caused
either laughter or a wet spot, I handed them a newspaper-
wrapped gift, trying to make sure a two-year-old didn't get
slippers made for a boy Trong's size. They didn't even wait
until they were off my knee before newspaper flew in the air
and shouts of "look see, look see, I got better than you" filled
the courtyard. Sister Tuan tried valiantly to keep up with the
flying newspaper but finally with ink-black hands gave up.

Thom and Trong were last in line for their gifts. Trong felt
he was too old for my charade and refused to sit on my knee,
taking his gift, flashing me the "V" sign with his fingers,
and moving away quickly.

Thom hopped up on my knee with her head down and one

hand over her mouth. She knew who was under the mo[p]
head. I took her chin carefully and turned her face towar[d]
mine.

"My friends told me you were a number-one special girl
so Santa Claus has a special gift for you." I said the word[s]
slowly so she would understand, then pulled her gift out o[f]
my shirt. She took the package in both hands and bowe[d]
slightly. She started to get off my knee but I held her an[d]
pointed at the gift, wanting her to open it in front of me.

Her slim little fingers pulled meticulously at the brown pa[-]
per. A look of surprised pleasure filled her face when she sa[w]
the snapshot of us, which Marie had taken without her know[-]
ing. I turned the picture over for her so she would see th[e]
small gold crucifix and chain I had taped there, then pointe[d]
at the three words I had written in careful Vietnamese . . [.]
"Chu Yeu Anh" (I love you). Nodding her head, she looke[d]
up at me and made our special sign, her fingers making th[e]
heart pattern on her little chest, then touched to my lips. Sh[e]
jumped off my knees and ran to show the picture to the nun[s]

Before I could stop her, Marie flopped down on my kne[e]
and put an arm around my neck.

"Well, Santa, what's you got for this little orphan fro[m]
Michigan?" she asked.

"I'm sorry to report, little girl, that Santa's checking ac[-]
count is a little overdrawn. But . . . maybe . . ." I said[,]
putting my arm around her waist.

"That's O.K., Paul . . . I mean, Santa," she said softly[.]
"Being with you and the children today and being you[r]
friend is quite enough. Besides, we exchanged presents las[t]
night, didn't we?" Her look and the tone of her voice sho[w]
me back to her candle-lit quarters. She was my first total sex[-]
ual experience with a woman and so was a fresh, very specia[l]
memory. She was more experienced and took me gently an[d]
erotically through foreplay, intercourse, and the tender mo[-]
ments of relaxation that followed. She was not quick to sho[w]
me the way out as I expected all women did or afraid of u[s]
being caught in the very carefully guarded nurses' quarters[.]
We treasured the warmth of each other's bodies as we talke[d]
until morning about the children, our work, each other, an[d]
this war that brought us together. It was the first time I ha[d]
ever told anyone the entire story of the orphanage. We

aughed together as I recounted the broken bag of powdered milk, and the incredible ride from Cam Ranh to Saigon. And we cried when I talked of the fiery end to the orphanage on the hill. It was the greatest feeling to speak quietly with someone who found what I was doing right and good.

"Santa, I think you'd better let go of me," Marie said, bringing me back from a most pleasant daydream. "We're being stared at."

A group of children stood in front of us, staring at the motionless Santa.

"Ho, ho, ho . . ." I yelled, scaring the children and Marie, "help Santa get to his feet, little girl."

I grabbed at the seat of my pants as Marie helped me to my feet and waddled up the stairs. About halfway up I let go of the pants and got the desired result. A courtyard full of hysterical children.

— 22 —

Dialogue with the Dead

The great happiness of Christmas seemed to power us al
through the next month or so. The population grew slowly
the orphanage ran smoothly, and our new friends kept the
supplies coming.

Everything seemed in balance until a week of horrendous
activity at the mortuary started me back toward Dexedrine
Monday, thirteen autopsies; trying to figure out which bag o
bones was a Vietnamese person and which were their American advisers. The aircraft crew had overloaded the firs
C-123 Gun Ship, turned over to the Vietnamese Air Force,
and it crashed on takeoff. Piles of burned humans waited fo
me in a convoy of gurneys after breakfast, lunch, and dinner.
The air force brass pushed for answers from us as we dug
around in the bags of char-broiled flesh. Legs and arms tied
in knots, no longer discernible as once human. "Jesus, make
sure ya'll don't send some slimy little gook home to Mrs.
Jones in Iowa," one of the air force ambulance drivers yelled
to me as I shoveled more pieces into a plastic bag. After
taking the X-rays on the tenth body, I sat down in the air-
conditioned developing room and fell asleep. Major Williams found me out cold on the floor and read me the riot act;
how could I be so careless, how could I shuck my responsibility so easily? I wanted to say, because I'm now working too
many hours here and too many hours at Hensler's wayward
home for orphans. Instead, I went back to Dexedrine.

Almost as if to balance the increased workload at the mortuary, big problems at the orphanage started to crop up.
With a sudden rush of twenty new children, everything from

the plumbing to meals, to space, to the nuns' ability to operate the bulging building, started to overload. The normal chores took several more hours each night and left me with no time for the children and not one minute for myself. Trong and I began to battle about almost anything, especially the fact that I was spending more time with Thom. He wanted to return to the old days of going to the black market with me where he negotiated our deals and once in a while drank a beer with his best partner. He was right, but there was no time to play, and Thom's adoption papers were more important.

After spending an afternoon wrapped in the local red tape of the Vietnamese Immigration offices, I was ready to try heroin. I thought adopting Thom would be a simple matter of filling out this form and then that one. It was more like pay some stupid girl a bribe just to find your forms. There were never less than a thousand people in line in front of me, all of them trying as hard as I was not to kill the girl behind the counter. G.I.s with their whore brides and arms full of babies added the last touch of madness to the room. Baby girls were easy to adopt, but when the skinny marine in front of me tried to bribe the Immigration officials into letting him adopt his illegitimate son, they smiled and said, "No way, Joe. You are holding a future South Vietnamese soldier." I had never seen a marine cry before that day and thought, so much for adopting Trong or any of the other boys. When I finally got to the counter, Thom was asleep in my arms. I was an hour late for work and the pretty young girl behind the counter smiled and asked me if I intended to marry Thom once I got her back to the States. I wanted to punch her right eye but instead started calling her names. I tried to apologize, knowing that my paperwork on Thom would now go to the bottom of the pile, but the woman refused to speak to me. Her supervisor, a wiry old man with a Ho Chi Minh beard of long whiskers, made my fears a reality as he shoved my request into a basket crammed with papers and forms and told me to come back in a month or so.

That same afternoon Major Williams threatened me with a court-martial for being two hours late for duty and warned that he knew I was up to something. Now I wanted to punch his right eye but instead pleaded innocence and promised to be good. The truth was that I was becoming sloppy and stupid in my stealing for the orphanage. Undetected so far, I had forged onward and was now scared sick that I had either left a trail back to me or in my drugged happy mind had forgotten to look before larceny.

My world was starting to collapse around me.

It started with an argument over no more children. I won, or so I thought, when the nuns agreed to keep the gates locked until I could build more chairs, tables, beds, cribs, and find more food, pots, rice bowls, diapers, slippers, schoolbooks, and steal more chalk, pencils, crayons, and powdered milk for the babies. One morning when the nuns thought I was still asleep, they tried to sneak two children, both of them tragically stricken with cerebral palsy, into the nursery. I was sitting in the kitchen with Thom as they passed the door.

"Excuse me, Sisters, but would you mind telling me where these children came from?"

"Oh . . . they been here long time," Sister Tuan chirped with a wide smile. "We just take them for walk with us."

"Bullshit, Sister. What about our agreement?" I said, getting up and walking to the kitchen door.

"Please, Paul. I do not like it when you talk like that," Sister Hoa said and started toward the nursery.

"Hold it, Sister. You didn't answer me."

"And I do not intend to!" she said, entering the nursery followed by a frightened Sister Tuan. It was now or never, I decided, and stormed into the nursery, slamming the door behind me.

"Sisters, this has got to stop. You lied to me. You told me you would not . . ."

"No more of this stupid talk," Sister Hoa shot back at me, stopping me cold. "We are a Catholic orphanage. Our job is to help those who cannot help themselves. These two children were evicted from another orphanage three days ago because the people running it were afraid of them. Afraid they would never be adopted. Sister Tuan found them yesterday, starving and cold, and did not tell me about them because she feared you. Now they are here," she said as she removed the children's soiled clothes.

"What is the difference if they starve out on the street, Sister, or starve in our pretty little orphanage? And what the hell makes you think we can get them adopted, when we can't even get the healthy children from our place . . .''

"Stop," she said, interrupting me again. "These two will live here and die here. They will never be adopted. They are the unwanted dust of life. Yes. That is what they and all orphans are called, the unwanted dust of life . . . So if there is no food for them I will give them mine. If that is not enough, Sister Tuan will give them hers. If you cannot see . . .''

"I know and understand what you are saying, Sister. But there has to be some organization to what we do here. You can't keep bringing in more and more children. You just can't."

"Please, Paul, we no can leave them in the street. They will die and your friend now bring us some food and they won't eat much. So we do what you say but . . ." Sister Tuan answered.

"But nothing. Not one more child comes through the gate or I'll leave," I said, raising my voice. "I'll walk out that gate and never come back. It's all of our responsibility to keep this place running. Not just yours, Sister. Remember that," I said and left the nursery, slamming the door again.

Thom had heard every word said and would not come near me. I changed into a clean uniform and came back down the stairs. The nuns were in the kitchen, starting the breakfast rice, and when I passed the door Trong ran out and grabbed my arm.

"Hey, Paul, why you make the Sister cry. They like . . .''

"It's none of your business, Trong, so go play," I said, pulling free of his grasp. His face looked like I had just slapped him, and he ran into the dormitory. Thom watched me from the far side of the courtyard, tears running down her cheeks.

"Thom. Please, come here," I called to her, but she ran into the dormitory and was almost immediately shoved back out the door by Trong. If he wasn't allowed in my room, she wasn't allowed in their room. I couldn't deal with it and drove out the gate.

It was a beautiful day, the sky clear and dark blue as I drove toward the mortuary. People who lived near the orphanage waved to me, saying good morning or the customary, "Hi, Joe." Even the air was fresh and cool, as I weaved in and out of the morning rush hour traffic. I took deep breaths, looked at the distant mountains, and smiled at the people I passed, but nothing could take away the persistent feeling that it was all going wrong and I couldn't stop it.

Waiting in traffic outside the 3rd Field Hospital, the happy memory of the three nights Marie and I had spent together put the smile back on my face. But as that memory continued, even it reminded me of trouble. Everything seemed right between us until she began to talk about love, and us, and relationships. Unfortunately, I was in the same situation with the topic of love as I was with sex, inexperienced. So as she told me of past relationships, some warm memories, others passed over, I listened intently. She was so mature and advanced in so many areas that all I could do was listen and pretend to understand. When she began talking about the feelings she had for me, I wanted to run, for I honestly felt nothing and could not reply. At the same time, I wanted the quiet sensuous nights to continue—for the thought of lovemaking until three in the morning was now one of the rare happy moments that kept me going at both the orphanage and the morgue.

As I approached the mortuary on my motorcycle, I wanted to just keep on going down the road, up the hill, and into Laos or Cambodia. If only once my CO would say, "Good morning, Paul, beautiful day isn't it. Listen, I know this is a tough job and I know how hard you work, but it's our assigned duty and we must carry on. If you ever need to talk, just let me know and I'll make the time."

Maybe he did say it, but I hated him and the army so much now, I probably didn't hear him. That's what is missing around here, I thought, as I walked into the identification room—emotion. Compassion for our dead, and a serious effort to stop the killing. Instead, everyone I passed was just doing his duty. Identifying, bagging, cleaning, dissecting, sewing up, writing up, embalming, and shipping home body after body as if they were sides of beef or rare fossils for a museum. This one goes to Illinois, this one to California, this one to New Jersey, and that one goes back in the reefer until we find his head. Paperwork piled up on case after case, crowding filing cabinet drawers with autopsy numbers instead of names. Clerks worked feverishly over DD forms

20, 1446, 90, writing the victims' names on flight manifests
s if they were preparing them for vacation trips to heaven.
Graves Registration packed the personal belongings of the
dead, reading letters, checking pockets, throwing away *Play-
boy* magazines and pornographic pictures bought on the
back streets of Vietnam.

And the war went on. The mortuary, like a well-run fac-
tory, kept its deadlines, met its quotas, and without fail always managed to fill the belly of an air force cargo plane.

And what could I do, I asked myself almost every day. And
who could I tell, I thought, as the face of another nineteen-
year-old suicide stared up at me from a bloody body bag.
The people who were running this out-of-control war machine knew how many were dying each day. A neat little list,
typed up by one of the mortuary clerks, landed on some
general's desk every morning at exactly the same time. In
alphabetical order were the name, rank, serial number, and
unit of each casualty. Next to each name was either a check
mark indicating that a medal was to be issued, or an asterisk
which meant suicide, the coward's way out of facing the
error of war. Two minutes later this morbid account of the
American progress in Vietnam was buried under another
list; the names of those invited to the general's cocktail party
for the Commanding Officer of the Vietnamese Air Force.

The only way I was going to make it through the rest of
this year was to stay high, cool, and too busy to deal with the
truth.

When I finally arrived at the orphanage that evening,
everyone was in tears except for Sister Hoa, who refused to
talk or look at me. It seemed like the same scene I had left
that morning, with Thom peering at me from our window,
the older children staring at me from the dormitory door,
and Sister Tuan sobbing in the kitchen.

"Now what's wrong, Sister?" I asked Tuan as I entered
the kitchen. She looked out the door behind me, as if
checking to see if someone were listening.

"Paul. Trong go away. He is very angry with you," she
said, wiping her eyes.

"Oh come on, Sister. He runs away all the time."

"No, no . . . this time he take his clothes and shoe. H[e] say he no come back. Please, you find him," she said. [I] sensed an urgency in her voice and in the way she was push[ing] me toward the orphanage gate.

"Sister, calm down. You know he'll be back for dinner."

"This time different . . . he say . . . please just go now."

"What did he say, Sister?" I said, grabbing her hands.

She looked around again and her eyes stopped on Thom who was right above us on the balcony. "He say you no lov[e] Trong, only . . ." she broke off again, her voice wavering.

"Only who? Only who, Sister?"

"Only Thom . . . and Marie," she said, lowering he[r] eyes to the ground. "He say he help you all the time, mor[e] than Thom. More than Marie. He go with you to black mar[ket], sell what you want, but you no care about him anymore[.] Maybe he die, go to jail. But he no stay with us anymore." Her voice broke as she spoke the last sentence. It was un[-]thinkable that Trong, their protector, their little comic, thei[r] man-child, was leaving them.

I looked up at the balcony but Thom was gone. "Goddam[-]mit! What's next in line, Sister, dysentery? Or an attack b[y] the Vietcong?"

I ran out the gate, cursing at myself, realizing I had hur[t] my little partner again. Between Thom's adoption paper[s] and my own problems, Trong had been inadvertently an[d] sadly neglected. He was my little hero and I loved him, bu[t] once again I had forgotten to tell him.

I ran faster now, down the side streets behind the orphan[-] age, through the small market, and back out onto the mai[n] road into town, praying, hoping that I would find hi[m] sulking on a curb and not in jail. Several weeks ago he ha[d] been caught in a chicken farmer's rope trap, whipped by th[e] old man, and then carted off to jail. The farmer knew whic[h] orphanage he was from and told the nuns he had turne[d] Trong in to teach him a lesson. Six hours later I found him i[n] a cell with fifty or sixty other little thieves, pimps, and prosti[-] tutes. He had been stripped, beaten, and humiliated by th[e] older boys, who laughed and poked at his small genitalia. Hi[s] angry eyes blazed, and his sinewy little body seemed to vi[-] brate as I paid for his release. He marched out of the jai[l] house stark naked and jumped up behind me on my motor[-]

ycle, refusing my fatigue jacket. I could feel him shivering
behind me as we sped through town—an olive-drab giant,
golden hair flying, with an angry, sober-faced brown boy
stuck to his back like an unblanketed papoose. With Thom
and Sister Tuan waiting at the gate for our return he relented
but only covered his front with my fatigue jacket as he
marched into the dormitory. With the look on Trong's face,
no one dared laugh.

A rush of Dexedrine and fear sent me running again, toward the area where Trong and I used to trade my beer.
Three blocks later and my lungs ready to collapse, I rounded
a corner and froze.

A short potbellied marine held Trong against a wall, yelling at him as he ripped through his pockets.

"You goddamned stupid little gook! You're all the same.
Ripping us off every chance you get," he screamed, shoving
his forearm against Trong's throat. "Now give me my
fuckin' watch or I'll break your skinny little neck!" The
man's red, puffy face was contorted with anger, and spit flew
out of his mouth like a mad dog. Trong was crying and shook
his head as he gasped for air. "Please, Joe . . . I no steal
watch!"

I crept up quietly behind the marine but not in time to pre-
vent him from backhanding Trong across the face and
knocking him to the ground. The crunch of the blow rang in
my ears, jarring me into action. Grabbing the fat marine by
the shoulder I spun him around and hit him hard in the middle of his face. His nose crunched under my knuckles and
blood spurted out and down his chin.

"What's your story, asshole? You into beating up little
kids? Is that your trip, you fat slob? . . . Come on, man, get
up and let's you and I get it on." It sounded like someone
else screaming at the shocked little man. I loomed over him,
fists ready, like a crazed, punch-drunk boxer. Trong was
staring at me with his mouth hanging open. Here I was, gentle, quiet, chicken-hearted Hensler, putting on a show I
never dreamed I was capable of acting out. I felt another rush
of power run through me, and I would have hit him again if
my hand wasn't throbbing so painfully.

The marine started to back away slowly, one hand over his
bloody nose, the other raised in front of him like a salute.

"Hey . . . I . . . look, man, that little gook stole my watch. I ain't got no gripe with the army."

"I no steal watch, Paul! He dinky dow!" Trong yelled at him, still holding his reddened face but no longer terrified.

"Shut up, Trong."

I dropped my hands and took a step toward the marine. "You didn't find your watch on him, now did you?"

"Uh . . . No . . . but he probably . . ."

"Bullshit, man!" I screamed and grabbed his sweat shirt, pulling him toward me. He clutched my right wrist to keep my hand from flying into his face again. "Let go of me, you pussy!" I said, shamefully enjoying his fear. "Now we're going to play Vietnamese street court. I find the kid innocent and your ass guilty. You lose, so how much money you got on you?" I demanded.

"What ya mean?"

"Just what I said. How much money in your slimy pockets?"

"I don't know, maybe fifty bucks."

"Give it to me," I said, tightening my grip on his shirt and drawing him closer to me. His hazel eyes widened and I could see the pupils dilate with fear. He pulled out the wad of soggy money and slapped it into my hand.

I let go of him and stepped back toward Trong.

"Now hear this, jarhead. This is my area of Saigon, you understand? My kids, the local MPs, and I work this area. So I don't want to see your fat ugly ass waddling up and down my streets. Now get the fuck outta here before I let the kid rip your face off." Trong looked up at me with a puzzled expression.

The marine half smiled and backed away warily, his face a mixture of disbelief and apprehension. I was now the mad dog . . . a battle- or drug-ravaged G.I. driven completely insane by an insane war. He turned around quickly and ran out of the alley.

Trong played with the ripped material of his pants pocket and then started to walk away. I grabbed him by the back of the neck and drew him toward me.

"Where's the watch, Trong?" I said, putting my bloodied hand out in front of him.

"I no steal watch. He crazy, maybe sick in head." He circled his finger at his temple.

"Give me the watch," I insisted, tightening my grip on his neck.

He reached deep in his pants and brought out an expensive-looking gold watch. After dropping it in my hand he tried to pull free of my hold. Grabbing him by the shoulders I knelt down so I could look him straight in the eyes.

"Now listen to me, Trong. This is a new rule. No more stealing from the G.I.s, ever. O.K.? Do you understand me?"

He tried to pull free again but I held tight. "Did you hear what I said? Do you want to go back to that jail or maybe go to the hospital? The next G.I. will be bigger, Trong, and break one of your legs instead of just slapping your face. O.K.?"

He stared down at the ground, shuffling stones with his bare feet. I shook him hard. "Goddammit, you little bugger. I want an answer," I screamed at him.

"I hate you, Paul!" he yelled back, looking at me with smoky hurt eyes. "You love only Thom. Not me. Not other kids." The words gushed from him and then stopped, but I knew there was more.

"And what else, Trong? Tell me it all."

His eyes filled with tears. "I numba-one man, work anything for you. Steal for you . . . you say nothing to me. Talk only Thom. I know now you hate Trong. Love only Thom."

"That's not true. I don't hate anyone. Especially not you."

"You lie!" he screamed back at me, tears now dropping onto his dirty shirt. "I see you and Thom together all the time. You love her, and Marie . . . and Sister Tuan too . . . I know Sister Tuan love you, but maybe you like . . . fuck Thom."

His words startled me, and a reflex, unleashed by my violent encounter with the marine, sent my hand smacking hard across his cheek. He let out a blood-curdling scream and spit in my face. "Why everybody hate me, hit my face? I . . ." He started to sob and I tried to pull him close to my chest, but his hands pushed me away.

"Trong, stop it!" I screamed back at him, shaking him

with my trembling hands. "Oh God, I'm sorry, Trong. I didn't mean to hit you, but you can't talk to me like that or say things that hurt people . . . I don't hate you . . . I love you like I love Thom and the Sisters and all the kids. And I said no more stealing because I don't want you to get hurt."

He wiped his eyes on his bare arm and looked me straight in the eyes. "I know you lie too much. You take Thom go America, not me, so you love her more than others."

His words stabbed through me like Sister Hoa's always did. How long had my little friend been waiting for me to ask him if he also would like to go to America. Trong had hope . . . he survived on it and an imagination that allowed a vision of a new life in a new country. How could I tell him it would never be? That all too soon his country would be calling on him to fight and die in their endless war.

"Thom is special. I want to help her speak again, and in America there are doctors who will know how to help her. Do you understand, Trong?" I asked, letting go of him, waiting hopefully for him to hug me and say he didn't hate me.

He didn't answer but stood staring at the ground.

"You ready to go back?" My heart was a cold lump of clay in my chest. He dried his eyes, then looked up at me. "I no go back. No one love me there. Maybe I go army, fight Vietcong . . . maybe I die."

"Well go ahead then. But I don't think anyone in the army will love you more than I do . . . and here," I put a dollar in his pants pocket. "You might get hungry on the way to the war." He turned and walked away, pulling the dollar out of his pocket and dropping it on the ground.

"When you feel better, come home and see me, I'll be waiting for you," I yelled after him.

"I never come back!" he shouted back.

By the time I returned to the orphanage the children had all been put down for the night. Halfway through the dormitory I stopped and stared at their beautiful faces, light shimmering off them from the pale glow of the kerosene lamp.

Sister Tuan stepped out of the shadows and moved quietly to my side. "I didn't see you, Sister."

"I say prayers . . . did you find Trong?" she whispered anxiously. The tiny bones in her face, framed by her white veil, were sharply accentuated by the almost iridescent light from the lamp. Suddenly I felt self-conscious. What was it that eleven-year-old Trong knew about women, and I did not? Was she really in love with me? And then I remembered Marie saying the same thing. I had only seen her nun's habit, her virtuous qualities of loving selflessness—toward the children and her God. But I really knew nothing of her as a person, as a human being. Sister Hoa had told me in Phan Rang that Tuan had been given to the nuns when she was nine years old. Her family, driven by desperation and their inability to feed eleven children, had left her as a maid for the convent. In return they were guaranteed that their daughter would be fed and cared for. To me she was still the innocent little girl I had met more than two years ago. "Paul, everything O.K.?" She touched my arm gently. I looked closely at her upturned face, her large black eyes reflecting light like sparkling crystal.

"Everything will be O.K., Sister. Thank you."

She smiled her cheerful smile. "Oh, that is good. I pray so hard you find Trong and everything fine."

I handed her the fifty dollars I had taken from the marine. "Here, Sister. Use this for food tomorrow."

"Thank you. We no have money for food. You very busy many days, very tired. Sister and I no like bother you too much." She looked at me hesitantly. "Paul, sometime you not like Paul before. You feel O.K.?"

"I'm fine, Sister . . . good-night."

"Good-night and God bless you," she said softly.

Back in my room I lit a cigarette and lay on my bed in the dark. Thom slept on her small platform in the corner, curled in a ball, breathing deeply. I flexed my swollen knuckles, feeling both ashamed and proud of myself. Going over the incident in my mind, I was still surprised at my bravado and a little frightened by the drastic drug-induced personality changes I was experiencing.

I heard a sound outside my door. For a moment the crazed thought that Sister Tuan had come to my room flashed through my mind. The screen door creaked open and a small figure slipped into my room. It was Trong. He had entered the inner sanctum and stood there shaking.

I lifted the corner of my blanket, inviting him in. He ran across the room and hopped into my bed.

There were several moments of silence while I waited for him to get comfortable. With the covers now pulled up under his arms, he let out a long sigh and I watched his eyes focus on me and then on the wall and back to me.

"I sorry I run away, make you mad, Paul. You know sometime I get mad . . . I no have mother or father."

"I know. It's O.K., Trong. Now go to sleep." I waited a moment before speaking again. "You know something?"

"What?" he asked, looking up at me.

"You're still my number-one black market boy."

"I no boy! I man!" he said, sitting up.

"O.K., you're a man. Now go to sleep."

He lay back down and cuddled up against me. It was true. He was an eleven-year-old man . . . and I was a twenty-one-year-old boy. He had shot from childhood to manhood, never experiencing the irresponsibilities of adolescence. I realized I was basically an adolescent who had never been responsible for anything, acting like a man. What a joke, I thought, as I put my arm around Trong. Someone else has always taken care of me, either my parents and then the army, and just this morning I had claimed shared responsibility for one hundred children. Now I had a good reason to be scared.

"I love you, Paul . . . you never forget, O.K.?" Trong whispered.

I felt a teardrop on my hand. I pulled him closer, not answering, and let my own tears slide down my cheeks. O.K., God, I said to myself, you and me all the way . . . Please!

The first clap of thunder came without warning. The ear-piercing noise shook the earth below us and rattled every window in the building. Trong's body went rigid in my arms, and then he shot upright in bed. I put my arms around him, trying to stop him from shaking.

"It's thunder, Trong. You know, *Tieng sam* . . . *Tieng sam*," I said softly, trying to pronounce the Vietnamese for thunder properly. Thom was awake now, kneeling on her bed, peering out of the bed cautiously.

"No. I think maybe VC come," he said, still shaking as he watched out the window.

"I'm sure it's thunder. Now lie back down," I said, pulling him back under the covers.

I heard screams coming up the stairs moments before my door burst open. Nine of the younger children ran into the room and scrambled for a space on or under my bed. Trong and I helped them find a space under the covers while Thom took a couple over with her.

"Dung co khoc, chi la Tieng sam." [Don't cry, it's only thunder], I said in my poor Vietnamese. They were still trembling and sobbing. "Trong, you tell them it's only thunder. No VC, only thunder."

The moment he said the words they quieted down. He repeated the words again, and then there was silence. The nights in Vietnam frequently erupted into bright light shows which fractured the torrid wet air with crackling, earth-shaking thunder. For the children the distinction between the sound of thunder and of bombs could not be made.

Finally my room was quiet, and now with only a skimpy corner of the blanket left to cover me on the crowded bed I wondered about sleeping on the floor. Either way I wasn't going to sleep tonight, because of the little bodies wrapped every which way around me, or the larger dose of Dexedrine I was taking that kept me wide awake and wired all night, or threw me into twenty hours of sleep without giving me one minute of rest.

As I listened to their peaceful breathing, I realized I had somehow lost that great feeling of being needed by these beautiful children. I felt frightened, that once again I was in way over my head. Frustrated that I couldn't run. And confused by all that was happening much too fast around me.

The weeks following my street scene with Trong were a sad succession of lost days, spread between the orphanage, mortuary, bars, whores, drunken nights, and drugs. Now instead of just falling apart quietly, in my head, everyone around me saw it. Kind voices, Marie, the nuns, and some angry ones, too, tried to help, advise, soothe, and warn me, and all I could say was, "You're crazy, I'm fine," or "Mind your own business!"

At first Marie welcomed my help in triage and the emergency room, where I worked diligently but would never fol-

low her to her quarters. I claimed fatigue, and a heavy mental workout each day in the morgue held back my interest i
sex. One night she brought me some coffee as a surprise an
caught me in the drug cabinet—the man I had been sutu
ing, writhing in pain behind me. She gave me three choice
talk it out with her, seek help from one of the docs who woul
quietly get me off the drugs, or be turned in to my CO fo
stealing narcotics. I agreed to talk to her and asked for a cou
ple of days to get my thoughts together. She agreed.

When I woke up the next morning I couldn't even re
member Marie's name, let alone my promise to her. I als
had no idea where I was until Thom entered the room with
steaming cup of coffee. When she motioned for me to stan
up, I saw the crucifix on the wall behind her and realized tha
I had crawled in and fallen asleep on the floor of the nun'
room. Thom took my hand and led me to the kitchen wher
she had prepared some eggs and rice for me. Sister Tuan wa
preparing breakfast for the children and watched me starin
at the food on the table.

"Paul, you must eat. You sick, so Thom make it for you."

"I'm not sick, Sister, I just can't eat . . . I gotta go." Th
smell of the eggs turned my stomach, and meaning only t
push the bowl away, I knocked it off the table.

"Paul, what is wrong with you?" Sister Tuan shouted a
she helped Thom clean up the spilled food. They were th
first angry words I had ever heard her speak. "Last nigh
you scare me. I think you are some crazy man, come t
my room . . . talking, talking, talking . . . and then you
cry. Sister Hoa tell you go away and you say things numba
ten . . ."

"I'm sorry, Sister Tuan. I . . . was tired."

"No, Paul, you cannot lie to me now," she said, sitting
down across from me. "I know you are sick with drug o
something, not tired."

Thom stayed at my side, massaging my arms and back,
hugging my shoulders in an effort to elicit some response
from my glazed eyes. She knew something was wrong and
seemed to understand. Every moment I was at the orphanage she clung to me, protective and caring.

But I couldn't answer Sister Tuan or Thom, who tried our
sign language. I couldn't explain to them that everything was

oming apart because the mortuary load was getting heavier
nd heavier, and the orphanage work had become unbear-
ble, and that I wasn't sleeping because normally sleep was
 period of rest, quiet breathing, but not for me. It was
ne continual nightmare of faces, blood, and their eyes—
creaming. Bring me back so I can reconsider. Each face was
 different set of circumstances, corroborated by their mili-
ary records and the men from Graves Registration. They
howed me letters from girlfriends, wives and lovers, that
aid they wanted out, up, or in with another man, and each
tter started the same way, "Dear John," a famous opening
ne that always meant the end.

And how could I make them understand that every time I
vashed the children it was just like washing the blood and
rains out of the blond hair of autopsy number one thou-
and. That when I saw one of the little girls holding a doll to
er chest it reminded me of the suicide case where the G.I.
lutched a pinless grenade against his chest, screaming that it
vas his Teddy bear. The men who lived in the tent with him
aid, "Sure it is," and dodged the flying body parts from a
listance.

"Paul . . . Paul, you O.K.?" Sister Tuan asked, tapping
he back of my hand. I looked across the table at her, then up
t Thom.

"Where's Sister Hoa?"

"She go to the market. Be back soon . . . you like to talk
o her?" she asked, her eyes brightening at my possible re-
uest for help.

"No . . . ," I said and started for the door.

"Paul . . . I ask God to . . ."

"What," I screamed back at her, scaring both her and
Thom, "you'll ask God to help me, Sister? . . . You must be
utta your fuckin' mind . . . either He's on vacation, or He
loesn't exist, and I think you should start thinking about
hat fact." She burst into tears and ran past me out the door.

Thom looked at me angrily. There were no tears in her
yes, just anger. Save your anger, my dear little friend, I
hought, for your country's screwed-up Immigration officials
who say denial of your adoption papers is only one signature
way.

I left the orphanage that rainy, dismal morning and staye away for the next ten days.

When I arrived at the mortuary, Major Williams w waiting for me. He had received a phone call from Marie an accused me of lying to her about my work, about myself, an about himself, and how he supposedly worked me too har He was furious, spittle forming at the corners of his mout as he warned me that I was on the verge of serious troubl He said nothing about stealing and I thanked Marie silentl for sparing me a term in Long Binh Jail. I listened quietl saying, "Yes, sir," and "No, sir," when I was supposed t then went to work.

Ten lost days. Autopsies, one after the other, paraded i front of me and I no longer cared. I woke up in bars, on th floor of my old quarters, and one morning in the gutter of th whorehouse district. But everyday I was on time. In a hal decent-looking uniform and stoned.

One afternoon I was alone in the morgue, preparing a su cide for autopsy. I looked down at the body on the autops table. He was a handsome, twenty-year-old, with dar brown hair, piercing blue eyes, and a strong muscular buil As I washed the dried blood from around the gunshot woun over his heart, I noticed the white untanned ring on his le hand where his wedding ring had been.

"Oh, Jesus, what is your mother going to say when yo come home like this?" I said to the dead man softly. "Di you stop to think about your new wife? How she'll feel, an what if she's pregnant? Now you'll never see your baby Now you'll never watch him grow . . . you look like a foot ball player, or a weight lifter. Your dad, what will he d when he sees you? Dead and gone. All his dreams and . . don't worry . . . I'll clean you up."

Five minutes later I threw up, shaking and heaving, bu there was nothing in me, only dry, cold fear. I was so fright ened when I realized I had been talking to a dead body that ripped my locker apart and threw away all the hash, dope and Dexedrine I had hidden.

That evening I climbed the wall behind the nurses' quar ters and tapped lightly on Marie's window. I saw a figure approach through the opaque glass, and then Marie opened the window a crack. When she saw me she started to close it again, but I grabbed the window's wooden frame.

"Please, Marie. You said I could talk to you if I needed help."

"It's too late, Paul."

"Please, oh God, please don't close the window," I pleaded. "Just for a few minutes and then I'll leave."

"You want to talk to someone, go talk to Sister Hoa. They're in trouble, Paul. There's almost no food left. Moses went home on emergency leave almost two weeks ago. I think you'll find her a little upset with you, and she's right!"

"I know . . . but what am I gonna say to her . . . I'm so sorry about everything."

"Don't tell me. Tell Sister Hoa and the two children who died yesterday from measles," Marie said, her voice a mixture of anger and sadness. I felt the air rush from my lungs. My legs turned to rubber and I fell in a heap on my hands and knees.

"Oh shit . . . what have I done to them?" Marie climbed out and jumped down next to me. "Get up, Paul. Stop acting like a goddamned child and get over to the orphanage," she said, pulling me to my feet. "You've been acting like a total ass, and no matter what you say, you've been wrong. Sister Hoa knows about your job. I told her. But they're not to blame for your drug problem, and neither is the mortuary."

"Have you ever seen the mortuary? Do you have any idea . . ."

"Don't hand me that bullshit," she said, interrupting me. "Just stop trying to make everything right and clear and understandable . . . it never will be, no matter who you ask . . . Paul, what happened to the guy that told me he was only trying to change the odds in their favor? You know, the tall, skinny blond American with the midget sidekick," she said, trying to cheer me up.

"I don't know . . . why."

"Well they needed you, Paul, and you weren't there. They still need you now, so get going," she said, wiping the wetness from my cheek.

"Will you come down and help?"

"I was there today. Just keep pushing the liquids, continue the ice baths and penicillin, and they'll make it . . . and yes, I'll come back when you've got the orphanage pulled together."

"Thanks, Marie."

When I arrived at the orphanage the gate was open, and I could see a few children playing in the darkened courtyard. I dropped my motorcycle on its side and walked toward the nursery door. The children stopped chasing each other and watched me as if I were a stranger who had just wandered in off the street. Thom, who was usually the first to greet me, was mysteriously absent, as was Trong and the older children.

Through the screen door I could see Sister Tuan and Sister Hoa moving back and forth, carrying children in their arms, and talking quietly to each other in Vietnamese. Both of them stopped in place when I entered the room but quickly returned to bathing one child after another in a washtub filled with ice water.

It was like my first meeting with them in Phan Rang as I stood there looking around the crowded nursery. Every crib had two or three sick children in it, and several of the older children were on floor mats against the wall. The nuns continued working feverishly, trying to cool the fevers that were burning them up and then out, and I couldn't move or talk or explain.

Sister Tuan passed by me and gently touched my arm, as if to say, welcome back, I understand, and after applying cold compresses to the children on the floor, Sister Hoa walked over and stopped in front of me. It seemed like years since I had looked her straight in the eyes, but I was ready for the inevitable confrontation that was about to start. Her eyes, set deep in her tired, lined face, were like penetrating black knives, stabbing at me with her stare, I was ready for the words, for the anger that had been building up, for the truth that she felt I must know, but was shocked when her sinewy arm shot out suddenly and her hand slapped me hard across the face. Her arm struck out with so much anger that the momentum of her swing spun her body around in a circle. Tears began flowing down her worn cheeks as she shook me angrily by the shoulders. I was so ashamed, so stunned, that I didn't hear her words but could only stare at her lips, moving, screaming, praying, and I wished myself away, back on the streets, drunk or dead. Thom had entered the room and was crying now, pulling at my arm to leave the room.

"How could you abandon us again, leave us helpless after helping so much?" Sister Hoa screamed at me as she let go of my shoulders. "You have broken your promise to me, shirked the responsibility you claimed was partly yours, and all because you are still a child and cannot admit it."

"You're right, Sister, and I am truly sorry."

"I thought you were different from your American brothers who are slowly destroying our country, fathering and killing our little children, and spreading a hatred for each other . . ." She stopped suddenly and put her hand to her mouth, frightened by her own words. All the frustrations, hard work, the war, malnutrition, and disease had finally worn Sister Hoa down. I was only the proverbial last straw. She had every right to be angry with me but was more frustrated with her inability to change their circumstances and make others want peace in her country as badly as she did. I had dealt with the same frustrations and anger with chemicals; Sister Hoa only had her God and prayer, and both had recently been as absent from her daily life as I had.

I grabbed her hands and held them strongly. "Sister, I can only say again I'm sorry. I was wrong and confused and everything else but I'm back. I'm here to stay. I promise you. If you want me to leave, I will." Our eyes were still locked as she gently pulled her hands from mine and with a listless hand wiped her brow.

"Oh, dear God. What is happening to us? Forgive me, Paul, as I forgive you. We have all suffered enough."

We worked through the night, a team again, all forgiven, each supporting the other in the struggle against immeasurable odds but sure once again of survival.

When we finished with the children in the nursery, Thom, Trong, Sister Tuan, and I began scrubbing the bathroom, kitchen, and dormitory from top to bottom with disinfectant soap and water.

At dawn, the worst seemed to be over. We found no new children with the prickly rash and had only lost one of the palsics and a new baby to the uncontrollable killer. I burned the last of the nursery linens and was about to take the two little bodies to the cemetery when Thom collapsed in the kitchen. Sister Tuan and Trong carried her to my room and placed her on my bed. Trong knew exactly what was wrong with her. She had continually given her meager share of rice to one of the other girls who was sick. My heart sank as Thom smiled up at me. She was every word in the dictionary that meant incredible, and I hoped as I gently moved the hair away from her eyes that it wasn't too late to get her adoption papers completed.

"I tell you, Paul," Trong said, leaning on my shoulder, "girls are too dumb."

"O.K., partner, I agree." Sister Tuan slapped us both on the shoulder. "Except for the nuns," I added.

"Sure . . ." Trong said with a smile.

"Sister, you fix Thom some rice and my partner and I are gonna go and do some heavy trading on the black market."

"Good, Paul. Sister and I already make a long list for when you come back." She looked at me and smiled. They never gave up hope.

—— 23 ——

A Most Tragic Mistake

Several weeks passed and I stood by my word, staying nights at the orphanage and working diligently at the morgue. Major Williams figured his threats had straightened me out, and a new pathologist, Captain Murry, found me the best technician he had ever worked with.

There was no way to explain to them what had happened to me. How one slap in the face had knocked me from a very naive twenty-one-year-old boy to a mature but frightened man. One conversation with a dead body had silenced my stupid questions forever. The important questions remained, but now in a new form, and with a patient guarantee that one day I would know and understand the answers. Sister Hoa's slap reminded me of a backhand delivered by my mother when I was ten or eleven. It was not the act of hitting me which made me so angry, for the pain went away quickly. It was the fact that my mother, a calm, gentle woman of great patience, never struck us unless she felt we needed to be stopped or shocked into comprehension. It never made sense at the time. The woman I loved more than anyone else in the world had hit me. But a week, a month, sometimes years later, I understood why. Lessons learned and never forgotten.

The orphanage was back to seminormal operation, with no new children being taken in until our food situation stabilized. With Moses gone, our storeroom of stolen supplies had quickly emptied. Trong and I traded everything we had and still we were only able to feed the children twice a day. Jarvis was a little help but, as usual, undependable and always late with his payments. A major new source of food, or goods tradable for food, would have to be found.

One afternoon I was washing down the autopsy room when Major Williams rushed in and told me that the outskirts of Saigon were being attacked by an unknown number of enemy troops. I was to go to my quarters and stay there until further notice. He and Captain Murry took off for the safety of their officers' quarters and I took off for the orphanage.

For several weeks now our neighbors around the orphanage had been talking about this attack, saying that one day the Vietcong would enter the city and maybe stay forever. No one seemed very concerned, though, for many times during the war and especially during the Tet offensive in 1968 the Vietcong had infiltrated the city. They caused havoc for a few days, blew up a couple of buildings, then disappeared back into the mountains. The Americans called it H & I, harassment and interdiction. The enemy called it "keeping them on their toes." It drove the Americans crazy in Saigon, never knowing what would explode in their faces or who among the millions of refugees was an empty sapper with a grenade in his basket of smelly fish.

I borrowed fifty dollars from one of the office clerks and stopped at the air base PX for my ration of beer and cigarettes. There was almost no food left at the orphanage, and I figured four cases of beer and five cartons of cigarettes would get us through the next two days. As I was strapping the goods to the back of my motorcycle, something hit the roof of the PX, filling the air with wood and metal debris and knocking everyone to the ground. An enemy rocket had just blown a three-foot hole in the roof, and because the PX was located in the center of the base, the Military Police and Security were terrified. There was no way that someone had just fired the rocket from a bordering area. The enemy had to be on the inside of the base.

I raced up to the Vietnamese Air Force gate, paid the guard my toll of two packs of Salems, and was waved on.

For the first time since my arrival in Vietnam the streets were totally empty. No motorcycles, carts, or cyclos passed me as I raced toward Gia Dinh and the orphanage. There as also no bombs or gunfire that I could hear, only a dark ack cloud of smoke climbing up over the China Town area, gering from the first attack. Even the squatters had pulled stakes and vacated the curbs and alleyways around the central market.

I was enjoying this rare unimpeded run through the city until a mortar hit the front of a building about two hundred ards ahead of me. Rocks, cement, and wood flew up the reet toward me, and before I could stop I hit a piece of cement and flipped over the motorcycle's handlebars. Putting my hands out to break the fall worked, but I left the skin of my palms and knees on the street. As I started to collect the eer and cigarettes, which were scattered all over the street, the roof of another building about three blocks away exploded. I picked up the motorcycle and took off. Bombs or no ombs, people appeared from nowhere and began fighting over my lost rations.

After zigzagging through narrow alleys and side streets, I nally arrived at the locked orphanage gate. I banged on it udly. A wild thought raced through my mind, they've fled the city. Suddenly Trong appeared from the shadows. His ttle black eyes looked like a cat peering around the corner of the building. Recognizing me, he raced to the gate and let me in. Gunshots rang out several streets away, scaring us as we raced into the dormitory.

The nuns had gathered all the children in the dormitory and spread them and their sleeping mats out in neat order on the floor. It was the first time all the children had been rought together in one place and also the first time I realized ow many children were in our orphanage. One hundred nd five little Vietnamese faces stared up at me as I walked to the center of the room, stepping carefully over tiny bodies. From thirteen to one hundred and five, and I couldn't remember how it all happened. Sister Tuan sat in one of the orners of the room, quietly singing to a few of the more rightened children. Sister Hoa sat against one wall with two quawking babies on her lap, carefully trying to balance hem and their bottles. The children tried to get me to sit ext to them, clearing a space and patting the tile floor with heir hands, but I moved over and sat down next to Sister

Hoa. She handed me one of the babies, who proceeded to w the leg of my pants the minute he arrived on my lap.

"That means he loves you," Sister Hoa said with a war smile.

"Do you think this will be over soon . . . I mean the stre fighting?"

"Yes, maybe tomorrow they will go. For now we must r main quiet and pray . . . What happened to your hand they are bleeding?" she said, putting the baby down an lifting my left hand so she could look at it.

"I fell off my motorcycle. They're O.K. . . ." I said, b she wouldn't let go. She called out to Trong in quick Vie namese. He jumped to his feet and ran out the door.

Thom entered next, carrying a welcome cup of hot coffe and a bowl of rice. Food was the last thing on my mind and shook my head no, but she pulled at the skin under my nec and pinched my stomach.

"Thom thinks you have become too skinny," Sister Ho said.

When Thom saw the abrasions on my hands, she hande the bowl of rice to one of the other children and began to ro up my sleeves.

Sister Hoa leaned over and took the baby from my arm: "Here, let me have the baby while your little friends tak care of your hands."

Trong arrived with some clean water and bandages, an for the first time since I met them, he and Thom worked to gether to clean and bandage my hands. It was like Genera Hospital, the children gathered around me in a large circle chatting quietly about the prognosis. As they taped the end o the gauze to my wrist, I looked around at the hundred littl faces, so serious and silent; suddenly they were grown up adults in children's bodies. They knew a bomb could dro and destroy the building, the nuns, themselves . . . the knew this and sat still, holding on to each other, arm wrapped around the child sitting next to them, seemingl unafraid and waiting patiently for what was to come. N other children in the world knew so much about death and expected it like these, I thought to myself. They never pla on tomorrow. Maybe that was why each child in the dormi tory had gathered around him the gifts I had given him a

Christmas, and any other possessions he owned, in case he was forced to run again. That was their secret, I decided, as I winked back at two beautiful little faces. They expected nothing of tomorrow, so they found overwhelming joy and happiness in the simplest acts of today, eating, bathing, jumping rope, and playing.

An explosion in the distance shook the building and the children fell silent. The smiles that had been scattered around the room disappeared. I couldn't stand the fear I saw in some of their faces and rolled into the children like a log, pulling as many as I could on top of me. The Tickle Monster had attacked, and suppressed laughter spread through the room. Trong gathered a few of the boys and whispered plans for a counterattack on the Tickling Monster that would render him helpless. I saw him out of the corner of my eye and rolled into the group, bringing them tumbling down in a pile. Even Thom joined the pile-on but made sure none of the children accidentally stepped on my face.

Suddenly the room exploded around us! The air, filled a moment ago with squealing laughter, was sliced by deadly flying glass, fragments of concrete and wood. It was total pandemonium. The candles had been knocked over, and children I couldn't see were screaming with terror and pain. As I looked up, all I could see were little figures running back and forth. When the debris stopped falling, I began crawling around, saying, "Quiet down now. It's O.K. It's O.K. We're all right." The children started to gather around me, grabbing onto my arms and back. As I felt my way around, my hands became wet and sticky with blood. The terrified screaming would not stop. They yelled my name and the Sisters', their cries piercing the dark room. In an effort to stop their panic, I yelled at the top of my lungs, "Quiet! Shut up now! Quiet!"

Sister Tuan and Trong finally found candles, and as soon as they lit them the children started to calm down. Thom was at the end of the room with an injured child in her arms, and the Sisters were tending several children with small wounds. It was a scene out of my worst nightmare; children with cuts from flying glass, sobbing and shaking with fear. Two little boys were dead, crushed from a fallen window frame. My brave little Trong was gathering the children who weren't hurt in one corner of the room, where he spoke to them quietly.

"Sister Hoa, go to the nursery and bring back all the bandages and tape we have," I yelled, then bent down, baptized one of the dead children, and began to wrap him in a bloody bamboo mat. Thom carried the limp body of a little boy, Kang, across the room and placed him next to me. He had a deep head wound and seemed almost unconscious. He and two others with bad cuts would require suturing and professional help. I bandaged them as best I could and laid them against the wall while I took care of the ones with minor wounds.

"Sister, I've got to take these three to the Army Hospital. They need suturing and someone to check their wounds," I said.

"Yes, go, and bring us more small bandages."

"No, you no can go out there," Sister Tuan yelled as she moved toward us, her hands and the arms of her habit covered with blood.

"That is enough, Sister!" Sister Hoa commanded. "Now help us with these children."

I checked the courtyard before we moved out the dormitory door. Something had blown a huge hole in the courtyard wall, and debris from the explosion had broken almost every window and door in the building. The three of us carried the children to my motorcycle, and Sister Hoa held baby Kang to my chest while I buttoned my fatigue shirt around him. Sister Tuan tied the other two children to the back of the cycle with knotted rags that went around them and then were tied at my waist.

"Please, Paul, we can wait for later. What will we do if you are . . ." Sister Tuan pleaded.

"Sister, go back to the others," Sister Hoa ordered.

"Sister, they won't live till morning without help. We'll be O.K."

"I know this, but I worry for you."

Sister Hoa sensed the younger nun's concern and put her arm over her shoulders. "They will be fine . . . Hurry back, Paul. We need you."

Trong appeared at my side, carrying the carbine I kept in

ay room. He said, "No worry, no sweat. I protect everyone
or you. If the VC come here, they die."

"Don't you fire that gun, Trong, or I'll break your neck.
ou protect them for me, but no shooting at the shadows."

"Sure," Trong said, slinging the rifle over his shoulder.

I started the engine and then took another look at the hole
a the courtyard wall. "Trong, cover that hole with some of
ae feeding tables. Get the boys to help you," I yelled as I
ulled away.

"Can do, boss . . ." he yelled after me, saluting and al-
aost knocking himself out with the barrel of the carbine.

It felt as if my heart was lodged high in my throat as I care-
ully navigated toward the hospital. One bullet was all it
vould take and we'd be in a pile on the asphalt. I prayed to
God, then Buddha, and anyone else who might have been lis-
ening, to help me get my precious cargo safely to the hospi-
al. The children were quiet and holding onto me so tight my
tomach ached. Baby Kang was too quiet, so I kept blowing
a his face. His eyes would pop open, then slowly close again,
ut at least I knew he was still alive.

When I arrived at the hospital's ambulance entrance, the
American guard refused to open the gate. I pleaded with
aim, telling him they were innocent children injured by the
ttack on the city, but he refused me again. He said his orders were that no civilians, hospital employees or otherwise,
vere allowed on the compound. He stood menacingly large
n front of the gate, his weapon ready to shoot if I tried to en-
er.

Marie's room was my last chance, so I drove into the alley
vehind the hospital and pulled up to the wall behind the
aurses' quarters. Putting one of the boys on my back with his
arms around my neck, and holding baby Kang under my
arm, I stood on the motorcycle seat and hopped up onto the
vall. That was the easy part. The motorcycle had given me
an advantage getting up, but it looked like fifty feet to the
ground on the other side. I tried lowering myself down
slowly, but with the boy on my back, and painful hands, I
couldn't hold on. My full weight landed on baby Kang. He
started to cry, so I knew he was still alive, and quickly put my
hand over his mouth. After one more trip over the wall, I
picked up all three boys and crept from building to building

until I found Marie's window. She opened it after the secon
knock and almost fainted when she saw the children.

"Jesus, Paul, what happened to them?"

"Something hit the orphanage . . . Kang's going bad.
can feel his breathing slowing . . . please, Marie, take them
Get one of the docs to take a look at them?"

"Paul, we're on alert. I only came back to change thes
bloody fatigues, and what if they're found . . ."

"Either you take them, or I'll walk into the emergenc
room and make someone take care of them at gunpoint."

"Don't be stupid . . . here give them to me. I'll get one o
the off-duty girls to help . . ." she said, lifting baby Kang i
through her window. "Are the others O.K.?"

"A lot more like this but none as bad . . . glass cuts
bruises . . ."

"If this ends, I'll come down . . . Are you O.K.? I mear
your hands?" she asked, taking the last child.

"My hands are O.K., and I'm O.K. . . . Thanks, Marie
I gotta get back."

"Paul, I'm sorry I was so rough on you that night."

"You don't have to apologize. You were right and you see
the little black and blue marks under my eyes?"

"Yes," she said, turning my face gently into the light tc
look.

"Sister Hoa was right too."

"Oh Jesus, you're kidding?" Marie said, laughing. "I'm
not laughing at you. It's just that I can't imagine Sister Hoa
belting anyone . . . Please be careful," she said, leaning out
the window and kissing me gently on the lips.

"I will. You take good care of them."

"No sweat, Joe . . ."

By the time I got back to the orphanage the nuns had all
the little ones bandaged and resting quietly. Trong was busy
playing doctor, putting fake rag bandages on others to keep
them quiet. The two dead children had been placed on one of
the sleeping platforms and covered with a sheet. When I en-
tered the room, Thom was lighting candles around the plat-
form and Sister Hoa asked me to join them in the rosary. We
never got through the first "Hail Mary," when someone be-
gan banging on the gate. We forced the children down on the

floor, blew out the candles, and lay silent, hoping whoever it was would go away. The noise continued for another few seconds and then stopped as suddenly as it had begun. I slid across the floor and after taking the carbine from Trong crawled out of the room. The courtyard was empty and the tables Trong had placed in front of the hole were still in place. Once again my heart sounded like distant mortar fire as I stepped slowly up the stairs. When I looked out over the edge of the roof, the street below and the area in front of the gate were deserted. I decided to remain on the roof where I could see everything and maybe scare off any future visitors. All of the gunfire and explosions I could hear seemed to be coming from the China Town area where several large fires leaped up above the buildings. Stay downtown, I prayed. Leave us alone, please God, tell them to leave us alone.

My prayers worked until about 2 A.M., when several large South Vietnamese armored personnel carriers rolled past, firing wildly ahead. Their fifty-caliber rounds literally tore apart everything in their path. In the headlights of the lumbering machines, I could see people running back and forth, firing at the impenetrable monsters.

A noise in the courtyard brought me crawling to that edge of the roof. I looked down in time to see the tables covering the hole fall away. Preceded by the barrel of his rifle, a small figure stepped through into the courtyard. He was wearing black pajamas and instantly I knew we were in trouble. The only people who wore black pajamas and carry weapons in Vietnam were the enemy. Pointing the carbine at him, I moved closer to the edge where I could get a clean shot. The man looked around the courtyard, then waved to someone outside the wall. At that same moment I heard someone starting up the stairs and slid over so I could see who it was. It was Thom, with a cup of coffee and another bowl of rice for me! I tried to get her attention, waving my arm in the air, but she was intent on not spilling anything and watched the coffee cup carefully.

Another noise in the courtyard brought me back to the edge of the roof. Now there were two soldiers getting to their feet, weapons ready. I was petrified. What if they saw Thom and fired? What if they missed Thom and fired into the dormitory? I knew gunshots were about to crack the silence surrounding the orphanage, but I had no idea what to do. I couldn't wait any longer and jumped to my feet, hoping the soldiers would see me first and run. One of them turned, as if his attention suddenly was drawn to something in the court-yard. Suddenly both men dropped to a knee-firing position and I screamed, "Thom get down. Get back." The minute I spoke, the soldier fired. I pointed the carbine at the first man, yelled as loud as I could, "Up here you asshole. Shoot me, shoot at me!" and at the same time closed my eyes and kept pulling the trigger until the magazine emptied. When I opened them again, one of the men was lying in a grotesque position on the ground, and the second man was diving back out the hole.

Suddenly I remembered Thom and ran to the top of the stairs. My heart stopped when I saw her lying in a pool of blood on the landing below. I dropped my carbine and taking three steps at a time jumped down to her side. Gaping wounds in her throat and chest oozed blood, and as I gently pulled her onto my lap I knew she was dying. I put my hand on the neck wound to stem the flow of blood, and at the same time could feel the warm liquid soaking my pants from a hole in her back. There was nothing I could do. Her life was slipping away, flowing out of her faster than I could think.

"Oh God, please, Thom . . ." was all I could say. Her eyes stared at my face. Unlike the darting eyes of the dying G.I.s in triage, she looked directly at me as she slipped to-ward death. She raised her bloody hand, touched my lips with her fingers, and then rubbed my chin softly. I could taste the salt of her blood, mingled with the cold tears run-ning down my face. I took her hand, holding it tight, and she closed her eyes for a second. When they opened again, I could feel her weakly pulling me down toward her. She opened her mouth when I was close enough, and I heard her faintly whisper, "Paul." She smiled at me, then quietly closed her eyes in death. I pulled her warm body close to me and held her until I felt the very last movement of her heart.

When I walked into the dormitory, Thom's limp body across my arms, both of the nuns dropped to their knees and cried out loud. Within minutes everybody in the room was gathering around, weeping and crying for our Thom. For the number-one girl in the orphanage. For the one who loved everybody the same. Three of the older girls wiped the blood from her face with wet rags and combed out her hair. Even Trong came over and wrapped his arms around my neck, tears streaming down his dirty face.

For what seemed like hours, we sat in a circle around her body. I was numb. Cold and numb, as I stared at Thom. My mind racing with what could have been, how she would have reacted to my family, and what had gone wrong. Over and over again I replayed the moments before the shooting. The soldiers' faces, the first man I had ever killed. It was done and could not be changed. No one could bring her back. I thought of Brian, the children in Cam Ranh, and the thousand faces I had seen in the morgue and triage. If only I could tell the other children that Thom was the last to die. That the war was over and soon they could play without ever being afraid again.

A little half-American, half-Vietnamese girl approached me quietly, stopping a few feet away, waiting for me to say come closer. She took another step and stopped again, this time stretching her thin arms out to me. Without even looking, I pulled her onto my lap and made her comfortable. She turned, stared up at my face, and began to speak softly in Vietnamese. As if carrying on a full conversation with me, she chattered away, wiping the tears from my cheek and pointing from me to Thom's body. When Sister Tuan saw her on my lap she moved over and tried to pick her up. It was the first moment I actually realized the little girl was there.

"What's wrong, Sister?" I asked, pulling the little girl back down on my lap.

"She talking. I think she bother you."

"No, no. She's O.K. What's she saying? She keeps pointing to Thom."

"Her name Tuyet. She want to know if you like her," Sister Tuan said, sitting down on the floor next to us.

"Tell her sure I like her. But why is she pointing to Thom?" I asked again. Tuyet began to talk again, but now she spoke to Sister Tuan and then pointed at me.

"No sweat. I tell you later."

"What's wrong with telling me now, Sister?"

Sister Tuan looked down at her rosary, then back up at me. "She say she love you, like Thom. She want to ask you if you take her . . . Thom is gone now, she want to go home with you. Be your baby.''

Little Tuyet's eyes bounced back and forth between Sister Tuan and me. Waiting for any response from me. As I was about to speak I heard the gate being opened, and with Tuyet wrapped around my neck I ran out into the courtyard. Before I could stop them, Trong and two other boys pushed the market wagon holding the dead soldier's body out the gate and disappeared into the dark night. I screamed for him to come back, but they were gone. Sister Hoa locked the gate and approached me, holding her fingers to her lips, wanting me to be quiet.

"They will be fine. Trong is very brave," Sister Hoa said, turning me back toward the dormitory door.

"Why did you let them go? Isn't there enough trouble already? If they are caught with a dead body, the enemy will come back. The whole place will be destroyed. Do you realize that?" I shouted angrily. Suddenly the enormity of what had happened—and could still happen—overcame me. It had to be a bad dream. Within the last several hours I had lost the first person who had taught me unconditional love; I had killed for the first time! And now Trong had bravely gone to dispose of the evidence that would have meant my death had the enemy returned.

"You don't understand," Sister Hoa answered patiently. "These boys are very smart. They know what they must do to survive."

"But I could have taken the body. It wouldn't have been so dangerous for me later."

"They're not just going to take the body away. They are also going to find food."

"Food! How can you think of food?" I asked, handing Tuyet to Sister Tuan.

Sister Hoa looked at me and shook her head. "You still don't understand us. You don't know yet. There is almost no food for the morning meal, which is only an hour away. The boys know where to go. We have some friends who will help us if they can. We must go on working, feeding and caring for the children. No matter what has happened, we must go on," she said and walked toward the kitchen.

I helped the nuns clear the broken glass from the kitchen

ounters and feeding area, nervously counting the minutes. I was just about ready to go out on my motorcycle and start looking for them when I heard Trong's voice at the gate.

"Hey, Paul, let me in," Trong yelled.

When I pulled the gate open, the three of them stood there, all smiles and proudly pointing at the wagon loaded with fifty pounds of rice, some vegetables, and two live chickens.

Sister Tuan pushed by us, picked Trong right off his feet, and hugged him tightly. I grabbed another boy, and Sister Hoa picked up the last.

"Hey, we man, no can do!" the boy in Sister Hoa's arms yelled, and she let him down.

"Where did you get this food, Trong?" I asked.

"Old man at the market say no sweat, we pay later. No business now . . . Paul, he say he send some box, I don't know how you say . . ."

"A coffin," Sister Hoa said, helping him.

"Yeah. He say he send tomorrow. No pay. He give you cause you like Vietnamese kid."

"Thanks, partner. Come on, I'll help you put this stuff in the kitchen."

"No, we mans can do," another of the boys said, and I finally realized it was Nick, Moses' son.

Trong and I sat silently on the roof until sunrise. Neither of us spoke, although I could feel Trong staring at me most of the time. Sister Tuan was washing the blood off the stairs and landing where Thom had died. They were cleaning up, preparing for another day of diapers, food, school, and the normal problems of running our orphanage.

"We go black market today? Just you and me?" Trong said as he wiped my carbine clean.

"We can't . . . Not with the Vietcong out there."

He said confidently, "No more. No more fighting. The VC *di di* [run] from the city."

"Then we'll go. Just you and me," I said, wrapping my arm around his shoulder.

"Paul, it lucky the VC no come back here."

"Why? Would you jump down and fight them with your bare hands, Tarzan?"

"No. You no have any more bullet," he said, looking up
at me with a big smile.

He was right. The clip was empty and I had no more
shells. "So, if they come back we'll tickle them to death. Like
this," I said, lunging at him. Instead of the many roosters
who jarred us awake in the morning, the loud high squeal of
Trong's laughter rang out from the roof of the best orphanage in Saigon.

Dear God:

In my whole life I only asked you for one thing . . . and he died. Then you gave me someone I didn't ask for. She became my life, and now, for some reason, you've taken her away, too. It's over. Faith sucks.

— 24 —

A Thousand Conversations

At about seven that morning, the old man from the market, along with two of his friends, carried a simple mahogany coffin into the courtyard. I watched from the window of my room as they helped Sister Hoa place Thom's body in the rough wooden box. On the top of the coffin was nailed a shiny tin cross, and it struck me that I didn't even know if Thom was Catholic. The nuns had dressed her in a beautiful white *Ao-dai*, the traditional dress of Vietnam, and wrapped a small white scarf around her neck to cover the wounds. Sister Tuan straightened her dress, arranged her neatly combed hair, then began to gather the children around the coffin.

Some of the children tossed paper money and brightly colored paper clothes into the coffin, articles they felt Thom would need in her next life. Other children reached in and touched her hands or her cheek, saying a final good-bye to their little friend. Next, an old woman that Trong and I had bartered with over stolen surgical tools brought an armful of long white gladiolas and placed them around the coffin.

The feeling of loss was deadening. Not just because I had replayed, a thousand times, Thom's first meeting with my family and the happiness I knew she would find in their love. But because of the many others who would never know the warmth of her revitalizing, unconditional love. In her happy and selfless devotion to all of us, she had been an example of unbelievable strength, equaled only by Sister Hoa. Sister Hoa had gathered the same strength in fifty years of service to her God and the children of Vietnam. Thom was only eleven years old.

Sister Tuan knocked on my door, then entered quietly. "Paul, we ready to go. The old man find a number-one place bury Thom," she said, adjusting the folds of her clean white veil.

"I'd rather not go, Sister," I said, still looking down at Thom.

"I no understand you, Paul. You no can change what happen. You know that. You be wrong if you no say good-bye to your friend. Cause she die, you cannot stop. You keep working like Sister and I."

"It's not that easy for me, Sister. My feelings, my reasons for helping the children, are different from yours. You keep working because of faith and God . . . It is your life," I said, turning to face her. She looked at me intensely for a few moments, then suddenly began to cry. She walked around the room wringing her hands and then stopped in front of me again. Silent tears streaked her face, now soft and sensitive.

"There is something I like tell you now." She took a deep breath and wiped the tears from her cheek with her sleeve. "For a long time I love you . . . like a woman love man, deep in my heart." She pressed her chest with her slender hands. "I dream so many night I marry you, have children for you, and you teach them like you teach and love children in our orphanage. I hope we fall in love every time I see you, and how nice to marry a man like you." She put her hands to her mouth, afraid of my reaction to her words, and shocked at her ability to speak them.

"I'm sorry, Sister. I didn't know how . . ."

"It is not for you to know!" she said interrupting me. "You think you should know everything before it happen . . . but something you no can know. Like when someone you love die. Or when someone love you so very much."

"I hope then, Sister, that I didn't do anything that made you think I was in love with you."

She waved her hands in front of me like fans, "No. You no do that, Paul. Only me love you. Since I first see you in Phan Rang I love you. Think and dream about us." The words tumbled out now, fast and breathlessly. "So many thing happen to me and I say, I must go on pray, keeping working. And I confuse when I feel my love for you is same-same, my love for God . . ." Tears of relief and no more secrets filled

her eyes, and a warm smile crossed her face. "Then I se
how you love our children. I see you grow, get strong, an
the same happen for me. My love now is strong for my Goo
my work, and the children . . . Like Sister Hoa, this is m
happiness now, and I think maybe forever."

"That's great, Sister," I said, taking her hands in mine

"When you leave us, maybe I forget you . . . but I n
think so," she said, gently pulling her hands away. "Com
with us now to bury your little friend."

We buried Thom in a lovely grove of trees at the edge o
the city. A small swing hung from one of the trees, and w
decided to bury her close to it. It was quiet and peaceful, wit
no city sounds or war for miles around. A soft breeze ble
across the bordering rice paddies, setting the swing i
motion. I imagined Thom sitting on the swing, talking-
telling me it was all right. I could almost hear her voice. I
was hard to know if I really heard her whisper my name wit
her dying breath, or if I had imagined it in those unforge
table moments. But I preferred to think that she had tru
spoken.

The old men and I patted the dirt down on Thom's grave
then stood aside so the children could place the flowers o
top. I had to get back to the mortuary but wanted a few mir
utes alone at the site. The nuns gathered the children in nea
lines and began the half-hour walk back to the orphanage.

I just sat and emptied my mind, breathing in the fres
smell of earth and lush green rice. The leaves above me
rustled in the afternoon breeze, the only sound penetratin
my still mind. I couldn't cry anymore, not for lack of tears
but because for some uncertain yet wonderful reason, I fel
that Thom's death was a new beginning for me. And all the
facts which made that feeling real were still confused excep
for one: the power of unconditional love.

Suddenly a withered flower appeared in front of my face
held there by a dirty little hand. I turned, following the arm
up to find Trong behind the tree I was leaning against. I too
the flower, then pulled him around onto my lap. We sa
quietly for a long time, and then he said, "I sorry abou
Thom."

"I know that, Trong."

"You believe I no hate her like I tell you. She good girl. I
d, too, cause she die."

Neither of us spoke again for a long moment. Trong
aned back, resting his head against my chest, then turned
ddenly, and looking straight into my eyes asked, "You
re you love? . . . Never forget me?" His eyes were vulner-
le, the eyes of the eleven-year-old boy he was and not those
the brave man who only hours ago had disposed of a dead
ldier's body.

I put my arms around him and said, "How could I ever
rget you—you're my number-one black market boy."

"Man!" he said, now grinning, and we both got up to
ave. I looked back to see the swing moving gently in the
reeze, and my throat tightened as I saw her sitting on it, legs
angling, waving good-bye to us.

"Good-bye, Thom."

Trong looked up at me understandingly, took my hand,
nd we walked away from the peaceful sanctuary.

Surprisingly there was no confrontation waiting for me
hen I arrived at the mortuary. Just a couple of brave but
angled pilots, a suicide, and too many bodies waiting to be
mbalmed. It was business as usual. The death of my sweet
ttle girl meant nothing to Williams, Murry, or any of the
eople around me. The mortuary personnel mechanically
ranked out one body after the other, with more dead being
nloaded as they worked. The war went on and would go on
orever, I guessed, here in Vietnam or someplace else. And
hildren would continue to be born into and die from its ha-
red, until peace and love became stronger than anger and
ggression.

I felt so different. As if someone had removed my blinders
r lifted an enormous weight from my shoulders. I was years
rom many of the answers and sad for the dead boy whose
hattered brain I held in my hands. But I now knew what the
otal effect of war was. It was the man on the table in front of
ne, who in one second of confusion, and with one unan-
wered question too many, destroyed his thoughts, memo-
ies, dreams, and all he was . . . or would ever be. And it
vas the little girl who died in my arms last night. And no an-

swer or reason in the world, no country or its territorial in tegrity, was good enough to justify any of it.

On my way back to the orphanage that evening I stopped at the nurses' quarters to pick up the children. Marie met me at the gate and we walked quietly to her room. The two older boys were sitting on Marie's bed, watching her television, but there was no sign of baby Kang. Marie went to make coffee and I flopped on the bed between the two boys.

"How's Kang doing?" I called to Marie, figuring they had put him in one of the wards for observation. Marie looked around the partition that separated the bedroom from the bath. "I'm sorry, Paul. He died a few minutes after you dropped him off. One of the docs worked on him for almost a half hour. He had a bad skull fracture, so I don't think he suffered at all."

"Thank God! . . . These two look O.K."

"They'll be fine. I'll take their stitches out in about ten days. How are you?" Marie asked, crossing the room with two mugs of coffee.

"Marie . . . Thom was killed last night," I said, taking the coffee from her. The two boys stopped talking and looked at me. Her eyes welled with tears and she said, "Jesus, Paul, what happened?" then noticed me looking at the boys. "Never mind . . . You seem pretty calm."

"There's not much I can do about it. It was stupid, but it happened . . ." I said, sipping the hot coffee. "Listen, I want to apologize to you. For being such an asshole . . . and . . . for using you." She looked surprised. "What do you mean," she asked as I moved from the bed to a seat next to her on the couch.

"You were my first woman, and so, something special. Something I wanted to continue . . . the sex, I mean . . . but the times we slept together I felt you were getting us involved in a one-sided relationship, because I didn't feel the things you did, and I wasn't in love with you."

She looked at me, smiling with her full lips and green eyes. "Now, Specialist Hensler, I'm going to tell you something that may sound a little shocking, but it's true. You were great in bed, and I can only hope one day to marry a man as mpassionate as you. But I was using you, too. We used ch other. That's all there is to it!''

Now I was surprised. "But didn't you believe it could go ? Become a relationship . . . that we were in love?"

"No."

I looked at her, speechless, and feeling stupid about my ig-rance. Marie sensed my embarrassment and continued. We needed each other, and we found each other. You now. A port in the storm, the war, and all that stuff. We're different than the docs and nurses around here, away om their husbands or wives for a year . . . Only we used ch other well. At least, I think we did . . . Don't you?''

"Uh, yeah . . . Does this change how you feel about the rphanage?" I said and wanted to cut out my tongue. "I ean, you'll keep helping them after I leave, won't you?"

"Of course I will. But you've got a few months left."

"Six weeks."

"Where the hell did the time go?"

"What'ya mean? I feel like I've been here for ten years."

"Don't worry. We'll keep the place together. Oh, by the ay, the doc who took care of Kang is gonna help, plus a ouple of others who met the kids this morning."

"They only have to meet these guys once and they're ooked. Thanks, Marie. You're really great."

She punched me on the arm playfully. "Hey, wait a min-te. I'm not doing all this just for you. I like kids too."

"Why don't you take a few home with you?" I said, pick-ng up the two boys.

"You can forget that idea. I want to have my own children irst . . . You want some help with them?"

"No. These guys are pros at riding through a combat zone vith me. You should see the fingernail marks on my stom-ch! . . . Thanks again for everything," I said as she opened he door for me.

"You sound like this is good-bye. I hope you'll make some ime in your busy schedule, Paul-san, for dinner and . . .''

"Yes, sir! . . . How about tomorrow night, sir?"

"You got a date, Private!"

"It's not Private anymore. Somehow, in the middle of all he madness out there, they promoted me to Specialist 5th Class."

"Oh . . . Sorrrrrry. Sergeant!"

"No, Specialist!"

"Whatever you are, tell Sister Hoa I'll stop by tomorro morning," she said, and after leaning out the door to chec the hallway, she kissed me tenderly on the lips. The two boy started to laugh and point at me. "Get going before I end u in the stockade," Marie said, giving me a gentle shove dow the hallway.

There was one more person I needed to set things straigh with, and a couple of days later I asked Sister Hoa if I coul speak to her alone. She suggested we go away from the or phanage where we would not be disturbed. I was pleasantl surprised, because we had never walked out the orphanag gate together, except to go to the market. We found a quie little hole in the wall soup stand and ordered two Vietnames iced coffees. It seemed strange to be doing nothing but enter taining ourselves for a few minutes. Relaxing in the coo early evening air. And I think Sister Hoa sensed my struggl to prepare what I wanted to say, for she remained silent an continued to watch the people pass on the street until I wa ready.

"I need to ask your forgiveness for all the times I hurt you and the children. For all the times I was more like one of th children than an adult. I did a lot of very stupid things, lik trying to run an orphanage without knowing how."

"Please, Paul . . ."

"Wait, Sister," I said, interrupting her, "I've been rehearsing this speech all day, so let me finish . . . I think know what you're going to say, but I still feel responsible for the deaths of those children in Cam Ranh and for Thom' death in a way. Maybe because I didn't understand the re sponsibility that I had taken on. If I had been trained to run an orphanage, there would've been no excuse for mistakes or the death of a child. But for a long time it was more a game for me, Sister . . . My reasons for coming to the orphanage were selfish. Because I was confused about my work at the morgue, and about myself, and drugs, I only wanted to play and not think about the truth . . . I know these feelings will go away someday . . . But right now I just hope you will say you forgive me and that you, Sister Tuan, and the children will remember the good times we had here, at the orphanage

Cam Ranh . . . and the Christmas party . . ." She
started to cry. She lifted the apron tied around her waist and
buried her face in it.

"Please, Sister, don't cry. Everybody's been crying, including myself, and I can't stand it anymore," I said with a
little laugh, trying to brighten the moment.

She sat up straight on her stool and said, "You still don't
know, do you? . . . You have seen the other orphanages
around us, Paul. Most lose children, not from the war but
from neglect or an inability to care for their numbers. Other
children die in the street everyday, here and in the country.
But not in our orphanage."

"I know that, Sister, but what about adoption, and birth
certificates, and papers, and real education, and the future?
It never changes for them. Their chances are no better . . ."

"You are wrong. In this situation there is no proper way
to run an orphanage like ours. There are no rules or laws.
You do all you can, as we will continue to do. If the war were
stopped today, that would be a change—but children—
orphans and their needs—will remain the same. We are not
the only warring country. And we are not the only country
with disease and starvation. In your future you will see worse
than here, and you will want to help them as you have helped
us. It is your way, perhaps. What you may call a career," she
said, drinking the last of her coffee.

"What can I do to help you once I get home, Sister?"

"Forget about us for a while."

"That's impossible . . . Why do you say that?"

"You must go home and forget. Forget the anger and
pain. Learn and grow, and when the time is right you will
understand how to use all your experiences to help others
. . . perhaps as a priest, or a worker with children, or a
teacher."

"I remember telling you once in anger that you had all the
words . . . I was right."

"And I believe I am right about you . . . Do you remember when I told you that I hated all the Americans?"

"Yes. In Cam Ranh, after the fire."

"Well, I want to change what I said. It is not Americans I
hate. It is man, for choosing war to answer his questions.
The Americans and Vietnamese who live aggression are

creating an environment of anger, and hatred, in which ou
children will grow. So if you want to help us, then learn how
to teach peace and simple happiness to every child you meet
Then maybe when they grow up, they will choose peace, an
not war . . . Do you understand what I mean?''

''I think so . . . You never answered my first question
Do you think they'll remember the happiness we all had to
gether?''

''Maybe not. The material things, your gifts, will be los
or broken. The food you brought will be eaten, and the toi
lets you fixed will jam again soon, I imagine. Your playing, i
made them happy for a moment . . . But your love—that i
the gift you gave and is what they needed most and will re
member.''

Now I was crying, but this time because of incredible hap
piness. All the confused thoughts were coming together i
my head, about Thom and about a new beginning. Sister Hoa
took my hand and pulled me to my feet. ''We must get bach
before Sister Tuan goes dinky dow,'' she said, and we both
laughed.

''I'm grateful for all you have taught me, Sister.'' I knew
we were saying our farewells. I still had four weeks left in my
tour, and I intended to make every day count as a bountiful,
happy one in the lives of the nuns and children. All the talking was done, life must go on, there was food to be found and
bartered for, baths to give, and one hundred and ten mouths
to feed.

As we approached the orphanage gate, she stopped and
put her hands on my shoulders. ''You came to us a boy . . .
and now you leave us a man. God bless you, Paul.'' She took
my right hand and pressed it to her cheek, then continued
through the orphanage gates. At the kitchen door, she
stopped and turned back to me. ''Don't forget we need rice
. . . and I told the children the Tickling Monster would be
coming tonight!!''

Dear God:
  Sorry about that last letter.
  You and me all the way.

Epilogue

For thirteen years after my return to the United States I tried to keep in contact with the orphanage in Saigon. A hundred unanswered letters, sometimes with a little money hidden in their pages when I could afford it, left me with a nagging, empty space. Like unfinished business, the fate of the orphanage came back at me, unannounced, questioning, memories good and bad. I would say to myself, "What can I do? What are they doing to survive? Are all the news reports about poverty and death on the streets of Saigon, now renamed Ho Chi Minh City, true? And why doesn't Sister Hoa answer my letters?" The answers were simple. No money, closed borders, no diplomatic relations between our country and Communist Vietnam, and the forward motion of my own life kept me from the thought of returning to Vietnam.

That was until April 27, 1983, when I boarded a Pan Am 747 jet for Tokyo, Hong Kong, Singapore, and then on to Thailand. There I would catch an Air France flight, the only service into Vietnam, and arrive in Ho Chi Minh City on April 30. We arrived in Singapore twenty-seven hours later, an aircraft full of bloodshot eyes and numbing jet lag. I made several calls to the United States Embassy in Singapore and was dissuaded from my plan to enter Ho Chi Minh City because of what they called strained relations with its Communist Government, and so, no protection if I ran into any problems.

The next series of calls to the North Vietnamese Trade Mission in Singapore was even less successful. After being switched from one non-English-speaking person to the next,

I was told that the borders between Thailand and Vietnam were temporarily closed. Strike two was the fact that the present government in Vietnam was quite upset with the "lies" written by some American journalists, and they were not allowing any more in. No matter what I said, the man on the phone could not be convinced I was a writer, not a journalist. I would have to meet face to face with the Vietnamese attaché in Bangkok. If I could convince him of my status and intentions, he might issue me an entry visa.

As the Malaysian Airlines jet banked sharply, beginning its final approach into Bangkok Airport, I looked down at the Thai countryside. Memories flashed up at me. Red clay, dark green mountains reaching into the clouds, small bamboo villages with children playing in their alleys, and even a little black-haired boy riding his family's water buffalo toward home. The scene, the colors, the heat waving up from the arid soil, reminded me of the day almost thirteen years ago when I left Saigon for the last time.

A similar countryside had raced by our window as we roared down the runway of Tan Son Nhut Air Base. I remembered the anxious moments as three hundred of us held our breaths until the chartered Pan Am jet was out of enemy firing range, and the last chance to die in the "Nam" was three thousand feet below us. The pilot's voice finally broke the silence as he spoke softly into the aircraft's intercom, "Pan Am welcomes you, gentlemen. Sit back, relax, and let us take you home." Shouts of joy and many tears happened that afternoon in 1970. But none of the three hundred Americans left Vietnam that day with more of a mixture of relief and sadness than I. For them it was over. They had survived 365 days in hell and were on their way home. For me it was a great new beginning.

In the last weeks before I left Vietnam, I continued working at the orphanage, concentrating most of my energy on stockpiling tradable black market supplies. A second task was to ensure that the orphanage would be watched over by other G.I.s. One fact I had come to realize through my association with men like Moses, Forbes, Stubbs, and Brian was the abundance of other soldiers whose minds and hearts were affected by the plight of innocent children, injured or orphaned by the war. Like myself, they could see the unfairness meted out to them and decided to help. They would make a difference in their quality of life, with food and laughter, a safe clean home, English lessons, medical care, and several new friends who would gladly sit in the doorway until they fell asleep. Marie and a growing number of volunteers would keep the orphanage going and promised me to hand on the responsibility to others after them.

So it was with a feeling of some comfort and security that I said my final farewell to Sister Hoa, Sister Tuan, Trong, and one hundred and twenty-five orphans. In the early summer of 1970, I waved good-bye to the orphan group as my taxi pulled out into the midday traffic . . . and I never saw or heard from them again.

After my discharge from the army in 1972, I began to search for the answers to a million questions generated by two and a half years in Vietnam. I thought it would be easy to put it all behind me and start looking at either school or career possibilities, but my thirst for information and explanations only increased as the war in Southeast Asia continued. Along with protest rallies across the nation, there was death on the campus of Kent State. Street fighting in New York and Chicago. New bombing raids on Hanoi and Cambodia, and a president who kept saying that PEACE was right around the corner. In this atmosphere of national frustration and anger there seemed no room for explanations, only a collective plea for an end to ten years of fruitless, unpopular war. Hardly the time to start telling the American people about the beautiful orphans of Vietnam, or a story of hope!

Two and a half years of preparation for the priesthood afforded me the time to carefully put all my past experiences in perspective. And while my feelings about a life of service remained strong, they lacked the necessary sense of direction within the Oblate Community. Their methods of dealing with children and the poor were far too unreal for me, no matter how directed by God their missionary work was said to be. So when I received the phone call from Dr. Chi in California, it might as well have been from Sister Hoa. Her words had come true. "Learn and grow, and when the time is right you will understand how to use all your experiences

o help others . . . learn how to teach peace and simple happiness to every child you meet. Then maybe when they grow
up, they will choose peace, and not war . . .''

After all the children from Camp Pendleton had been
placed with foster families in the Southern California area, I
moved on to work in the motion picture industry as a Vietnam technical adviser. The money I made allowed me to
continue visiting some of the children from Pendelton, send a
little to Saigon, and help several Vietnamese families I had
met in the camp.

The list of films I worked on concerning Vietnam began to
fill my resume: *Apocalypse Now, Who'll Stop the Rain?, A Matter
of Inconvenience, Heroes, the Exterminator, More American Graffiti,*
and others. All of them were great learning experiences, but
at the same time I knew none of them were the truth for me.
Yes, a scene here and there may have occurred in Vietnam.
But film after film perpetuated the belief that nothing good
ever happened in America's longest war. National guilt,
stereotypical drug-crazed soldiers with no true leadership in
Washington or the Pentagon, and our final physical and
moral defeat in Vietnam seemed the only story ideas the
major studios would consider. I could find no one who was
willing to listen to another side of the Vietnam story.

Although the facts were all there, studied and discussed in
the greatest of detail, they were still not my experience of the
Vietnam War. I had seen the results of the moral confusion
and fighting every day, in triage, on the hospital wards, and
most tragically in the mortuary. But I was also a painful wit-
ness to the suffering of the Vietnamese people and their children. No filmmaker or novelist had yet directly confronted
the Vietnamese point of view, how they suffered and died.
Two and a half million Americans served in Vietnam; of
those, 57,939 died. The Vietnamese, conveniently and continually depicted as the villains, lost millions fighting for
their equal right to freedom.

In 1978 a now famous film director told me the one sure
way to tell my story of the children of Vietnam would be to
write both a script and book myself. With a script I might be
able to find financial backing, produce the film, and if it were
successful I would then be able to help some of the children
still in the refugee camps. In a little more than eight weeks I

completed the first draft of a screenplay entitled *Don't Cry, It's Only Thunder*.

My agent and I tried valiantly to sell both the script and its possibilities as a book but found the film and publishing companies unreceptive. The major studios, along with the larger publishing firms, were still only interested in blood-and-battle stories from the war. A compassionate story about children, hope, and love had no place on their lists of would-be hits.

After hearing of the tragic problems of the boat people in Malaysia, several friends financed my journey to the refugee camps outside Kuala Lumpur. Old documentaries about the death camps in Nazi Germany were the only visual memory that could parallel the horror I found in the Malaysian camps.

On the island of Pulau Bidong, about a mile off the coast of Malaysia, ten thousand Vietnamese boat people were packed into makeshift huts constructed to hold two thousand. Tuberculosis, pneumonia, dysentery, malaria, and forced beachings of sinking boats kept the grave-digging detail hard at work. Children as young as two years of age, unaccompanied and uncared for, wandered through the squalor begging for food. Their stomachs were swollen with worms and the hunger sickness, their noses running with pus from viral pneumonia. I worked in the camps, bucking the local authorities for medical supplies and food until I became ill myself.

When I returned to the United States, I carried in each arm a child who needed a new home, a list of refugees who were in desperate need of sponsors, and two new refugee families to watch over.

After several more rewrites and the addition of the research from my Malaysian trip, I was finally able to find an independent production company to finance my film. And so, in October 1980 *Don't Cry, It's Only Thunder* began filming in the Philippines. The cast was led by Dennis Christopher, Susan Saint James, two Vietnamese child actors found in a refugee camp in the Philippines, and hundreds of extras who were themselves Vietnamese refugees.

I knew the film and this book, started in 1980, could not possibly eliminate nine years of moral predicament over the

Vietnam War. But by telling my story I was able to present another reality of Vietnam, another view of the Vietnamese as a humane, compassionate people, and a first-time look at the many heroic American soldiers who were the embodiment of the human spirit we all know exists in our country. I could call attention to the brave men who died on the battlefields, to people like Moses, Sister Tuan, Brian, Sister Hoa, and many others all over Vietnam. There were enlisted personnel and volunteers who rebuilt schools, churches, hospitals, orphanages, and lifted the spirits of the poor, wounded, and dying. They were examples of the universal goodness—of both Vietnamese and Americans alike—who transcended the destructiveness of a war which nearly destroyed a country and the spirit of another.

In that sense *Don't Cry, It's Only Thunder* was a total success, seen by both critics and those who saw the film to be a most compassionate plea, mirrored by the suffering and death of innocent children, for an end to all war. Many people across the United States asked me why Vietnam was so different from our country's past wars. And until I wrote this book, I did not have an answer. Now I can say, especially after reliving my time in the U.S. Army Mortuary, that it was not the war that was different but the people fighting it. We were so changed a generation of men and boys fighting in Vietnam. We were more educated, sensitive, aware of life and death, and more conscious of moral decisions and their sometimes tragic results. And so, the trigger was no longer easy to pull, simply because someone identified a race of people as the enemy. And death was no longer a secret, a stage of suspended spiritual animation before the journey to heaven or hell. Death in Vietnam was final and tragic, whether the victim was Vietnamese, Filipino, Australian, or American.

After checking into the Oriental Hotel in Bangkok, I drove toward the North Vietnamese Consulate, preparing myself for the threatened uphill battle. Although very gracious, the attaché argued, parroting the man in Singapore, that devious, double-faced American journalists were not welcome in Ho Chi Minh City. After six cups of bitter tea, a picture-showing session, and two hours of careful diplomatic placation, the suspicious wiry old man jumped to his feet and said, "O.K. I will do what I can." I was to return in three days.

Although the wait would automatically extend my Thailand visit because of infrequent flights to Ho Chi Minh City, it would be just enough time to complete the second reason for this trip.

In early 1983 the Vietnamese Student Union from the University of California at Los Angeles had used the film *Don't Cry, It's Only Thunder* to raise money. Half of the four thousand dollars raised was sent to the rescue boat *Akuna*, which still sails the South China Sea aiding the boat people and the other half I was asked to deliver to a Thai priest, Father Peter Prayoon Namwong. Father Namwong has been the faithful guardian of a group of abandoned Vietnamese children in one of the larger Thai refugee camps. Caught in a dangerous and heated political argument over the continual flow of refugees, these children were being threatened with immediate deportation. Their status of being abandoned or unaccompanied by adults was just too complicated for the Thai Government, who were at present trying to end the entire refugee problem. The money I was carrying would hopefully buy some time for the children so I could get all the facts and try and help once back in the States.

And, once again, on April 29, 1983, I found myself surrounded by Vietnamese children. This time I was inside the Unaccompanied Children's Center of the Sikiu Refugee Center (or the Sikiu Prison Camp, as it has just been renamed by the Thai military), about three hundred miles north of Bangkok. Crowded around me are sixty unaccompanied children, not forty, as I had been told in the States.

The biggest problem facing these children is the fact that most of them cannot be adopted because their parents are still alive in Vietnam, nor can they be legally sponsored because they are minors. For each child that has no living relative in a receiving country (outside Vietnam), a new set of rules must be written. Finding foster homes, an already lengthy process for American children, is almost impossible when the child has no family paperwork or history and is twenty-five thousand miles away. There's no time to exchange pretty photographs so an American family can decide whether they like this child or another. And very few American foster homes are prepared for the problems of these special children.

All they can do now is wait. At night they cry for their parents. During the day the little ones play or go to school, while the elders worry about the increasing Thai threat to send these troublesome children back to Vietnam.

What an incredible horror. Parents who have raised these beautiful children with love, sending them off, saying goodbye for what they know is the last time! And why? FREEDOM! It's really that simple. Even the children know and understand why they have been sent away from the parents they love and miss. Their parents also know that in the United States, or wherever they end up, they can get a good education and perhaps someday return to Vietnam and work toward or fight to free the country they love . . . Now their children are here, crowded into a refugee camp built to hold 2,000 people and whose present population is 8,300!!

To make matters even worse for the refugees, the Thai military run the camp with enough bureaucratic bullshit and bribery to choke a horse. I bought about one hundred dollars' worth of candy, crayons, and books to give to the children. Following the camp rules, I left the goods at the Thai Camp Commander's Office to be inspected. Less than half of what I brought was eventually given to the children. I can just imagine what happens to money, medicine, or other things brought specifically for the refugees. Even though I have found this a normal practice in all the Southeast Asian camps I have visited, it's still hard to accept.

I was only allowed to visit with the children for fifteen minutes my first morning in the camp. The Thai military seemed afraid of me, not one of them daring to enter into a conversation beyond hello and good-bye. They could not understand why a single American had come so far just to see the children. One of the Vietnamese camp coordinators told me later that the Thais were afraid I would write nasty letters about the treatment of the refugees and their children. And once again, no matter what I said, including showing them the entry pass Father Namwong procured for me, they decided to limit my entry into the camp. When the Thai Deputy Commander came by to inform me that I would be allowed to attend the afternoon children's mass, I asked him why they had changed the name from Sikiu Refugee Center to the Sikiu Prison? He said they were hoping that by treating the refugees like prisoners, with rationed food, water, and medical attention, the message would get back to Saigon, "If you come to Thailand, you'll go to prison." The Thais are very much like the Vietnamese people. Warm, family-oriented, and friendly. But they, like the Malaysians, can no longer feed and house an endless stream of Vietnamese refugees while the poor and needy of Thailand go hungry. I did not like the way they were treating the people in this camp, but I agreed with him that it must end soon. The United States is the only country which still has its doors wide open to these unfortunate people, and even we are beginning to lower our quotas again. The struggling Third World countries like Thailand, Malaysia, and the Philippines have enough internal problems of their own and have been caring for these refugees for almost ten years. The commander's final statement to me was very clear. Unless the United States or some of the other sponsoring countries increase their allocations, the Thai military would have no other choice but to force these people, including the children, back across the border into Vietnam.

The children fare a little better in the camp, thanks to Father Namwong. For the last six years he has kept a special watch over the orphans and unaccompanied children of Sikiu Camp. The Military officials don't like him because of his attention to the medical care and continuing education of these children, called the offspring of Communist criminals, and so he is only allowed in the camp on Sundays to say mass. Several of his helpers have made friends with the military and are now able to carry out his work for the children. Even Father Namwong's scant supplies, clothes, pencils, and school books are halved by the front office, but he and his co-workers continue with a smile.

The two masses Father said that afternoon were incredible experiences. The first mass, in Vietnamese, was for the adults. Two thousand people filled the small church and spilled out into the center courtyard of the camp. Grown men and women wept out loud as prayers for peace and an end to the Communist regime in Vietnam were said. The children's mass was at three, and I cried too when they started to sing,

heir voices taking me back to the orphanage and Christmas
Eve in Saigon with Marie.

Two of the Vietnamese seminarians then secreted me back
into the children's center so I could see them one more time
before we left. It was 112 degrees inside the dorms, my
clothes were soaked with sweat, the air was almost unbreath-
able, and I just sat there watching them bounce around the
room with endless energy, crowding in close to look, touch,
and listen. I felt as if I was back in the courtyard of the orphanage in Saigon, or in the doorway of the nursery, waiting
for them to fall asleep. And from Thom, Trong, the children
in Saigon, Camp Pendleton in 1975, Malaysia and Singapore in 1980, my children in Los Angeles, and the little ones
who waved good-bye to me from the gate of Sikiu Prison, I
have heard and keep hearing the same requests over and over
again—"Take me away with you. Will you be my daddy,
my sponsor, my friend? . . . I miss my mother and father
. . Will you love me?"

I kept saying "YES" . . . and yet there was so little I
could do. If I had the money, time, and power to cut through
the red tape, I would have brought every one of them home
with me. Found them families even if I had to walk the streets
of Los Angeles with a child under each arm. And it was dou-
bly sad that I didn't have a suitcase or large pocket with me
then, or I would have smuggled the greatest little boy out of
the camp with me . . . Instead I carried only another long
list: two partial artificial legs for a couple of boys in the center,
vitamins, powdered milk, supplies for Father Namwong's
Sikiu School, underwear for the little girls, and families to
find for some incredibly beautiful children.

The following day I returned to Bangkok and immediately
reported to the Vietnamese Consulate . . . Two more hours
of waiting and then their answer, NO! . . . The valiant
troops of liberated Vietnam are returning from their victory
at the Chinese border. There will be parades and celebra-
tions in Ho Chi-Minh City to which I was not invited.

As I walked back toward the hotel, I found myself disappointed and at the same time somewhat relieved. When I began this trip back to Vietnam ten days ago, I was both
excited and terrified. The thought of seeing Sister Hoa, Sister Tuan, Trong, and maybe a few of the original children

kept me awake almost every night. But running parallel to the excitement was the very real fear of arriving at the orphanage gate and finding them gone. It had nothing to do with the long journey back or the money spent but only with the emotional bond that still connected me to them. Thirteen years of hopes and memories I did not want changed. I could not have lived with the reality of finding them destitute or dead! And so, it was almost better that I went on believing the nuns and Trong were okay, surviving as only they knew how, and perhaps at that exact moment the orphanage courtyard was filled with laughing children.

On May 5 I stood at the Pan Am counter at Singapore International Airport. Gathered around me were eighty-six frightened Vietnamese refugees whom I would escort on the last leg of their journey to America and the beginning of a new life. They were so excited to have made it from Communism to Freedom that many wept openly as I handed them their boarding passes, unashamed of their tears in front of the gawking, richly dressed tourists around them.

During the long flight the tired, frightened refugees began to talk, sure now that they were on their way to freedom. No longer afraid of being silenced by the Thai military, or their Communist oppressors in Vietnam. They wanted me to know how long they had dreamed of this day, how many people died before their dream came true, and how many people continue from behind the Communist borders to cry out in prayer for freedom.

After saying good-bye to the last of the refugees in Honolulu, I walked toward my waiting friends, tired and ready for a week of Hawaiian rest and recuperation. But I could not rest because inside me I carried another story, the outcome of which becomes more frightening as each day, week, and month race by. About my fears for children—yellow, black, red, or white—who desperately need freedom, homes, and families before they forget what love means. Before they begin to hate; before that hatred turns indelible; before the "Dust of Life," the unwanted, the war orphans from around the world, are battered by their miserable environment into revolutionaries and fascists—the executioners of tomorrow.

Hawaii was as beautiful as I remembered it from many previous visits. But this time I could not enjoy Paradise. Not

hen, at the same time, sixty children needed help before
ome tired, underpaid, and overworked Thai official mind-
ssly sent them back to Vietnam and, for most, back to their
eaths!

It might be too late to save all of these children. But it is
ot too late to save many others, to protect their innocence,
eir ability to love without fear, and their belief in a God
nd goodness in the world.

That hope is what draws me back to them over and over
gain, whether they are here in the United States, Thailand
r Malaysia—that hope . . . and Thom's lessons of uncon-
itional love.

Thoughtful Reading from SIGNET and MENTOR

**Buy them at your local
bookstore or use coupon
on last page for ordering.**

MENTOR and SIGNET Titles of Interest

**Buy them at your local
bookstore or use coupon
on next page for ordering.**

MENTOR Books of Related Interest